HEART WIDE OPEN
A True Story

Janae Thorne-Bird

iUniverse, Inc.
New York   Bloomington

Heart Wide Open
A True Story

iUniverse books may be ordered through booksellers or by contacting:

iUniverse
1663 Liberty Drive
Bloomington, IN 47403
www.iuniverse.com
1-800-Authors (1-800-288-4677)

ISBN: 978-1-4401-8576-2 (pbk)
ISBN: 978-1-4401-8577-9 (ebk)

Printed in the United States of America

Library of Congress Control Number: 2009913128

iUniverse rev. date: 2/16/2010

**For John, Nolan, Kurt, Patrick, and Brad. And for all lovers past, present and future.
**Special thanks to Jim Catano for his stylistic edits.

Our nakedness is a metaphor for our willingness to expose ourselves to the light…and become enlightened. J. Bird (naked as a)

Contents

Keep it Steady, Cowgirl

High, wide and handsome
Down from the great white north
More than enough and then some
Swept her up on his horse

Tumbleweeds were meant to
Get stuck up on a fence
Heaven must have sent you
You've got no wire to roll against

Keep it steady, cowgirl
Don't let go of the reins
You are ready now girl
Never mind the growin pains

Worlds out there are waiting
Big and wild as the sky
No more hesitating
It's now or never, do or die

Keep it steady, cowgirl
Don't let go of the reins
You are ready now girl
Never mind the growin pains

As hard as you imagined
It being without me
We'll both be wishin
It were that easy

Don't give me a pull
Give me some room
When this roundup is through
I'll be comin back home

Wide open spaces
Between these two prairie hearts
Wonderin where their place is
In a world so far apart

Keep it steady, cowgirl
Don't let go of the reins
You are ready now girl
Never mind the growin pains

Keep it steady, cowgirl
Don't let go of the reins
You are ready now girl
Never mind the growin pains

(Words from John Denver's *The Flower that Shattered the Stone* album)

Introduction

Life *is* relationship. The only thing we do in life is relate. It's the only thing that brings us our reality. Our eyes relate to our surroundings giving us sight. Our ears relate to the sounds around us giving us hearing. Our bodies relate to every bit of sensory stimulation, which gives us our perception of life. How we perceive the world is determined by our ability to relate to it. If we are open and willing, our relationship with the world can be extraordinary. If we are closed and shut down, our world can be fearful and terrifying. And so it goes with our personal relationships with people.

If our hearts are wide open, our personal relationships can be rich and expansive. If our hearts are closed because of past pains and disappointments, our relationships will follow this same pattern until they become open again. To have our *hearts wide open* means to be fully present in each waking moment—in every situation. Yes, this means we *can* and *will* experience every emotion possible—including pain—but relating to *all of it* is truly the richest experience we can have in life. *It's what's real!*

This book is about relationships. The names have *not* been changed to protect the innocent—because we are *all* innocent! We simply are acting according to the programs we've chosen for ourselves. We *can* and *do* change our programs at will. That's the beauty of life. We are totally in control of our reality, and *that* reality can change as we make different choices. We learn wonderful things about ourselves by making choices. There are no good or bad choices—there are just choices. Some consequences of our choices may not turn out the way we'd like, and so we may choose to make different choices in the future. That is the way we learn. Some of us are quick learners; some of us are rather slow. It makes no difference. We're all headed for the same place—enlightenment—and even though some of us will arrive there sooner than others, it's all about the journey to our *own* enlightenment.

This book is a sequel to my first book *Heartsong,* so if you haven't read it, much of this one may not make as much sense. I suggest you pick up a copy of *Heartsong* before embarking on reading *Heart Wide Open*. *Heartsong* was written as a fantasy novel but based on reality with some situations consolidated or embellished for continuity. The names were changed to protect "the guilty," but since there really are no "guilty," I've chosen in this book to include real first names and to make the information as accurate as possible. The reader must understand, however, that in any non-fiction novel, reality is only the perception of the author.

So this is *my* perception of *my* relationship to God, to Mother Earth, to myself, to family, to friends, to lovers, to jobs, to books, to experiences, etc. I hope you will enjoy my journey into relationships and if at any point you relate to it—fantastic! Then we will have become one, too.

Chapter One—God

Many religions including the religions of the Native Americans teach that you can experience God directly without the assistance/interference of a spiritual mediator. The first century Christians practiced this and were described as Gnostic Christians—Gnostic meaning "to know." Through Native American ceremony and Gnostic Christianity, I've enjoyed incredible experiences contacting God directly through sacred ceremony and prayer. The following describes one of these experiences, which I loosely term "vision questing."

It's early spring—1998—when I climb the sacred summit seeking vision. We named the summit "Marriage Mountain" because of the numerous marriages we'd performed there and because it was one of Kurt's (my husband) and my favorite spots to make love. It was also an energetic vortex where hawks and eagles would circle in an amazing aerial display.

I'm breathless as I reach the plateau. Pausing a moment to catch my breath, my eyes span the panoramic horizon viewing the entire Ninemile Valley. It's beautiful this time of year dressed in its verdant spring embellishments. I'm drawn to an area of soft lichen-carpeted earth, inviting me to spread out my ground cover. I sit and pause for a moment until four medium-sized rocks beckon me to form the four directions—north, south, east and west. I place them with deliberate care, and then fill in the spaces with eight smaller rocks to create a sacred circle or Medicine Wheel. This was something I'd learned from Patrick (a Shaman friend) years ago.

My clothing falls gently to the earth before entering the sacred circle. It's a traditional metaphor for entering sacred space—naked and vulnerable. No secrets. No resistance. I'm completely open before my Creator to know as I am known. I came into this world seeking to join spirit with flesh, now in Vision Quest, I seek to join flesh with spirit. With heart wide open, I surrender myself to the Great Spirit as I sit in silent meditation. My eyes close to shut out the sensuous beauty surrounding me. I focus the intent to pour out my innermost feelings to my Creator in a passionate heartsong—a melody-drama filled with love, devotion, desire, and pain.

So many voices call to me—drawing me out to teach the wisdom which has become mine by learning to surrender to Spirit. Which ones should I listen to? Those of my own flesh and blood who need my constant care and whom I enjoy serving? Or those of a desperate world crying out for the healing wisdom I may offer? Always being pulled apart in different directions, I desire to know what's the most important direction. I'm confused—not together. I need to get an answer from God.

How can I deny the previous revelations I'd received in Colorado years before during my last two-week Vision Quest? I was told in no uncertain terms that I was the prophetess who many prophets had foretold would come to heal the planet. The Christian world was waiting for the return of Christ in a male form, but Native Americans spoke of a female prophetess and gave her the name White Buffalo Calf Woman. Their prophecies told of her return to perform a final ceremony with the sacred pipe to join together all people in a rainbow vortex and to open the fifth dimension. It would be then that peace and love would reign throughout the Earth. Was I that White Buffalo Calf Woman? Or was I simply an archetype or perhaps even a wannabe? I was prepared for an answer.

I mentally reviewed the evidence as I meditated. When I first moved to Montana I connected with a Mountain Man who built willow furniture. I couldn't even recall his name because it had been so many years before. He told me he felt impressed to give me a book called *Mother Earth Spirituality* by Ed McGaa, Eagle Man. It described the Native American paths to healing ourselves and our world. The first chapter described the coming of the White Buffalo Calf Woman and the sacred Peace Pipe. I was fascinated, intrigued by the story. But even more, it resonated deep inside me in a way that was truly mystical and sublime. I knew after finishing the book that I was a pipe-carrier and needed to obtain my own personal peace pipe. I sent this intention out to the Universe and it wasn't long before the Universe responded.

Kurt, at that time, sold vacuum-sealed food processors which took him to various cities in the Intermountain West. On one trip, he met a Native American selling peace pipes made from catlinite—a red stone from quarries in southwestern Minnesota and reserved for this sacred purpose. It was a week or so before my birthday, and Kurt knew of my fascination with Native American folklore. He said that one of the pipes actually spoke to him, in spirit, telling him that this particular pipe was to be mine—that it had been designed especially for me. He noticed that it had a buffalo embossed on the beige leather surrounding the stem, representing the White Buffalo Woman—the original pipe-carrier. But the pipe was quite pricey, more than

Kurt had anticipated paying for my birthday present. He couldn't justify the expenditure with so many mouths to feed with our large family, and so he walked away. Again the pipe beckoned him, so he returned to renegotiate. When he explained his reasons for wanting the pipe suddenly the Native American seller softened and asked Kurt how much he could afford. It was half what he was asking, but the seller settled on the price and presented it to Kurt, seemingly honored by the transaction.

Kurt placed the pipe in the trunk of his car for safekeeping, but that evening while he was in bed in the motel room, the pipe spoke to him again. It told him how disrespectful it was to leave the pipe in the trunk. Kurt tried to ignore the prompting, but it persisted. Finally, he surrendered and brought the pipe inside where it spent the night next to his pillow and continued to speak to him and energize him.

These stories and more Kurt brought home with him as he presented the curious pipe to me on my birthday. It was then that I told him about my intention to obtain a peace pipe after reading about the White Buffalo Woman. We were both astonished. I felt its deep importance at the time, especially after we smoked it together in sacred ceremony and received blessings of peace and empowerment. But it wasn't until later that it all made sense.

Nearly ten years afterward I met Speaking Wind, a Native American Shaman from the Pueblo People, and my experiences with him totally shifted my awareness of the spirit world. After reading his book, *When Spirits Touch the Red Path,* I had the opportunity to ask him some questions concerning shamanism. After he answered my first question, "What is it like to be spiritually one?" other questions kept pressing upon me like, "Who was I and what was my Indian name?" He'd indicated that *he* couldn't tell me—that *that* information was sacred and I needed to go directly to God for the answers. He did, however, state that I was one of the "Ancient Ones" who'd been sent back to heal the planet, and he kept saying over and over again, "I can't believe you are here!"

I invited Patrick (which is what he preferred being called) to come to Montana to perform sacred ceremony and to bless our land, Higher Ground. When he petitioned Spirit about which ceremonies he'd be allowed to perform, he was astonished to find that Spirit had given him full permission to perform the most sacred of all ceremonies—the Seven Steps to Returning to Oneness. We then made preparations for me to go to Alabama and meet many of the chiefs from many of the Native American tribes in a large gathering of tribes. After that they would follow us to Montana to Higher Ground to perform the sacred ceremony that was guaranteed to shift the planet.

But then everything came to a dramatic halt as Kurt, in a fit of jealousy, went to war with Patrick. When Kurt threatened Patrick with his life, Patrick cancelled the trip—and the ceremony. The last words Patrick spoke to me were, "I'm sorry, little one, but things are not in balance to perform this sacred ceremony right now. We must wait until things can come into balance." That was over two years ago and Patrick had not contacted me since.

And so now it was that I was seeking God for answers.

Hours pass as I sit in deep meditation, closing out the many voices that call to me so I can listen to the One True Voice. The sun beats down upon my naked body causing me to grow weary from its persistence. Attention flagging, I curl up on the ground cover for a short nap and moments later slip into a deep sleep. I am startled awake when a black wasp stings my right foot, which has slipped beyond the boundaries of my sacred circle. I cry out in pain, knowing it is a message from the Creator. I have strayed from my purpose here.

I resume a seated position inside the Medicine Wheel and continue the meditation. My long golden hair, bleached from the sun and dampened from perspiration, cascades across my shoulders protecting them from the burning rays. Time passes slowly and I decide to open my eyes to gaze upon the wonderland around me. Blue lupine, Indian paintbrush, and golden sunflowers form a delightful rainbow display. I then notice some unusual butterflies I'd never seen before flitting about the wildflowers. Their tan wings have markings that resemble eyes opening and shutting as they flap. I laugh as my mind does a play on words. These butterflies see with real eyes—they "realize." Again the words come. They are like the children of Israel—they see what "is real." I enjoy the play on words as I laugh to myself.

Then I notice the black wasp flitting about them. A feeling of concern sweeps over me as I'm reminded of the sting on my foot which is beginning to swell. The black wasp represents darkness and evil, and I grow concerned for the butterflies' safety. I spiritually call to them, beckoning them to come inside my sacred circle for safety, but they continue to flutter about among the colorful flowers unaware, it seems, of my presence or of the dark presence.

With a touch of resignation, I return to my meditation. Silently I bring myself into harmony with the purpose for which I am here. Cleansing myself of my own desires, I center myself upon the desires of my Creator and just listen. Suddenly, I feel a slight tickling in my cupped hands resting in my lap. I open my eyes and gaze down to see two "children of Is-real" butterflies resting gracefully in my hands. I smile in delight as I receive the sublime message from the Creator—so this is the gathering of Israel.

And just as if the Creator acknowledges that the message is received, the two beautiful butterflies—resting in my hands—merge together in mid-flight to form an energetic vortex spiraling them to heaven. I sit for a moment, awestruck, feeling profound messages from heaven flood my soul. My heart swells and my eyes overflow with the majesty and intimacy of God's love. I say a silent prayer of thanksgiving and know that my vision quest is complete.

I carefully return all of my stone sentries to their original positions. I dress and fold up my ground cover. These ordinary tasks seem illuminated by the radiance of my newfound knowledge. I know now that I must write my story and call it *Heartsong*.

When I get back to our log cabin, I am excited to tell Kurt about my experiences vision questing. He does not share in my enthusiasm as I disclose my own interpretations of the deeper meanings I've received. In fact he mocks me with searing skepticism, claiming it is a product of my own wild imagination. I retreat to my room and cry painfully. As has happened before, I've allowed him to steal away something precious from me. I pray to God for more answers and enlightenment—and perhaps more signs and witnesses. Miraculously they come.

The following week as I'm finishing up making a pair of boots for our neighbor, Andie McDowell (the actress), I notice something interesting. As I sew on the last item—a buffalo-head nickel fashioned into a button—I get a strange feeling of deja-vu. I know I've seen the same image of a buffalo somewhere before. Then I look down at the bottom of my bare left foot that for most of my life has born a strange mark. It started as a large black mole when I was young, but as I grew older it turned into a large, skin-colored tag. I used to joke with people that I'd know my soul-mate because he would have a similar skin tag. My children used to try to pull it off as it looked to them like a piece of gum.

It also opens up my *kundalini* energies when I massage it. But now as I look down on it for seemingly the first time, I notice something extraordinary. *It is the image of a white buffalo.* When I place the buffalo-head nickel next to it, the similarities are striking. I'm nearly overcome by this new revelation. I dare not tell anyone about it, especially Kurt who continues to mock me for my strange intuitions.

Then, over the course of the next few weeks, another remarkable coincidence occurs. I receive two cards in the mail—one from my mother for my birthday and another from a dear friend, Shara, letting me know she is thinking of me. My mother's card has the image of an Indian smoking a peace pipe. Shara's has a picture of three buffalo in an open field. Coincidence? I don't think so.

But again I'm careful not to share these experiences with anyone, thinking they would think I'm crazy! And perhaps I am a bit crazy as the mind has a

Chapter Two—Paul and Rose

I went over early that morning to deliver to Rose her moccasin-boots. "Rose" was Andie McDowell's real name and how I knew her as a neighbor and friend. I often wished she was more open so I could share with her some of my more sacred, intimate experiences, but she kept herself at a safe "celebrity" distance. I wished Christy, my sister-wife, was around as we'd become close to where I could share practically anything with her. But Kurt had sent her away to Lovell for the summer as he and I tried to heal our strained relationship. Deserae, my second oldest daughter, had moved back from Logan for the summer to help me with her seven younger siblings, and it was nice to have her back. I'd missed her immensely while she'd been living with her Grandma King while going to high school, and I was anxious to get to know her again.

I knocked on Rose's rustic back door avoiding the stain-glass rose inlays. Rose and Paul Qualley (their actual names) were particular about architectural details that reflected a warm and inviting Adirondack atmosphere. Rose thanked me and paid for the moccasins and then came outside to enjoy the spring morning. She tiptoed through her daffodil garden picking a handful of various blooms. "How sweet," I thought, as she handed them to me.

"Rose, I have a favor to ask you?"

"Sure, Janae, what is it?"

"Well, I have this great idea for a book, but I don't have any way to write it. You know we don't have any electricity, and my manual typewriter would take me forever to type it on, let alone edit. Is there any way I could use your computer for the project?"

She thought for a moment, her brunette curls reflecting in the morning sunlight. She was stunningly beautiful—more so in person than on screen. A part of me felt such a connection with her which I yearned to have realized.

"I don't see why not. Let me ask Paul if he'd be okay with it. He uses the computer quite a bit, but I think it'd be all right when he's not using it. I'll let you know."

The next morning Kurt went to work out with Paul on the heavy bag in their personal gym. He was teaching Paul some kickboxing moves he'd learned in L.A. from studying with "Benny the Jet," a champion kickboxer. When Kurt returned home he mentioned that Paul had said it was all right for me to use their computer. I was delighted and determined to start first thing in the morning. Deserae and Ariel had both agreed to help tend the younger children while I wrote. Summer in the mountains was a wondrous time and the children always found plenty of things to explore. I knew they would be well cared for with Kurt while he was cutting firewood and building fences.

The next morning I arrived at the Qualley's and knocked on the back door. Rose greeted me and said that Paul was already in the office above the gym doing some work on the computer. She didn't think he'd be too long and told me to make myself at home over at the gym until he finished. I felt a little awkward—a bit like an intruder in spite of Rose's outward hospitality. It was probably just me being nervous around a celebrity. I drove my white Subaru across the large parking area and parked next to the gym—a two-story nearly finished rock-faced building. I walked past the indoor pool and up the stairs leading to the office in back.

I could hear Paul in his office speaking a foreign language I didn't recognize to someone on the phone. It sounded like he was doing some stock exchanges—but I couldn't be sure. Paul's voice sounded straight out of a foreign film, so I listened outside the door for a few moments fascinated. Then I thought he might think that I was eavesdropping, so I took the opportunity to find the bathroom. It was at the end of the long balcony of ivy-clad rod-iron rails. The bathroom was quaint with a hand-thrown pottery sink and inlaid leaf-print tiles along the counters and splashboard. Paul was a stickler for detail. I could feel the love for Rose that had gone into it.

After using the bathroom, I decided to kill time by looking at some books in the hallway outside their personal library. Wadsworth, Emerson, Dickinson, Bronte, and more—original hard-back editions lined the shelves. I was impressed. I didn't realize Rose—or perhaps Paul—was so well read. I envied their collection compared to my condensed version of "The Great Books" series. They were celebrities who could afford such luxuries, but how could they ever find the time to read? I grabbed an Emily Bronte book of poems and sat down. Then I noticed a guitar sitting in the corner. I wondered whether it was Paul's or Rose's. I picked it up and started tuning it, but it must have been played recently because it was already in tune. I began playing some chords to my song "Even Now" my fingers fumbling as it'd been some time since I'd played.

"You play the guitar?" It was Paul. He'd finished his phone conversation and heard me playing.

"I used to—but it's been awhile." I set the guitar down and tried not to stare at Paul in his bathrobe. He was a hunk, no doubt. One of those babes that you see in the fashion magazines who you don't think you'll ever meet in person. You just had to avoid eye contact with Paul. If you caught a glimpse of those piercing baby-blues—it would be all over. You might lose yourself in them…

"Well, I'm done with the computer, if you want to use it."

I nodded. "Thanks. So who plays the guitar around here—you or Rose?"

"Oh, I used to play in a band in England in my younger days. That seems decades ago, but I still fart around on the guitar once in awhile. I taught Rose how to play that song she sang in *Michael*. Did you see the show?"

"Oh yea, I remember—'Sittin' on the Side of the Road in the Middle of Nowhere'." We both laughed. I didn't tell him that I thought Rose wasn't too good at singing or playing the guitar. Instead I remarked, "You did a good job teaching her to play. The guitar isn't just something you can pick up overnight."

Paul sat down and started playing the guitar, and I thought it best to move to the office so if Rose showed up she wouldn't think there was something going on between Paul and me. That was Rose's greatest fear she'd confided to Kurt and me—that Paul would fall in love with another woman. But I knew from my conversations with Paul that he was totally devoted and in love with her. She was and always had been the woman of his dreams. But celebrity life was tough on relationships, so I didn't want to give Rose any extra grief. I kept my distance from Paul.

And so I began my new adventure at writing a novel. I decided to write my life story as a fiction using the character of Grandma Jesse—me at seventy—as the narrator. That way I could be free to mix fact with fantasy for the sake of continuity. I also wouldn't be making any claims about who I may or may not be. I chose to take the archetype approach rather than actually claiming to be the fulfillment of the White Buffalo Woman legend.

As I entered deeper into the bowels of my book, however, I got deeper into the bowels of my own soul. I knew I was writing not only to express myself publicly but for my own healing. I knew Kurt would read it, so I left out parts I thought might offend him. Yet I knew some of the issues concerning our plural marriage relationship needed to be explored regardless of his feelings.

The book, *Heartsong*, took nearly the entire summer to write. I finished it the day Rose and Paul decided to sell their place and move back to Rose's home town in South Carolina. I tried to talk them both out of moving as we had all become good friends, and I hated to see them go. Paul had put so much effort into creating a paradise for Rose, and I hated to see them give it all up. From his custom-made rose inlaid floors in her bedroom to all of the custom rockwork Paul had painstakingly hauled in rocks himself for—it seemed like a labor of love that wasn't fully appreciated. I wasn't surprised to learn they divorced shortly afterward—just about the same time I left Higher Ground and got a divorce from Kurt.

After my first manuscript was written, I didn't know what to do next. I knew it needed editing before I sent it to publishers, but I didn't know what the next step should be. I felt prompted to travel to Salt Lake and give several unedited versions to my sister, Wendy, and a few to her friends. I also mailed a copy to my sister, Cheryle, in San Diego. I knew, somehow, that I also needed to travel to Alabama and give Patrick a copy. I felt anxious about him like perhaps he was in some type of danger. I knew Kurt would never approve of such a journey.

Then Kurt felt compelled to bring Christy back into the relationship. We ended up in a huge fight that turned violent. He knocked me to the floor in front of the children after I slapped him with a dishtowel. Afterwards, I bolted and left everything behind except for a few clothes and Ariel, my teen-aged daughter. Ariel wanted to attend high school in Salt Lake City, so we both ended up at Mom's. The other children were forced to stay with their dad and Christy as everyone felt that this would be best for everyone involved. (Except for me of course! I was shunned and labeled "an apostate" and left to my own devices.)

The white Subaru I was driving broke down a few days after my arrival in Salt Lake, and so I was stuck at my mom's whether I liked it or not. Fate or Destiny (also the name of the daughter I'd left behind as the oldest) had her way with me as usual.

Chapter Three—Cheryle

Shortly after I arrived in Salt Lake, my mother's family held a reunion, which included a Native American tribute to her family's charitable foundation set up to help send Indians on Mormon missions and to college at the BYU (Brigham Young University). A group of young people from the American Indian Services performed ceremonial dances in traditional costumes to the percussive beat of a drum circle. It was a dazzling demonstration which I thoroughly enjoyed, although I couldn't agree with the politics and practices of the American Indian Services. I did believe that they had good intentions to help Native Americans receive a higher education but to have them convert to Mormonism in order to go to the BYU was quite offensive to me.

As far as the LDS Indian missionary program; I believe Native Americans have far more authentic spiritual beliefs and teachings than Mormons do especially regarding the power of the spirit world. These teachings and ceremonies were given to them by the White Buffalo Calf Woman during the same time period that Christ was ministering on the Eastern continent. I felt this was to create balance in the world between female and male energies... yin/yang, right brain/left brain, passive/active. Unfortunately much of that knowledge was lost during the dark years of American history when the Christian influenced government conquered, destroyed or converted most Native Americans to their brand of Christianity.

And then Joseph Smith arrived on the scene along with the Book of Mormon—a fraudulent history of the so-called "Lamanites" described as a fallen and cursed or "darkened" race. Thus the spiritual practices of the Native Americans were further discredited and discarded as "barbaric." Later I learned that the Book of Mormon was stolen and plagiarized from the fictional novel "Manuscript Found" written by a Baptist preacher named Solomon Spaulding. His beliefs, along with Sidney Rigdon's, a Cambellite preacher, formed the foundation for the Book of Mormon and consequently Mormonism. Granted, both were based on the premise that the Christian church had fallen from truth and grace, but to introduce a fabricated religion based on deception was further insult and injustice to the Indians. Incidentally, Mormonism is my religious heritage back four generations through all four grandparents.

My investigation into earlier forms of Christianity—like Gnosticism— supplied many answers in my own spiritual quest, but I believed that the Earth-based Native American beliefs supplied even more. Unfortunately, many of the original "organic" elements of Christianity had been eradicated when first-century Essenes and Gnostic Christian "heretics" (Cathars) were slaughtered and their written works destroyed.

It's interesting that the relatively recent discovery of the Dead Sea Scrolls and the Nag Hammadi Library have been publicized much to the chagrin of organized Christian religion. Although English translations are readily available, few Christians have yet to take the time to study them. Perhaps the well-established churches discourage their study because it may upset their apple cart as those "heretical" teachings are based on "Gnosticism" which means to "know God for oneself" and without the need of any "medium" or "mediator."

I often wondered if I was purposefully sent down to this time and this heritage to heal the broken spiritual circle which had occurred throughout the centuries. If so, then oh, God, I needed help!

After the Indian tribal celebration, my oldest sister, Cheryle, and I got together. She'd flown in from San Diego and had brought gifts for everyone, which is her usual style. She's a practicing Shaman and Wiccan, and has followed her own spiritual path for many years. There was always a fertile conversation when the two of us connected—the two Geminis of the family. I'd sent her a copy of my *Heartsong* manuscript and she was full of questions. It wasn't until we got to Mom's house that we found some private time to talk.

"I really enjoyed your book, Janae, especially the part about Patrick. I've just been studying about spirit-journeying and have done some journeying of my own."

We then launched into a fascinating discussion about spirit-walking and soul-retrieval. She shared some interesting and intimate discoveries she'd made about herself and her past lives. I then showed her the strange mark of the white buffalo on my foot.

"I'm not sure what it all means, Cheryle, but I'm sure it's part of my spiritual path. My life's been filled with strange coincidences and I've always felt that a Divine Source has been leading me the entire time."

"You can say that again! Speaking of coincidences—or maybe intuitions—I saw these two books at a used bookstore. I felt prompted to buy them for you." She handed me the two paperbacks—*You'll See It When You Believe It* by Wayne Dyer and *Journey to Center* by Tom Crum.

"Didn't you mention something about Tom Crum in your manuscript? I thought you'd enjoy his latest book. Also, the spirit told me to give you these to help you along your journey." Cheryle handed me a large plastic bag filled with her handcrafted jewelry that was worth hundreds of dollars. I felt it was too expensive a gift and tried to refuse it.

"No, take it," she insisted. "I wanted to give you something to help you on your path and I thought if I gave you cash you might give it to Kurt and the kids. I know how you are. This is just for you. Use it however you feel necessary." My eyes filled with tears as I gave Cheryle a heartfelt hug. She was truly my spirit-sister, too.

Wayne Dyer's book was fascinating and explained a lot about why I was experiencing so many strange coincidences in my life. I was *seeing* what I was *believing!* But still I wondered whether it was just in *my own* head—*my own personal coincidences*—or was it bigger than that? Was God the divine force behind all of these extraordinary synchronicities and just witnessing his or her manifestations *through* me? Wayne Dyer seemed to have a lot of the answers I sought, and I truly connected with his way of expressing himself in the written word. He was a word mechanic like me using a lot of play on words. I hoped someday I would connect with him on a personal basis so I could ask him a few personal questions about my life's incredible manifestations.

As I journeyed into Tom Crum's book, *Journey to Center,* I reconnected with the delightful humor of one of my favorite mentors. When I got to the chapter called "Back in the USA," a couple of stories really hit home in another strange sort of coincidental way.

As John Denver's bodyguard, Tom dealt with a lot of crazy people. (He probably thought I was one, no doubt.) But I guess there were some John Denver fans who were even crazier than me. You really need to read Tom's book to fully appreciate Tom's sense of the absurd, but I'll try to paraphrase two of his stories, quoting their introductions.

> People can be different. I never knew how different until I was invited to work with John Denver as his bodyguard. In the mid-seventies John was one of the top entertainers in the world, doing two shows a night to packed houses of 18,000 people in the Madison Square Gardens of the world. I figured that it would be good basic aikido training to protect him from adoring fans, control drunks or disorderlies from

time to time, and spend some private time helping John
develop the skill of centering to create peace of mind in the
crazy world of celebrities. What I did not count on were
all the irrational folks out there who were trying to get to
him for one reason or another. I'm speaking of people who
inhabit other realms of reality, forcing me to rely not on
normal negotiation skills but on creative thinking. I needed
to jump into their world without questioning whose reality
was right.

His first story was about a man who had walked his two mules clear from
Missouri to Aspen just to talk to John Denver in person. His journey took
him two months and considering that amount of effort, I don't see why it
didn't earn him at least an audience with John. Tom negotiated with him,
thinking he was crazy of course. The Missourian told Tom that he was on
a "mission from God" to bring John a message. Tom politely told him that
John was out of town, but he would gladly deliver the message. He wanted
to let John Denver know that it was important that he not hide the truth from
the world anymore—that he was John the Baptist. He needed to declare it
to the world.

To make a long, very humorous story short, Tom asks the man, "Is John
the Baptist a true man of God?"

"Of course," came the emphatic reply, "a very important one."

"Well, then, as a man of God, he must be constantly speaking to, and
listening to, God for guidance. It must be incredible what John knows that
I don't know, with all that direct connection to God."

"Yep."

I could see him nodding with approval.

"Then there must be a reason for John Denver to withhold this kind of
statement. God is guiding him to do this for a reason. It all must be for a
good purpose. It's just that the purpose is yet to be known. God works in
mysterious ways…"

After Tom convinced the man that God was in charge and was keeping
the information from the public, the man was satisfied and left. I love Tom's
final statement: "I *am* glad he didn't ask, if that was the case, why the heck
God sent him to Aspen via mules."

His next story began with the introduction. "One other case took a
number of years to break through. It all started with a series of love letters
to John. No big deal—it was happening by the bagful in those days—but

if they got too insistent, bizarre, or voluminous (book-size), J.D.'s secretary would toss them in the "outward-bound" file and send them to me."

Tom then made the mistake of responding to one such case. And then the writer started writing to him instead of to John. He became her confidant. She was convinced that she and John were lovers, and that he had proposed marriage. At that point in the book I was nearly convinced that Tom was writing about me as I'd shared with Tom some intimate information about my intriguing coincidences with John's song lyrics. I was relieved to find that Tom had not publicly disclosed our correspondences but was telling a story about another lady who he considered "on the fringes" as she continued to send Tom personal items like her lace underwear.

Tom concludes: "I realized that different realities are as plentiful as cockroaches. The reality with the most advocates gets to be the standard for society. Who's to say that these fringe realities are *all* wrong?"

Tom's book was a tonic for my soul. I laughed out loud at myself and others who may be as crazy—or even crazier than me. But as Tom so generously offers—"who's to say that these fringe realities are *all* wrong?"

Chapter Four—Family of Friends

"Friends—I will remember you, think of you, pray for you,
And when another day is through,
I'll still be friends with you."

"There are those in this life who are friends from our
heavenly home."

"For a time between storms in the side of a mountain,
With another man's family—family of friends."

I know, I know—you don't want to hear another John Denver lyric, but *Oh God*, how can I help it? (Remember the movie?) He says everything I want to say so articulately. How I wish you were still alive, John!

Anyway, I'd hooked up with a family of friends in Salt Lake before I'd even thought about leaving Kurt. After Ariel and I arrived safely at Mom's, I called Joe—one of my best friends—to see if anything was going on for the weekend.

"Hey, Janae. You ought to come over to my apartment tonight. We're having a small gathering with a few people and this guy David is going to talk about some really far-out stuff. I think you'd really be interested in what he has to say."

Joe gave me the directions to his apartment and I hopped into the Subaru. It began snowing those big, juicy flakes you see at the beginning of snow season that stick to the ground like mush. My car was running lousy and had bald tires, so I wasn't sure if I would make it. I prayed as I pulled into the parking lot of K-Mart to get my bearings in the snow. I knew I'd missed the turn-off Joe had mentioned so I called him from a pay phone.

"Oh, you're right across the street from where we're at. Just drive straight east and you'll find the apartment complex."

I followed his instructions and landed on his doorstep just as a bolt of lightning struck a few hundred yards away.

"Wow! Did you see that!" Joe exclaimed as he opened the door. Of course, I had. It nearly knocked me off my feet!

Everyone inside was in a stir as the lightning bolt had been visible through the window.

"You must be one powerful lady to produce that kind of energy," commented the dark, handsome man standing in front whose presentation I'd interrupted. "Hi, I'm David" he said, grabbing my hand and pulling me into his embrace. The energy between us was electric.

"Sorry, I didn't mean to interrupt your meeting," I apologized.

"No problem. We were just getting started."

David then launched into an interesting conversation about awakening the twelve strands of DNA that we all have in our DNA structure. He explained that most of us are functioning on just two strands, but he'd learned a process of awakening the other ten strands in order for us to be fully awakened. People weren't fully awake and aware until all twelve strands of DNA were functioning. He then talked about the products he was promoting—precious metal minerals that helped awaken the strands of DNA. Some were made from ionized white gold and silver that had been chelated so the body's cells could readily accept them. He had brought some samples for all of us to try. We passed the minerals around in a circle and David offered a kind of prayer to help awaken our DNA. He also let us try a new formula he'd brought called GHB. He warned us that it powerfully brought on a loving state of oneness, and he couldn't guarantee what would happen after that.

I felt warm and cozy as everyone started to leave after the meeting was over. Elizabeth, one of my good friends who had also been a polygamist wife, left early as she wanted to spend time with her boyfriend. Her son, Joe, whom I'd met before and who was a real hunk stayed. David and his brother, Robert, and the my other friend, Joe, lingered for awhile after everyone else left. I was feeling rather expansive and more than a bit seductive from the GHB. I allowed myself to fantasize about how erotic it would be to have a sleep over with these four gorgeous men who'd stayed. As if they'd read my mind, they all encouraged me to stay the night. But I soon came to my senses (or not) and asked if any of them would follow me in their car so that I would make it home safely. David quickly volunteered, and I soon distanced myself from temptation realizing it may become one of those unfulfilled fantasies I would regret in the future. But I was still married to Kurt and my personal integrity always got in the way of my sexual explorations.

At Mom's house, I invited David in to warm up for a bit. We immediately got into an interesting conversation about health, Native American practices, and energy vortexes. I knew we had a lot in common—I'd never met anyone I could relate to so readily on so many different subjects. We got really deep, really fast. It almost frightened me. As he left, I offered him my *Heartsong* manuscript to read. He said that he was very interested in my life's story and looked forward to reading about it. I told him he could get to know me quicker and better if he just read my book. He kissed me tenderly on the hand and held it for a moment before leaving. Again I felt a bolt of electricity move between us—like when I first walked in Joe's apartment. Lightning does strike twice!

Chapter Five—David T.

During the next few days, I helped Ariel get registered and settled into my old Alma Mater—Highland High School. I was shocked at how much it had changed since I'd left 20 odd years ago. The atmosphere had changed from a cliquish, white, preppie school to a melting pot of racial diversity. I was startled to see blacks, whites and Chicanos wandering the halls in their distinctive cultural garb. Some displayed attitudes of gang members, and I began to have second thoughts about sending Ariel, who'd been home-schooled and sheltered all her life, to what I perceived as a threatening environment. But her enthusiasm prevailed, and she was excited to begin her new adventure of high school.

Mom had traveled to Yuma, Arizona for the winter, which left the large house on Dallin Street empty except for my older sister, Marsha, who was living in the downstairs apartment. Ariel moved into my younger sister Wendy's old bedroom, and I occupied Mom's room. My old bedroom had been turned back into a library with its large glass windows all around. We had stuck frosted sticky paper on all the windows when we'd first moved in so that I could maintain some privacy. The library was now cluttered with Mom's nick-knacks, which included an assortment of Native American artwork given to her as tokens of appreciation from the American Indian Services.

That Friday after Ariel and I had settled in, David called and invited me to spend Saturday with him in Payson where he and his brother, Robert, lived. I told him that my car wasn't running very well so if he wanted me to visit him, he'd have to pick me up. He agreed. Ariel said she'd be fine as she wanted to hang out with her older sister, Aubrey, who was living with her new husband, Mike, in Salt Lake. I gave David's home phone number to Ariel—in case of an emergency—as we left for Payson the next day.

Before going on to Payson, David wanted to show me something up Big Cottonwood Canyon and seemed full of anticipation as we drove part way up. He stopped at a pullout, and we both got out of the car. We went for a short walk in the fresh snow. I had my moccasin-boots on as if anticipating such an occasion. David had on smooth-soled street shoes, and I had to keep him from falling a couple of times. When we finally came to the designated spot, David pointed across the valley to a rock formation.

"Can you see it? Can you tell what it is?"

I followed his arm and extended finger to view the rock formation indicated. It was almost too obvious. It was the form of a buffalo. I smiled and nodded. "That's so cool! It's a buffalo!"

"No, look again," he whispered in my ear. "Notice the snow on it."

I laughed as I got the gist. "It's a white buffalo!" I exclaimed.

I turned around to meet the passion in David's eyes. It sparked passion in my own heart, a passion I hadn't felt for a long time—perhaps never! The intensity frightened me. We both stared at each other for an eternal moment.

"May I kiss you?" His words were unexpected but sincere.

My heart skipped. I was still officially married to Kurt, and I knew how he'd feel if I'd made such romantic advances. He'd nearly beat up Joe in a restaurant when he'd found out Joe had given me an "innocent" kiss. Even though doors seemed to be closing on Kurt's and my relationship, especially after the blow-up the day before Christy came back, was I ready to start a new romance with someone I'd just barely met and with my current life so up in the air? But the desire in David's eyes was pulling me in like a magnet. What harm could there be in just one kiss? I felt my body melt as he pulled me into him. His warm lips met mine, and my whole being exploded as fire ignited the passion between us. It was more than either of us could handle. A few moments later I pulled away in bittersweet resistance. How could I have opened this door? Oh, but it felt so good to step inside.

We walked back to the car warmed by the passion between us. We headed toward Payson and during the next two-hours we shared our hearts. I told him of my conflicted feelings concerning Kurt. He understood. He had gone through a painful divorce a few years before when his beliefs about Mormonism split his relationship with his wife. The split from his five children was painful. It still was. Divorce was not the answer for reconciling differences. But the feelings between us were real—very real. How could it all be reconciled?

David showed me around Payson and took me to one of his favorite spots—a warm springs. He said he and his brother, Robert, spent many a childhood day skinny-dipping there. He dreamed of someday owning it and of building a healing retreat. I shared one of my own dreams about building a healing retreat at a warm springs. I'd hoped it would be at Higher Ground in Montana—but presently I was open to almost anything. I was amazed by how synchronized our visions were. David inspired me, and I was tempted to strip off my clothes and hop in the warm springs naked and let nature take its course, but the temperature of the water versus the air was not conducive. It would have to be an adventure left for a warmer day.

It was getting late and David offered to show me the place he shared with Robert—a drab basement apartment fit for a couple of bachelor brothers, but it was cozy. David showed me his makeshift lab where he concocted his mineral formulas, and we got into an intricate discussion of the chelation process. I knew the person who produced his formulas for him and understood the principles behind the "vortex" process. David was amazed that I had enough background for the conversation. I had become interested in the process years before for building purposes—using chelated minerals mixed with adhesives to pour into forms that would look like marble. He said if I stayed the night he would take me over to our mutual friends' production plant to show me the whole process—equipment and all. How could I refuse such an offer?

David pulled out a bottle of wine he'd been saving for "special occasions" pouring us both a glass. We each took a sip and smiled. He led me into the living room and onto the couch and said he wanted to try something fun if I was game. After a few more sips of wine, I was game for just about anything. He filled his mouth with wine and then pulled me close indicating he wanted to kiss me. I obliged him and he gently spilled his mouth full of wine into mine during an intimate and erotic French kiss. I felt our lips getting wet with excitement. The fire between us was igniting, and I wanted to let go completely and be consumed by it. It felt warm and wonderful.

Just then the phone rang, quenching the mood. David rose to get it in the other room and when he came back, he said it was for me. My heart sank as I thought Ariel might be in trouble. Instead Kurt's voice boomed from the receiver.

"Janae, what the *hell* are you doing at some guy's house! I need you back home right now! Andrew's got a high fever and he needs you *bad*. We all need you *bad*. Everything's fallen apart since you left. You need to come home right now before you get yourself into any more trouble!"

Kurt's demanding and controlling voice rattled me. It still had a powerful effect even though he was 500 miles away.

"Kurt, I would love to come home if things were different—if you hadn't brought Christy back. Besides, my car is nearly broke down and it would never make it back to Montana even if I wanted it to."

"But Janae, Andrew is *really* sick. He needs you. How can you just leave all of your children and me behind? What kind of spiritual path are you following anyway?"

"Kurt…you'd never understand. Don't even try. Tell you what. David and I will say a prayer for you and Andrew… and all the kids. That's all I can offer right now. You're going to have to deal with it…with Christy."

Kurt tried to respond, but I hung up the phone before he could get his hooks any deeper into me. I felt empowered—maybe for the first time—in my relationship with Kurt.

I rehearsed the conversation as I slid in beside David under his arm.

"Now where were we?" I concluded.

I was exchanging my mouthful of wine with David when the phone rang again. "Don't answer it—or better yet—take it off the hook," I suggested. David complied.

Now we were truly alone as Robert, David's brother, had mysteriously disappeared. I felt my head spinning and the room spinning as I felt myself falling deeper and deeper into some unknown energy vortex. I wanted to lose myself in David's soul, but I knew if I did I would never find my way back. But maybe that wasn't such a bad thing. How could it be when it felt *so* good…*so* right? But still in the back of my mind was Kurt's voice scolding me…making me wrong. David sensed my confusion. He got up from the couch, and I noticed a bulge in his pants.

"Janae, let's take a break, before things get totally out of hand," he remarked and I agreed. He went to his bedroom and brought back a bundle of red cloth. "I wanted to show this to you when you came down. Maybe now is the right time. He sat down on the floor and crossed his legs, and I did the same across from him. He unrolled the red bundle to reveal a beautiful Native American peace pipe. The awe inside me escaped in a sigh.

"David, how beautiful!" It was more than just beautiful—it was magnificent. I was awestruck by the intricate totems carved into the stem and bowl. My own peace pipe paled in comparison. I wanted to know all of its history—the story behind it. I knew I wouldn't be disappointed…and I wasn't.

David had been inducted into the Navaho tribe by a well-known Mormon author, who specialized in Native American and Mormon folklore. She was one of my favorite authors and had taken a liking to David. (I couldn't imagine why.) David had miraculously climbed the precarious Native American totem pole because of his gifted spiritual prowess and been pronounced a pipe-carrier—a very high honor for a white man. He'd been gifted with a sacred ceremonial peace pipe in honor of his spiritual advancements. David took his role as a pipe-carrier very serious—as did I.

I so desired to smoke his sacred peace pipe with him and, as if he'd read my thoughts, he began to prepare for the sacred pipe ceremony. He carefully placed carved totems of a wolf, a bear, an eagle, and a buffalo in all four directions. He then lit some sage to dispel any negative energy in the sacred medicine circle. He loaded the pipe with some ceremonial tobacco and carefully lit it. He puffed on it until puffs of smoke were circling above his head. His voice was filled with resonant spiritual power as he pronounced prayers upon Kurt, Andrew and all of my other children at home who were suffering in the absence of their mother. He then said prayers for me as tears filled and flowed from my eyes. I wept for the first time in weeks at missing my children…and my home. My silent prayers joined his as the smoke from the peace pipe swirled around the room. I knew that God would hear our prayers and honor our requests for healing Andrew…and all of us.

After the peace pipe ceremony, we were both exhausted. We collapsed into David's bed where I relieved David of his excruciating hard-on with a hand job. "Perfect size," I thought to myself as we both drifted off to sleep.

The next morning we were awakened by the phone ringing. "I thought you took that thing off the hook last night," I sighed groggily.

"I did," replied David as he pulled himself out of bed. "Robert probably put it back on when he got home last night."

I dozed off to sleep to the muffled sounds of David in a heated conversation with someone on the other end of the phone. I assumed it was some business deal that had fallen through. David's hand coming around my waist awoke me the second time. "That was Kurt. He's mad as hell that you spent the night with me, but I was able to calm him down. I told him nothing happened."

I sighed. Well, technically nothing really did "happen" but I couldn't deny the intense feelings of love I felt for David and the strong connection we'd felt lying together in bed that night. I knew he felt it, too. It was something neither of us could deny.

"So what did you do—promise him that nothing would *ever* happen between us?" I queried sarcastically.

"Exactly. I really do believe Kurt loves you *immensely* and I wouldn't want to come between you and him and your children. Janae, believe me, you don't want to give up your entire family, your entire life for some romantic fling with someone like me. I love you *too* much to do that to you. You don't realize how much I've suffered since I divorced my wife and left all my children…. you just can't even imagine the pain. I wouldn't want that for you." David's voice faltered.

"David!" I shouted attempting to stir him from the delusion he was in. "Don't even start! How can you deny the deep connection we felt? I've never felt that way towards anyone, and I know I never will again. It was magical! It was incredible! And we were just kissing! Can you even imagine what it would be like to make love!"

David's resolve weakened with the thought of making love. "Well, who knows? Maybe I can work something out with Kurt if he realizes how much *I* love you, too. I mean he still has Christy up there with him and maybe a second man in the relationship could help balance things out. Perhaps if we could all get through our issues, this whole idea of community could really work."

"Thank God," I prayed half silently.

The ride to Salt Lake was awkwardly silent. David shared a bit about his previous attempts at community. He'd lived with a retired movie star in a so-called "cottage" up in Cottonwood Heights, not far from Mom's. A group of them enjoyed the freedom of unrestrained sex for several months until David began feeling like a gigolo to a bunch of older women. Very few men lived in the community, and the unbalanced sexual energy finally drove David away. He realized that there needed to be a balance of male and female energy for the dynamics of community to work. He thought maybe there was a chance for it up at Higher Ground in Montana—if Kurt would open up to the idea.

I was hopeful as David walked me to the door. He made no attempt at kissing me, as this was part of his agreement with Kurt. I was impressed by his honesty and integrity. But part of me wanted to throw up at the thought that Kurt had gotten his hooks in him.

The next morning David called. I could tell from his voice that he was more than a little upset. He had just talked with Kurt for over an hour attempting to console his fears and offering him a solution. David had even offered Kurt the gift of his sacred peace pipe in exchange for peace between them. Kurt had responded violently with the remark that if David even attempted to show up on his property with his peace pipe that he would, "Shove it up his ass and shoot him on sight."

"So much like Kurt," I said in disgust. "So much male ego energy. When will it ever stop!"

"I'm divorcing him," I told David resolutely. "That's the only way he will ever learn his lessons. He will have to lose me in order for him to be humbled. It's the only way."

"Well, that's your choice, Janae," David responded sadly. "I don't wish that for you or anyone else—but only you can know what's best for you. It's your spiritual path."

"Well, I'm filing for divorce tomorrow, David, because I feel it's the only answer. I hope you can support me in this. I really need your support."

David agreed to support me but made it very clear that we could have no sexual relations until after the divorce was finalized. This was the agreement he'd made with Kurt. David would honor our marriage—or what was left of it.

That morning I wrote Kurt a five-page letter explaining to him why I needed a divorce. I was clear and to the point. I could not live plural marriage the way we'd been living it. It was impossible to maintain peace in an imbalance of male and female energy. If Kurt would not accept David into the relationship, then I would have no other choice but to divorce him. I was not impressed with his responses to David's offerings of peace. His impudence concerning the peace pipe was not only offensive to David and me—but offensive to God. He needed to repent of his impudence and offer David a sincere apology. I would not to put up with his brutality any longer. I was finished. It was over and the only thing left was the paperwork. I was willing to have Kurt write up the divorce papers there in Montana, and I would then sign them here in Utah. I would agree to whatever terms he offered (which I would later live to regret). I was *that* adamant. I then signed the letter, sealed it and sent it off in the mail.

A few days later, Kurt called. He had received my letter. He begged me to come home and try another attempt at monogamy. Christy was willing to leave the relationship and go back to Lovell to live with her parents. Kurt just wanted me back home with him and the kids. Andrew was recovering, but he and the other kids were really missing me. How could I even think of leaving them for another man?

I told Kurt it was too late. I had fallen in love with someone else. The idea of going back to him and living the old life-style up in the back-woods had no appeal for me. Yes, I loved my children and would miss them terribly, but my heart was giving me no other choice. I felt this was the best decision for all of us. I asked again, if he would consider allowing David into the relationship, but Kurt replied that too much damage had been done to his heart. He was afraid that he would want to kill David if he ever met him. He still couldn't believe I had violated our marriage like that.

I was dumbfounded. Violated our marriage? Who had violated our marriage? Who was up there sleeping with another woman probably in our own bed? Who had brought a third woman into our marriage bed against my wishes and then had all three of them violate all of our marriage promises? Who had stepped out on me with two other strange women and then kept it secret for over ten years? Who had knocked me to the floor when I protested bringing Christy back and threatened to leave with all the kids? Who had violated our marriage? Me? Because I had fallen in love with an honorable man who loved me enough to offer in peace the object that was most sacred to him in an attempt to make an expanded relationship work? OH MY GOD!! Was Kurt on a crazy ego trip or what?! I hung up after mumbling, "Just send me the divorce papers so we can move on with our lives, Kurt. This is insane."

David visited me later in the week with a gift—a beautiful necklace with a large, Tourmaline stone pendant. He told me about how he'd found it in a pawnshop in Sedona, Arizona several years before. It had called to him and told him that the green stone was designed for a special type of healing. He couldn't figure out how to use this stone for healing but thought he would loan it to me to see if it could heal the damage that Kurt and my relationship had suffered since David felt somehow responsible for part of it. But I assured him that the relationship was over way before he had come along.

That night I went to bed feeling totally disgruntled with men. I had the wild thought that Kurt had somehow conspired with David as males to destroy all females—especially me. Right now I needed David's love more than ever to see me through the traumatic process of divorce, but he had become progressively more distant during the past few days. Was I imaging it—or was David falling out of love with me already? Maybe my aggressiveness in getting the divorce was a huge turn-off for him considering how he hated divorce. But couldn't he see the intentions behind this one? I loved David enough to sacrifice everything I held dear—even my own children! Couldn't he see the love that I had for him was *real?*

I was about to doze off with these discouraging thoughts rampaging through my mind when I felt a stirring within me which originated from the Tourmaline pendant that lay on my mother's dresser across the room. It drew me out of bed to pick it up and bring it back to bed with me. The full moon outside the window illuminated the green crystal with an eerie iridescence— the large stone reflecting the moonlight as I turned it over and over again in my palm. A startling thought passed through my mind—it wants to make love to me. Goose bumps shuddered throughout my body and erupted over my skin as I embraced the thought. Suddenly my pussy became warm, wet and inviting. I shimmied out off my underwear and brought the green stone down next to me. My clitoris was aroused, anxious for the stimulation. I gently rubbed the green stone around and around my clit, feeling the sexual energy of the stone getting me more and more aroused. Images of David came to mind as I continued to excite myself with his green stone. With the chain still attached, I slid the stone up inside my pussy as I continued masturbating my clitoris to full orgasm. I hadn't felt this sexually stimulated for years, and I felt *Kundalini* energy exploding inside me—just like with Patrick. Thoughts of Patrick and our *Kundalini* experiences together aroused me even more. My body recalled the time he had made love to me as the four elements—fire, water, earth and air—igniting each energy within me. Now it felt like the green stone was making love to me—as the moon element—and I wondered if Patrick had anything to do with it. But again my thoughts were drawn to David and the sensual feelings of love I'd experienced with him that first night, and it ignited the passion within me. They'd been so strong and the images of us in bed together were now flooding me with the same excitement until I exploded into orgasm after orgasm. Oh, God, how I loved David! Oh, God, how I loved Patrick! Oh, God, how I loved God!

I left David's green stone up inside me all night long. I felt it was healing me from some ancient wounds inflicted upon me during past lifetimes. I could feel the stone's energy vibrating into my womb, healing my uterus from the damage of this lifetime of eleven pregnancies. It was vibrant…and so real!

The next morning I called David and described my experience with his green healing stone. I didn't leave out any of the details. That afternoon he drove up to talk to me personally about my experiences with the stone. I could tell he'd had a change of heart as I graciously placed the stone in his hand. He stared at it for a moment—then breathed in its aroma.

"I hope you didn't wash it," he said.

"I didn't," I replied.

I hadn't heard anything from Kurt for about a week, and I was beginning to have doubts. I missed my children intensely, and my love for them began to weaken my resolutions about divorce. On Sunday I would fast and pray for some answers. Ariel was with Aubrey that day, so I spent the morning by myself in bed praying and reading the Bible. So many apprehensions filled my soul. Was God going to damn me to hell for my thoughts of "fornication" with David? I couldn't believe that God could be so cruel to inflict such pain on women as happens in polygamy. How could King David justify marrying hundreds of women? How could God justify such an abomination to women? I couldn't relate to a God who could be so unkind to women. Did he hate all females or just me? Why did I have to suffer so much pain as a woman? Would the pain ever end? God *must* be male to have made things the way they were. Where was the feminine aspect of God? Could the God I was raised to believe in ever understand a woman's heart? My heart was shattered as all of these questions and feelings passed through me. When would all of this be resolved so I could find peace within my soul?

Just then the doorbell rang. I sprang from my bed thinking it was David. I opened the door to find a Federal Express driver with a registered letter for me to sign. I signed it thinking it was unusual for Federal Express to deliver on Sunday. I opened the letter to find Kurt's rendering of the divorce papers.

They were official enough but absolutely ridiculous. He asked for full custody of all of the children with supervised visitation at his discretion. He also stated that I had "willingly abandoned my children" and that this was the reason for supervised visitation. I shook my head in disbelief. I couldn't believe the extent of his delusions. I knew I couldn't sign the papers "as is," but what were my choices? He wanted me to fight him so he could buy time. In the meantime, he would keep me from visiting the children, but, oh, how I missed them!

I knew he would use the children as pawns to get his way. It wasn't beneath him to use any tools to try to control an outcome. The holidays were coming—in fact Thanksgiving was the following Thursday—and I wanted to get this over so at least I'd be able to spend some time with my children. I prayed for answers. Just then the phone rang. It was Kurt calling to see if I'd received his letter. I could tell he was gloating thinking he had one-upped me. He knew I wouldn't sign the divorce papers.

"Well, you really think you have it over on me don't you?" I began. "I mean what's this bullshit about me 'willingly abandoning my children.' Is that the kind of lies you want our children to believe about their mother? That I willingly abandoned them?!"

"Well, that can always be changed later. But if you want to see your children at all for the holidays, you will have to sign it 'as is' so my lawyer can process it before the holidays. Otherwise it will take another few weeks to draw up another set of papers," Kurt bluntly stated.

"You mean, if I sign these papers, you'll make sure I can see my children for the holidays?"

"I don't see why not—but I can't make any promises. Salt Lake's a long way from here, and I don't know if I'll have the money to make the trip. I have to pay the lawyer, you know."

"Well, if I agree to pay the lawyer's fees and sign the papers as is, do you promise I can see the children?" I knew I wasn't thinking clearly, but the urgency to see my children after three long weeks was driving me insane. I felt Kurt could be reckoned with after he came to his senses—perhaps during the holiday season.

"Sure. I promise. The lawyer's fees are going to run about $500. You can send a check along with the papers in the mail tomorrow. The sooner I get them the better. Christy and I have had enough of your adulterous spirit. We just want to put this all behind us, too."

I had only $300 left to my name from the jewelry that Cheryle had given me to sell. But I knew that my mom's dividend checks from the oil companies would be arriving before Christmas. It usually came to a few thousand dollars after dividing it among my siblings. I told Kurt that I'd try to get all the money to him but was a little short. I would definitely get it to him when he brought the children down for Christmas. He told me to send what I could.

The next morning I reluctantly signed the divorce papers, folded up my last $300 in them, and mailed them off—regular mail. When I told my brother, Bruce, what I'd done, he had a fit. He said I had signed my own death sentence and would regret my decision for the rest of my life. I should have waited to talk to a lawyer before giving Kurt full custody of the kids, and that it was a big decision to make without legal counsel.

I knew he was right, but I had given up hope. I'd tried contacting Tapestry for Polygamy to see if they could provide free legal services, but they told me that since the children were in Montana that I would have to seek legal counsel in Montana. There was nothing they could do to help me there in Utah. I also asked my sister, Marsha, who was living in the basement apartment of Mom's if she might possibly move out and allow me and my children to live down there until I could secure a place for them. But she refused to help me and told me that it would be too hard on Mom. I knew if I could secure a place for them that Mom would loan me here Lumina van to go after them in Montana. But without the support of other family members or the Mormon Church (I'd even gone to Mom's bishop for help) that I'd have to settle in giving Kurt custody of the kids.

And I was so emotionally embattled that I'd given up the fight. I just wanted to be free of Kurt and all the drama of that relationship. I wanted to start a new life, and I felt that my children were probably better off right now in a stable environment with Christy as their mom. I could trust Christy, if not Kurt, to take good care of my kids. They knew her as their "other mother," and she'd always been good to them. Her whole soul was domesticated, whereas mine—I was like a wild bird trying to find somewhere to land.

I called David and told him what I'd done. The papers were signed and notarized, and as far as I was concerned I was divorced. I needed a shoulder to cry on as my emotions were running high. I needed the comfort of David right now.

David came up with his brother Robert that evening. I was a bit disappointed that he was with Robert as that meant he couldn't stay the night. I wanted so much to spend some intimate time with David even if it just meant holding him close. But David was adamant that he couldn't break his promise to Kurt—that as long as I was married, David would have no sexual contact with me. We would have to wait until the divorce was finalized. The three of us visited for a short time, and then I invited David into the library alone for some privacy. We sat down on the couch.

"David, I really need you to stay the night just to be with me. I am so missing my children and Thanksgiving's coming up the day after tomorrow. I've never spent the holidays alone and I don't know if I will survive."

"Janae, I know how difficult this must be for you right now, but I've really done some serious thinking about it. I've decided that if you really want me, then you'll have to marry me. I'm done playing this game of community and "free love." I'm really convinced that the only way community can work is by starting with a strong monogamous relationship and then expanding outward from there. All of the other scenarios just cause a lot of heartache and chaos. People need to form and maintain committed relationships before community can work. I know it's the only way, and I feel that the love between us is so strong that we can begin that process."

I was stunned. I didn't know what to say. David was proposing marriage to me, and I was filled with such mixed emotions. Sure, I loved David, but I still loved so many other men and wanted to explore intimacy with them. Patrick, Vaughn, Warren, Joe and even Ed came to mind. How could I jump from one monogamous relationship into another when I didn't even believe in monogamy? It seemed so restrictive—so unlike me. I needed time to think about it—time to explore my innermost feelings. I sat in silence, and I could tell David was a bit disappointed by my reaction to his proposal. He got up and went over to the shelves and pulled down a vase from the top shelf. I'd never noticed before, but it had a picture of a white buffalo on it. He looked at it then handed it to me.

"That's weird. I've never noticed this vase before in my mom's library. It's kind of pretty, isn't it?" I turned it over in my hands noticing the blue sky and clouds as the background to the white buffalo. It was similar to the portrait my mother painted of me as a child with blue sky and clouds in the background. It was hanging on the opposite wall of the library along with portraits of my brothers and sisters. She said I always had to be outside and I could never sit still very long for her to paint. It sounded so much like me—a Gemini—an air sign that just can't sit still. I then turned the vase over to see if the artist's name was on the bottom. Sure enough it was—and I was stunned. *It was David's last name.* I showed it to David. He laughed. "Well, *now* are you convinced? Isn't that enough evidence for you to know that we belong together?" I winced. The sign was striking yet I hesitated at the thoughts of being again trapped in a marriage.

"Let me think about it for a few days, and I'll get back to you," I said.

We went back into the living room where Robert was sitting. I invited them both to a party on Friday night that my group of friends was having. It would be at Penny's, a girlfriend who lived a short distance away. She had a Jacuzzi and we were told to bring swimsuits and our own booze. It promised to be fun. I knew all of my friends would be there. David and Robert assured me that they would try to make it if they could. It was Thanksgiving weekend and they had been invited to their own family gatherings, but by Friday they thought they could be free. Ariel was driving up to Montana on Wednesday with Aubrey and Mike to spend time with the family there. This meant I would be spending Thanksgiving alone. My heart sank at these thoughts as David and Robert got up to leave.

"Are you sure you can't spend the night with me, David?" I whispered in his ear. "My emotions are running so high, I don't think I can make it through by myself. Please stay with me."

"You're strong, Janae—you'll be fine. I'm afraid my emotions are running high also, and I don't think it would be wise. I'll see you on Friday. I promise."

Then he and Robert left.

Chapter Six—Only Women Bleed

The next morning I started my period—another indication that God is a man and hates women. What female God would create such an inconvenience every month? I thought it had the makings for a great song, so I decided to put my feelings into words just to pass the time. I was also reminiscing about how my grandmother died and how my mother still talks about that experience. She had left my grandmother alone on her deathbed to come up to see me in Paradise, Utah because I had just delivered my fourth child, Ariel, at home there. I always felt she regretted her decision to visit me that day, because it was that day her mother died. She bled to death of uterine cancer. And so I wrote this song about the legacy of women.

Only Women Bleed

> Hey, young girl, you're a woman now,
> Your breasts are full, your heart's on fire.
> The boy next door gives you a smile,
> It's not for you, but your friend by your side.
> And you bleed, only women bleed, girl…
> Only women bleed.
>
> Bobby comes home for a romp in the sheets,
> His college pals drag him off for some drinks.
> You sit home alone, wondering why,
> Those old time movies always make you cry.
> And you bleed, only women bleed, girl…
> Only women bleed.
>
> The sun coming up always makes you sick,
> And you wonder how you'll ever get through it.
> A look in the mirror for the things to come,

A Volkswagen figure makes you want to run.
And you bleed, only women bleed, girl…
Only women bleed.

Why didn't they tell you, why did everyone lie?
How could they explain the way it hurts inside?
You want to die, you try to die, why can't you die?
It's a girl they then lay next to your side
And you bleed, only women bleed, girl…
Only women bleed.

You sit all alone, watching her grow,
She looks like her daddy, will he ever know?
How long has it been—can't keep track of the years,
Or the tears, or the fears, oh, the tears.
And you bleed, only women bleed, girl…
Only women bleed.

She sits next to you and watches you die,
The sheets are stained and she wonders why.
The doctors never warned you it would be this way,
But both of you know—soon it will be okay.
And you bleed, only women bleed, girl…
Only women bleed.

That evening the doorbell rang. My heart leaped along with my feet as I hurried to the door. Maybe David had reconsidered. To my surprise and even greater delight, instead of David, there stood Vaughn. I hadn't seen him since Wendy and I had visited him in prison several years ago. I'd heard he'd gotten paroled for good behavior. I was astonished that he had come to me with such perfect timing. Of course Vaughn's timing was always perfect when it came to our synchronistic meetings.

"Vaughn!" I declared in delight. "What brings you to this neck of the woods? I thought you were all settled in Grand Junction, Colorado."

Vaughn's face was jovial and his eyes twinkled with mischief. He'd put on a few pounds and was shaved bald. He had the outward appearances of an ex-con, but I could tell a heart of gold still beat within him.

"Well, actually my son doesn't live too far from here, and he invited me to spend Thanksgiving weekend with him. I came up a few days early and drove by your house and noticed the Montana car in the driveway. I took a chance you might be down for the holidays, too."

I invited Vaughn to sit down on the couch with me as I poured out my heart concerning my life's adventures since we'd last talked. Hours went by as we caught up on all of the details of each other's lives. As we shared, the time and distance between us melted, and we both felt the yearnings to be close. I needed the comfort of a good man to hold me as I concluded the story of what had just transpired the past few days.

"You know I always thought Kurt was an asshole the way he treated you. I knew someday you'd wake up and smell the bullshit and get out of that relationship. It's about time."

Vaughn's arm came around me as he lifted me onto his lap. He cuddled me close, holding me on his lap, as I allowed my tears to express how much I missed my kids. Andrew was only a year and a half old, and I couldn't even imagine the fear and confusion he was feeling with his mother gone. I knew Jenny and Kelsey were probably both crying every night for me to come home, not to mention Jonathan and Jordan who probably couldn't understand why I would ever leave them. None of it made any sense to a child's mind. I cried for them and their feelings as well as for my own. Vaughn seemed to understand. He'd left his own two children when he'd gotten divorced. That was years ago, but I knew the pain would never go away—it might soften, but it would never leave.

On the other hand, how could I ever go back to Kurt and try to work things out? He was a belligerent, bull-headed patriarch who would never compromise. I never got to express my feelings with any guarantee of him hearing them. Most of the time, he shunned me thinking that women are just emotional basket-cases and that their feelings are invalid—especially when they're having their periods. I wished Kurt could be a bit more like Vaughn who seemed to be so present with my feelings. As we cuddled, I could feel the sexual energy rising between us and Vaughn's hands went up my shirt to caress my breasts. It felt so good to be touched in that way, and the sexual woman inside me awakened. As his hands ventured further down to my crotch, I cringed as I realized I was on my period.

"Sorry, it's that time of the month," I interrupted.

"Oh, I'm sorry," he said somewhat disappointed. I knew he felt my disappointment at his disappointment. "That doesn't mean we can't cuddle in bed, does it?" he replied consolingly.

"Not at all." I lead him into Mom's bedroom. I slipped off all my clothes except for my underwear. Vaughn did the same and we both slid into bed. His firm body saddled up against me as he spooned me underneath the covers. It felt so good to have a strong male body next to mine, and we both quickly fell asleep.

As the morning light filtered through my mother's sheers, I quietly slipped out of bed to change my pad. I was glad I hadn't had an accident that night with Vaughn in bed with me. Vaughn was still asleep as I slid back next to him. He stirred for a moment as my hand accidentally slipped through the slit in his boxers revealing an enormous hard-on. I wondered if he was aware of it—or was he just finishing up with a sexy dream. Nevertheless, it really turned me on. I couldn't believe how stroking his dick turned me on so. Again Vaughn stirred and opened his eyes. "You better be careful with that thing because it likes to play," he whispered.

"Well, if it doesn't mind getting bloody, I wouldn't mind playing with your one-eyed serpent. What do you say we try?"

"I don't know," replied Vaughn a bit wearily. "I've never screwed a woman on her period."

"Don't worry. It's not as bad as it seems. Kurt and I used to do it all the time. He was always such a horn-dog. Besides I'm not flowing much."

Before Vaughn could offer any more resistance, I climbed on top of him and gently slid his hard cock into my wet pussy. It felt *so* good. My body had a way of climaxing that only required a stiff cock underneath me. Vaughn became the passive partner as I went for it and exploded in a full-blown orgasm. I could tell that we orgasmed at the exact same time. "His timing is always impeccable," I said to myself as I carefully slid out of bed to grab a wet washcloth. The blood on the sheets was minimal and it was well worth it. I felt that I needed to put closure on my relationship with Kurt—and open up relationships with other men. I wondered what David would think when I told him. Would he be mad? I couldn't think any more about David when Vaughn was lying warm and wonderful next to me. He had always shown up for me and for now—that was all that counted.

Vaughn and I showered together and then he had to leave. He needed to spend time with his daughter and help get things ready for Thanksgiving weekend. He said he'd love to go to the party with me on Friday if I thought it would be okay. I told him I would be looking forward to it. He said he'd pick me up around 7:00.

I spent the next while cleaning up Mom's house. Wendy called and invited me to spend Thanksgiving with her and her husband, Jay. I filled her in on all the details concerning David and Vaughn. She warned me that I was getting myself into water that was way over my head and hoped I wouldn't regret it later. I told her that I felt like I was in a current that was drifting me exactly were I needed to go. Whatever spiritual path I was on was perfect for me at that time. I needed to learn the lessons these experiences were going to teach. Besides, the freedom I felt was exhilarating!

That afternoon the doorbell rang again. I couldn't guess who it could be this time—and I certainly never would as I opened the door. It was Warren, Wendy's former fiancé and my old publisher. I hadn't seen Warren in a coon's age. He only lived a few miles from Mom's house, and I wondered why he was here. He said he was looking for Wendy and wondered what had become of her. I invited Warren into the living room and we sat on the couch and talked. I told him that Wendy was currently married to whom she considered her "soul-mate," Jay. I could tell by the expression on Warren's face that he was a bit disappointed. He was one who was slow at expressing himself, which was one of the reasons Wendy had broken up with him. He just wasn't sure he wanted to commit himself to another relationship when his past marriage had turned so sour. He'd always felt that community was the way to go as it freed him up to express himself more authentically. Marriage seemed to exact from him things he wasn't willing to give. It made him accountable to another person for his time and whereabouts—and that didn't work for him.

As I shared my feelings concerning community and my vision in my book *Heartsong* (I was hoping Warren would publish it) he began to see the vision. I told him about my experiences with David and my spiritual connection with Patrick and how it made sense to me that the more free we are to express ourselves in the moment, in the passion of the moment, the more real we can be with each other. This idea really turned us both on. We then started to freely express the love we'd felt for each other over the years. It had been suppressed as we'd both been in other relationships—him with my sister, me with Kurt. But now, we were free to express those passionate feelings of love we'd held hidden that we'd never been able to express before. And those authentic feelings were hot and intense and it wasn't long before Warren and I were stripping off our clothes and making mad, passionate love.

It was some of the most wild and crazy sex I'd ever experienced and neither of us was concerned about the blood. It was so real and so spontaneous that I later remarked to Wendy—it was like a blood at-one-ment! To hell with the cross! I'd rather spill my blood in an erotic sexual encounter in order to create oneness then splatter it hanging on a cross. And so I did—twice in one day with two different men! And with no regrets!

Friday evening came and Vaughn arrived to pick me up for Penny's party. He declined the offer to make love before we left. It was a little too much blood for his vegetarian liking.

When we arrived at Penny's impressive home, many of my "family of friends" were already there. Joe and Pam, Gary and Natalie (Gary was a chiropractor), David G., Ross, Ed and Sharon, Elizabeth and her two sons,

Joe and Don (who resembled Brad Pitt). They were all situated in various sections of the house, sipping drinks. Vaughn had purchased a bottle of wine, and he took it into the kitchen for Penny to open. I could tell by the look in Vaughn's eyes that he was immediately star-struck with Penny; and by the look in Penny's eyes I could tell the feelings went both ways.

My heart sank, but I knew I had to let go of my jealous feelings if I were to survive at this game called "free love." But I still couldn't hide the hurt around Vaughn being so open with another woman when I had come to the party with him! Part of me hoped that David would show up, but part of me was terrified that he would. I hadn't talked to him about my previous day's sexual encounters. I didn't know if I dared. I knew it would break his heart and I still really cared about his feelings. I realized Wendy was right—I had really gotten myself into some deep water—without a floatie.

Wendy and Jay arrived a little later, and when I told her what had happened with Warren she couldn't help being irritated with me. "What are you trying to do, Janae, screw *all* of my old boyfriends?" Her and Jay left soon afterwards because the party was turning more wild than they could handle. About the time Wendy and Jay left, David and Robert arrived. I could tell that David was a bit out of sorts, and I didn't know whether or not he'd been drinking. I finally figured out he'd been downing some GHB and was in high spirits. He practically ignored me as he flaunted himself about with all the other women at the party. I was a bit perturbed with him, so I tried to make him jealous by sitting on Vaughn's lap. As he watched Vaughn fondling me, I think he got the picture. I could see the hurt in his eyes, but part of me didn't care. We seemed to be at war, and it was anyone's guess who would be the victor. I went for another drink, and Vaughn followed me into the kitchen to hit on Penny. They went into the bedroom and closed the door. I immediately got the picture.

Someone put on some dance music, so I decided to distract myself by dancing. I grabbed another David—David G—to dance with me. He was game. We danced for a few songs, and I felt a strange sort of connection with him also. Was I caught in some kind of spell in which all the men I came in contact with were sexually appealing? Was this what it meant to have my heart wide open? In a sense it felt good to be so open and responsive, but in another sense I could feel the painful drama I was creating that was ready to explode into something horrific. I didn't know if I was prepared for *that* melodrama.

Pam, Joe's girlfriend, had been dancing the swing with Don, Elizabeth's son, the Brad Pitt look-alike. Don had just gotten in from LA where he'd been doing some acting. He was in his early twenties, and I could tell that Pam was trying to get her hooks into him. I tried politely to cut in, for his sake of innocence, but Pam exploded at me and told me to get my own *damn* dance partner. She was having fun with Don. Don then used the opportunity to excuse himself and left with his brother, Joe, as they didn't want to get caught up in the drama. I didn't blame them. I didn't like the scene either.

I went upstairs and sat down next to Joe who was crying in his beer, so to speak. Pam wasn't paying any attention to him, and he'd witnessed her nasty reaction to me which bothered him. I asked Joe to dance, but he simply wasn't in the mood. Then someone suggested that everyone get into the Jacuzzi. Joe's eyes brightened as he offered to get in with me. I told him I didn't bring a swimsuit and he said it wouldn't be a problem—he didn't think anyone had brought suits. Most everyone ended up naked whenever they went hot-tubbing. I wasn't sure I was ready for that being on my period, so I declined.

Penny was still in the bedroom with Vaughn, and I wondered if she would be upset with everyone heading to the hot tub without her permission. No one seemed to object as Joe, Pam, Gary, Natalie, David and Robert filed downstairs to jump in naked. The rest of the party sat on couches and tried to ignore the orgasmic sounds reverberating through Penny's house. I curled up on one of Penny's couches and cried bitter tears, as I knew what was up with David and Vaughn—the two men I thought I loved! I figured I was being punished for my recent indiscretions—because God was a man, too!

Ross came over to me while I lay on the couch crying and offered some comfort. He was safe, and the warmth I felt from him was genuine. "Janae, just remember one thing—and one thing only. *You are perfect.* Everyone else in your life may seem a bit screwed up right now, but you, my dear, are perfect."

How could anyone, least of all Ross who hardly knew me, think I was perfect? I felt like I had literally screwed up my entire life in one felled swoop and had no idea how I would ever unscrew it. Maybe that was the key word here—*screw.* Why is it *screwing* always *screws* things up?

After about an hour or so of excruciating agony, the pulsating music ended and both David and Vaughn showed up on the scene. Vaughn asked David to take me home, as he wanted to spend the night with Penny. I conceded, as I just wanted to get home any way possible—as soon as possible.

David and I drove home in stark silence. No words were spoken. There was nothing left to say. David walked me to the door and the only words left in me were—"I never, *ever* want to see you again."

"As you wish," he replied and stepped off the doorstep into the night.

Chapter Seven—David G.

Vaughn went back to Grand Junction without even saying good-bye. The next time I saw Warren was about a week later, and he was a bit conflicted about the whole sexual freedom idea and wanted to take a step back and examine his true feelings. He shared David's views about starting with a committed relationship and expanding outward—but he wasn't sure if he was ready for such a commitment—especially with the sister of his ex-fiancé. In the meantime, I wasn't going to push any sexual agendas on anyone.

He did, however, hook me up with a friend who gave me a job in a Native American novelty shop at the Cottonwood Mall. This guy (I won't mention his name) is what I call a wanabe Indian and a real nut case. He first asked to know if I wanted to get paid commission on my sales or strictly an hourly wage—$8.00 per hour. I told him I preferred being paid by commission, and we agreed on 15% of my sales. I knew I was a good salesperson, and by mid-afternoon I had sold more than he usually did in a week. I had well surpassed my hourly wage, but for some reason that didn't make him happy. He tried to renegotiate my wages, but I wouldn't budge. It was about that time when David G walked through the door.

David was looking for some Native American Christmas cards to send out to his family and friends. I didn't realize that David was into Native American folklore until that moment. He said he wanted something with a picture of the White Buffalo Woman on it. I thought it was quite an interesting coincidence *that* he was in that store on *that* particular day asking for *that* particular item. But if you haven't guessed by now, my life runs on co-incidences or "incidences bringing people together." I showed him where the Native American Christmas cards were and together we found a perfect card set with a beautiful depiction of the White Buffalo Woman stepping forth from a white buffalo holding her sacred peace pipe in both hands. David was delighted with the find.

"If you don't mind me asking, David, but what makes you so interested in the White Buffalo Woman?" He then proceeded to tell me the following story.

One day when he was sitting at his office desk there was a knock at the door. When he opened it, there was a Sioux Chief whom David had never met. The chief told David that he'd been directed to him specifically because he had a pure heart. He invited David to go on a journey with him to where the sacred peace pipe that the White Buffalo Woman had brought was being kept. It had been passed down through the generations by a sacred clan called the "Pipekeepers" of the Lakota Sioux tribe. They were located in Green Grass, South Dakota, which is where the chief took David.

Although he was not given the privilege of seeing the sacred peace pipe— no white man has ever had that opportunity—David was told that he would someday be given the honor. The day would soon come when there would be a healing of all the tribes on the earth and the fences between the tribes would be broken down and all would live as one tribe. In that day the White Buffalo Woman would return and claim the sacred pipe and perform the sacred ceremony of returning to oneness.

I was dumbfounded as I listened to David tell his story. Then as his final comment he stated, "The Pipekeeper shared a curious prophecy before I left. He told me that I would soon be dancing with the White Buffalo Woman."

This sent shivers up my spine as the image of David and I dancing together the previous weekend was brought to mind. I remembered the mystical energy that had surrounded the two of us as we danced. I wanted to share with David some of my own experiences with the White Buffalo legend, but I knew with the storekeeper keeping an eye on me, that this was not the time or place.

It wasn't until years later, when the same Sioux Chief paid us a visit at our healing center in Draper that the story was brought up again. But that is another story for another chapter.

By the way, the storekeeper fired me the next day after I asked for my commissions for the previous day which amounted to over $200. (I really needed the money.) He told me he couldn't afford me at that price. A few months later his store went out of business. Go figure.

Chapter Eight—Patrick

The next time I saw Warren I was struck with some unexpected tragic news. He first asked me how my job was going at the Native American store. I told him I'd been fired after the first day of work but it was fine as the reason I'd been sent there was made pretty obvious. I didn't go into any details about my meeting with David G, as that kind of thing is a bit hard to explain without an exhaustive history. I then asked Warren how I could get a hold of Patrick as I felt it was timely that I contact him. I had a premonition that his life was in danger.

"Don't tell me you haven't heard?" Warren acted surprised. "Patrick was killed a few weeks ago. Everyone thinks he was murdered shortly after he was aired on the Art Bell show. Some of us believe he said too much and was taken out. Others say he simply died of a heart attack. I suppose it's all up for debate."

I was stunned. I couldn't believe it! I'd known after listening to some tapes of one of his lectures (that a mutual friend of ours had loaned me) that Patrick was in deep trouble. According to the tapes, Patrick's brother, Cheeway, and a group of archeologists had been murdered in a mysterious cave-in somewhere near Mexico City. I felt that after the holidays were over, I would travel to Patrick's home in Alabama to warn Patrick of the impending danger I'd sensed. I tried several times after leaving Montana to contact him at his old phone number, but all I got was his answering service. Now it was too late, and I was devastated. "How could this be possible?" I questioned more to myself than to Warren.

I then told Warren how I'd met Ginny (the mutual friend of ours) in Sugarhouse Park the previous summer. She'd generously loaned me some tapes she'd received at a seminar Patrick gave. She told me that they were "unbelievable" but that I might be interested in them since I knew Patrick. No one knew how *well* I knew Patrick, as some of the spiritual experiences we'd shared were very personal and hard to explain to anyone who had no concept about how the spirit world works. For many years I kept the story private until I finally shared it in my book, *Heartsong*. Although I've shared it with a select few, the manuscript (to this date) has yet to be published.

Patrick's tapes which Ginny loaned me were mind boggling. They were right out of a "Raiders of the Lost Ark" movie—but for real! His brother, Cheeway, and a group of his archeologist colleagues had gone to the Yucatan Peninsula to investigate some ancient temple ruins. Patrick believed that certain temple sites and pyramids were built on natural vortexes or doorways. The shamans or holy men knew this and also knew the process in which they could be opened. Patrick believed the shamans left writings on the temple walls containing these instructions. Cheeway and his colleagues were determined to take home, in the form of charcoal rubbings on large pieces of paper, the instructions to be later translated. But then came the rest of the story.

As they are doing their work of obtaining the rubbings, they notice a man dressed in the robes of a Catholic Priest following them. He seems to appear at every archeological site, carefully observing their every action. Patrick states in his tapes that he believes the priest is part of the infamous "Illuminati." How he comes to this conclusion, I have no idea. A few days later, Patrick is called home on a family emergency. While he's gone, the entire party is killed in a mysterious accident—one of the temples collapses on them. Patrick suspects foul play and desperately tries to get this information out to the public to save his own skin. In a desperate attempt, he goes on the Art Bell radio program. I'm not sure what he says, but a week later, Patrick dies of a mysterious heart attack although he has no history of a heart condition.

I asked Warren if he knew where I could get the tapes of the Art Bell show. Warren tells me he can get them for me, which he does. I listened to the tapes but couldn't put my finger on anything that would implicate Patrick's involvement with the Illuminati or the Catholic Church. He does, however, advertise concerning his seminars where he offers to give further information to anyone who is interested. I supposed he was trying to play it safe even though it still got him killed.

Although I was unable to contact Patrick in the physical world, I still maintain contact with him in the world of spirit. I know he is one of my spirit guides who are directing my every move. He is presently involved with the writing of this book as I feel him now as I'm writing about him. Thank you, Patrick, for your life, your spirit, and your message of oneness to the world. I'm sorry that Kurt burnt all your books and tapes in his rage of jealousy, but I pray that this type of energy will be dispelled so that the truth of our oneness can exist, once and for all. I love you—forever!

(Note: Patrick's son, White Raven, later on published Patrick's manuscripts concerning his last few years on Mother Earth. The books are part of "The Red Path Adventure Series" entitled *The Watchers of the Shadow and the Light, The Brotherhood* and *Lumen*. All Patrick's books can be obtained through Heartsong Healing Center or iuniverse Publishing Co.)

Chapter Nine—Ed

It wasn't long before the word was out that I was divorced and available. Every available man in our group of friends—and even the unavailable ones—seemed to want to "date" me. For several days after my ungracious encounter with David T (who I never saw again until after we'd both remarried), I went into recovery from the "screw-ups." But Ed kept calling me to go to lunch with him, so I finally gave in. He took me to an oriental restaurant just up the street from Mom's and basically cried in his egg flower soup. He'd just broken up with Sharon, who tried to kill herself on a weekly basis, and said he was fed up with all the drama. He called me because he needed a shoulder to cry on and felt I would understand after my recent divorce from Kurt.

The first time I'd met Ed was at a meeting I was asked to give at Alan's (the ex-husband of a good friend) apartment. A mutual friend, Mary, had asked me to do a presentation on my book *Becoming One*, as the principles in the book, she thought, would be beneficial to our "family of friends." Ed, who was half Native American and half Mexican, heckled me throughout the entire meeting. It almost got to the point of being rude, so I asked him to leave if he didn't have anything positive to say—which he, Joe and Pam did. The rest of the audience finally "got" what I was trying to put across—that multiple relationships needed to be done honestly and in the open for them to work.

Now as Ed was expressing himself concerning his recent break-up with Sharon, he finally "got" what I'd been trying to say at the meeting. I told Ed that I'd be glad to loan him a copy of *Becoming One* if he wanted to better understand the principles of oneness. He said he'd probably like that. I didn't have another manuscript of *Heartsong* as David hadn't given back his copy, and I wasn't sure Ed was ready for it anyway.

The following Saturday Ed called to see if I'd be interested in coming to dinner at his place. He told me that one of his favorite things was to cook for people and promised to put out some real Mexican fare. I'm a sucker for good Mexican food, so I agreed to come over, although in the back of my mind I was suspicious. Ed assured me that there wouldn't be any "funny business" as his teenaged daughter, Alene, was living with him. It was merely a dinner between friends.

Ed picked me up at Mom's since I hadn't gotten the Subaru fixed yet. Besides, I had a tendency to get lost in big cities having spent the last 15 years of my existence in the woods. I could trail blaze like Daniel Boone in the wild, but to negotiate the streets of Salt Lake—I was lost. I guess it wasn't one of the programs in my mental computer God blessed me with. It's a "girl thing," I must confess.

Ed introduced me to Alene who was in the midst of cleaning up poop from her new puppy. The dog was cute—the messes were not. I didn't want to get involved in the clean-up, so I made myself comfortable on the couch while Ed served me a glass of red wine. He told me to relax while he finished preparing his "Mexican Fiesta." He'd prepared tamales, enchiladas and tortillas—the real Mexican way. As he served one dish after another, my stomach soon got "fed-up." The food was excellent and the wine intoxicating, and Ed knew he had me in his power. He joined me on the couch and offered a foot rub—something else he enjoyed doing for people. With one bare foot in his lap—I was putty in his hands. And of course Ed didn't just stop at my feet. As soon as Alene was safely in bed and out of hearing range, Ed offered to finish the massage in his bedroom. I was too inebriated and feeling good to refuse. Besides, the last full body massage I'd had was from Kurt back in Montana. And I must admit—I'm a massage addict.

Well, the rest is just the history of man and womankind. Man sees woman. Man wants woman. Man gets woman drunk. Man gives woman massage. Man gets his way with woman. I guess we, as women, shouldn't complain. I mean, look at all the work we put men through just to get what *we want, too*—to be fucked. I mean is fucking such a bad thing? Maybe for some women who are still in the Ice Age, but for modern women who have come to know the value of orgasms—it's not such a bad thing. I guess it's just the stigma attached to fucking that gets us all into a guilt trip. I mean if we were just in our own natural state of being—fucking would just be another biological function—like taking a shit (as Joe describes it). But somehow, once you've opened the door to fucking, the dynamics of the relationship changes. Somehow ownership of the relationship comes into play, and attachments, control dramas, and all the little games we humans seem to want to play with each other get in the way. Wouldn't it just be easier if we were like dogs? I mean dogs have such a sweet, simple life. I even thought of a list of ten reasons why dogs rule.

Ten Reasons Why Dogs Rule

1. Dogs can roam wherever they want without the fear of being arrested for trespassing.

2. Dogs can poop wherever they want and have someone else clean up their shit.

3. Dogs can pee anywhere, anytime and not have to worry about it.

4. Dogs can screw any bitch in the neighborhood and be considered a great stud.

5. Bitches can screw any dogs in the neighborhood and not worry about being called a "fucking bitch".

6. Dogs don't have to worry about what they are going to wear every day. In fact, they don't wear anything and don't worry about getting arrested for indecent exposure.

7. Dogs get fed every day without having to cook or clean up after themselves.

8. Dogs can express their feelings freely with only the threat of being sent to the doghouse.

9. If they're sent to the doghouse, they don't have a problem with it.

10. Dogs can give and receive pure unconditional love freely without any strings attached.

So who are the real masters of this planet? The ones at which end of the leash? Just some questions to ask yourself.

For the next month or so, I played the dog's life and screwed every Tom, Dick and Harry that came along. Of course their names weren't Tom, Dick, or Harry—but I'd better not mention names for the sake of discretion. Actually there weren't that many and it only lasted a few months until Valentine's Day—when I didn't receive a darn thing from any of them. Go figure. I wasn't special to any of them—just easy. I guess there was a need in me to sow the wild oats I'd never sown in my younger days. Or maybe I was playing the part of the "fucking bitch" and just getting back at every dog in town. It was freedom to the max and good fun—until it wasn't. Or until I woke up and found that there were other things in life besides fucking. And fucking became old after awhile, especially when the dramas came into play.

Chapter Ten—Joe and Pam

And so along came the Joe and Pam drama—or should I say "the never-ending drama." Let me first give you a brief background so you know how it all started.

It all began when Mary, (an older woman with an agenda to start a "holy order") got my sister Wendy, Alan, Joe and herself involved in a "foursquare marriage." For those who don't understand fundamentalist Mormon lingo, a foursquare marriage is simply *a menage a quatre* (four people fucking). Well, this meant a lot more to Mary and Wendy than it did to Joe. I'm not exactly sure what Alan's take on all of it was, as I never had a conversation with him about it. But according to Mary and Wendy, the four of them were committed in a marriage relationship and had all the rights and privileges of a "married foursome."

Several weeks after the foursquare marriage was consummated, Pam came along and stole Joe's heart. At least that is the story she tells everyone. It was a "mystical experience" according to her. She was down and out, depressed in her bed, when the "spirit" told her to get up and go down to the local bar in Bountiful to find "the man of her dreams." And there was Joe sitting at *her* usual table with some friends. Immediately Pam was taken by Joe and asked him to dance. I'm sure she was wearing one of her "come and get me" outfits, which all men fall victim to. It wasn't long before Pam had cast her spell on Joe and had her way with him. Her hooks in him were deep and menacing; and when Joe tried to free himself from her to return to Wendy or Mary, Pam made it very clear that this wasn't going to work for her. Joe was *hers* and *hers* alone—and that was that! She even convinced Joe that they were "soul mates." That's always the final nail in any relationship coffin.

This all happened, by the way, while Wendy was still in a relationship with Jay, her "soul mate." How she figured *that* was going to work as part of the expanded relationship, I never quite understood. I think Jay and her were on the outs, and she was just getting back at him for not "getting it" about expanded relationships. I'm not sure that anyone "gets it" including me, but it all just seems to make sense somehow to those "in the know." Anyway, Wendy told me how Pam and she got into a huge cat-fight at a local dance club after Joe tried to dance with Wendy. Finally, Jay and she left after Wendy got upset that Pam verbally attacked her in the ladies' room

So this is the background I had when I meet Joe and Pam for the first time. Wendy also believed that Joe is the "Joe" in John Denver's song, "Joseph and Joe," so I was quite curious to meet him. Well, the first time I met Joe we experienced an incredible connection, as we seemed to be on the same page and speaking the same language. We related deeply to each another and thus began our "relationship". But then, along came Pam on the scene who is more than a bit concerned about Joe and my connection (even though they'd only been dating for less than a month and Joe had been clear from the start that *he* was *not* monogamous, Pam clearly was). So when Joe makes a pass at me at one of Alan's gatherings at his apartment, Pam bristles and shows her claws. I'm not sure how I feel about all of this either since I'm still married to Kurt and not ready to get involved with another man even though Kurt is still with Christy *and* Sandy.

But a few months later, after my divorce from Kurt and my false-starts with David, Vaughn and Warren, I'm ready to pursue a more intimate relationship with Joe, in spite of his attachments with Pam.

So Mary comes up with a plan. Joe is renting space in her one-bedroom apartment, which seems to work out nicely until Pam enters the picture. Pam insists that either Mary or Joe move out so she can know that Joe isn't sleeping with Mary while he's in relationship with her. Mary resents Pam's manipulating request as up until now, things have been working rather well between Joe and Mary.

One night Mary calls me on the phone and tells me that Joe is interested in hooking up with me, and that she will be out of the apartment that night. I'm being set up, but I realize that I, too, have my own axe to grind with Pam. (I still held a lot of resentment towards her and the way she treated Joe and me at Penny's party in the hot-tub scene with her and David also involved. I suspected that they'd had sex together in the Jacuzzi, which I never took the time to validate. I admit it was my own story but I was sticking to it, which was creating a lot of resentment towards Pam.)

And so that night I showed up at Mary and Joe's apartment, looking for some action. Joe is all too willing to comply. In the midst of our "love-making," the phone rings and Joe insists on answering it. It's Pam. She wants to make sure Joe isn't up to "no good." He assures her that he is being *very* good (yes, he is) but Pam suspects something is up and keeps calling Joe and he keeps *answering the damn phone as if Pam is his conscience.* The whole scene is troubling for me, and I vow never to return to a sexual space again until things are cleared up between Joe and Pam. Joe assures me that he will take care of it. That he really wants to be in an open, *honest* relationship with both Pam and me. It's just that Pam isn't "getting it."

A week or so later, Elizabeth and I decide to go visit Joe at his apartment. Again, Mary has set up the whole thing to break Joe loose from his relationship with Pam. Of course, we're all doing it for Joe's sake as we all feel he's trapped in something he can't get out of on his own. The three of us, Elizabeth, Joe and I, end up in a *menage a trois,* (which I find out six years later he never tells Pam about). I realize that this whole relationship dynamics doesn't work, and I tell Joe that until he comes clean with Pam about his and my relationship that sex is off. He agrees, and a month or two later, he invites Judy and me (Judy's in my next chapter) up to his cabin for a work project.

Of course Pam is invited, too, and after an icy encounter, she, with her usual dramatic flair, tells me, "You'd better leave Joe alone—OR ELSE! Aren't you woman enough to get your *own* man because Joe isn't the slightest bit interested in you sexually." I didn't want to burst her bubble and tell her that Joe and I had already been sleeping together on several occasions, but that Joe isn't man enough to *tell it to her face.* I knew if I'd revealed that tidbit of information, she might erupt into the "OR ELSE" mode and we'd end up in a cat-fight, which is *so* unladylike. Joe frankly wasn't worth it at that point anyway.

During the following seven years I watched Joe go from a spiritual, health conscious, physically attractive male to a smoking, drinking, drug-addict. (I know that's a harsh observation, but I call it how I see it.) Pam had finally succeeded in bringing someone down to her level so that they could enjoy some sort of "oneness" together. During those years, we got together occasionally, and each time Pam shared with me her latest drama concerning her children, Joe's kids and his ex-wife, or her latest catfight with another woman because of Joe's sexual indiscretions. I learned to keep Pam at a safe distance to avoid all the melodrama.

For example, there was the "Mary's books drama." Mary had generously donated all of her books to Joe as a gift to the "family of friends." It was an extremely large collection of books, including a selection of spiritual reference books like the Baghavad Gita, the Tao Te Ching, the Dead Sea Scrolls, the Nag Hammadi texts, the Kama Sutra, the Vedas, the Torah, the Zohar, etc. There were boxes and boxes full of books, which Joe stored for a long period in a storage unit. For a while they were displayed carefully on shelves at our Higher Ground Healing Center in Draper, but that was short-lived. I volunteered to put them in my storage unit when I moved to Las Vegas, but Pam insisted that they keep possession of them as Mary had placed them in

Joe's care. So they were stored in some large storage crates in Joe's basement for another year or so.

Then I receive a call from Joe out of the clear blue. He is getting rid of Mary's books and do I want some of them? *Of course I want some of them!* I want *all* of them, which is what I'd said to him before I'd moved. I told Joe that Brad (you'll meet him in a later chapter) and I were moving back to Salt Lake in the next month or two and could he wait until we moved back to move the books. I heard a background conversation with Pam. No, that wouldn't work. Pam wanted the books out of *her* house *NOW!* I told Joe that I would be up in a week or so and if he could possibly put them outside in the protected crates that I would be glad to go through them when I was up next. Again I hear a background conversation with Pam. Joe then tells me that they would "go through the books 'by the spirit' and separate out the ones they felt I would be interested in." The rest would be going to the dump.

I was dumbfounded and started to react emotionally to Joe about how valuable many of those books are and that I would be glad to take *all* of them off of their hands as soon as I could. Pam then grabs the phone. "Janae, can't you take 'no' for an answer?" Somehow this triggered something deep inside me that hadn't been healed from my past. An avalanche of reactive words was building inside me ready to explode, but instead, I simply said, "No," and hung up. A few minutes later Joe calls back and talks with Brad about how it would be fine for them to leave the books by the side of the house until I could go through them. A few weeks later I do just that. As I'm loading the last box of books into Brad's truck, Pam comes out carrying a copy of my *Heartsong* manuscript which I had painstakingly copied and given to them to read. As a final slap in the face, Pam hands it to me and remarks, "Sorry, Janae, we don't have time to read this one either."

The books that I now have in my possession are valuable gifts from God—or should I say from Mary—bless her heart. (Joe said he talked with Mary who said she didn't want them back as she had no room in her tiny home.)

Then there was the time Joe and Pam were coming to Vegas (where we were living at the time) to get married and didn't even invite Brad and me to their wedding. I got my feelings a bit crushed as I thought we were considered some of their "closest friends." But then we found out that the wedding was just another excuse to have one of their ecstasy parties, and we were glad that we hadn't been invited. The whole drug scene was definitely the turning point in our relationship with Joe and Pam as Brad and I were very clear that drugs would not to be part of our life. Our lifestyle is based on health and wholeness, and as I watch Joe and Pam struggle with health problems, (Pam struggles with fibromyalgia and female problems; Joe with severe back pain),

I realize that our lives are the reflection of our choices. Our choices are how we learn—and sometimes we make poor choices with poor results.

But I still love Pam and Joe dearly and (believe it or not) consider them some of my closest friends. I must admit that Pam's gifting me with Wayne Dyer's book, *The Power of Intention* on CDs was a turning point in my life. I really learned to apply these principles of intentional creation, and began to realize that the clearer our intention is—the clearer our creation. Also, Brad and I have learned so much from their relationship dramas, which have helped us see ours more clearly. They are our perfect mirrors. Sometimes our greatest learning comes from observing the relationships of others. And only time will tell whether or not we will ever get past the drama and into a place of unconditional love.

Chapter Eleven—Jerry and Judy

Jerry was one of those choices that I wasn't sure was a good or a bad one. Of course, if it wasn't for Jerry, I wouldn't have met Judy—who was a *real* sweetheart.

I met Jerry at an MLM meeting that Wendy's ex-husband, Richard, dragged me to. (Don't even ask me about Richard—*that one was definitely* on the "poor choice list.") I got convinced about the MLM product line after Richard demonstrated one of the lotions on me as having properties that turn women on. The Eucalyptus oil in the lotion definitely had warming qualities and Richard definitely took advantage of them. (Yes, I know what you're thinking—but it's just another one of my "hound-dog" stories.)

Jerry, sporting shorts, sandals and a beret, was the MLM presenter. For a man in his seventies, he emitted his own kind of sex appeal. His long white hair was neatly tied in a ponytail and he looked like an ancient born-again hippie. His free spirit was attractive, and as he dazzled his audience with his bullshit, the thought entered my mind, "Can he still get it up?"

As if Jerry had heard my thoughts, he made a beeline for Richard and me after the presentation. Richard and Jerry were obviously friends as they shared with each other their recent MLM exploits. Jerry was curious about Richard's new female friend, and when Richard introduced me as his ex-sister-in-law, Jerry figured I was fair game. He followed Richard and me back to Mom's and the three of us talked for a short while in the kitchen. He wanted to know all about my background and history, so I handed him a copy of *Heartsong* (by then I had made other copies) and told him to read it as it would be the quickest and easiest way to get to know me (and what he was in for).

He stayed up all that night reading it. I was impressed. The next morning he called and invited me to attend Unity Church with him the following day—Sunday. I told him I had a date that night with Ed (The Mexican Fiesta Night), and told him I would meet him there the next morning. He offered to pick me up, but I knew by the address that it wasn't far from where I lived.

That morning Ed offered to drop me off at Unity after he prepared some authentic chorizo egg burritos for breakfast. By the time I met Jerry at Unity,

I was so sick to my stomach on Mexican food that I was ready to vomit. My system was not used to all the pork and spices (including the hot tamale Ed shared in bed with me that night) and I was on system overload. A member of the congregation found me in the ladies' room puking my guts out and offered to do some Reiki on me, which really helped. I knew my energies were *way* out of alignment, but still, I was up for a new adventure with Jerry.

I enjoyed Unity's easy-going atmosphere, which included a live band and guided meditations; so different from the anesthetic Mormon worship, which included organ funeral music and cryptic tirades. After the meeting, the Unity members enjoyed a coffee break gathering, where they could actually socialize. This was new and exciting, and Jerry introduced me to a few of his friends, bringing me into his Unity circle.

After the coffee break, Jerry offered to take me to his place so that I could meet his sweetheart, Judy. This was the first time he talked about a "sweetheart." I'd assumed (assume means making an "ass" out of "u" and "me") that Jerry was single. He then explained that Jerry and Judy enjoyed an "open relationship." That they had evolved beyond their jealousies and were both free to experience whatever relationships "spirit" drew them into. Now this was a refreshing thought. But by now I questioned the meaning of "spirit" realizing it probably meant "man's natural tendencies toward horniness."

To make a point of how "open" Jerry and Judy's relationship was, as soon as Jerry got me into his small trailerhouse, he started to undress me. I could see Judy out of the corner of my eye on the phone in the bedroom. "What the heck," I thought. I was willing to "go along with the spirit" especially after Jerry's hard-on came up along side my naked thighs. It was enormous! "Wow," I thought to myself. "This will be an unforgettable experience!"

Jerry did me standing up and then finished me on the couch—in full sight and hearing range of Judy. It was quite erotic, but I could tell by the look on Judy's face, that she wasn't as "free a spirit" as Jerry led me to believe. She told him to come into the bedroom—alone—so she could talk to him. I knew he was in trouble. For a few minutes I sat alone on the couch wondering, "Why do I get myself into such shit?"

But when Jerry came out, he had a smile on his face. He must have been convincing as he invited me to join Judy and him in bed. We all cuddled up in the king-size bed that spanned the entire bedroom. Judy insisted on being in the middle, which was perfect, as she was even more cuddly than Jerry was. By morning Jerry was ready for a romp in the sheets. He did both Judy and I until we were completely satisfied—and then some—and then had an enormous orgasm of his own, which sent him into something resembling an epileptic fit. I thought we'd killed him and got up to call the paramedics. Judy assured me that he was okay—that this was his normal way of expressing his orgasms.

I wasn't sure I could deal with *that* kind of expression on a regular basis, so I soon passed on any more sex with Jerry in the future. Besides, I wanted to respect their relationship dynamics as I felt that Judy wasn't *really* okay with Jerry and my sexual relationship. But we all got along famously as friends to the point that the four of us (which included Ed) celebrated Christmas together. (And I *almost* got my Christmas fantasy of having two men at the same time; but Judy kind of put a kybosh on that one.) Then Jerry, Judy and I moved to St. George, Utah after the first of the year and rented a six-bedroom home with Wendy and Jay. This was to be the start of the first Heartsong Healing Center in St. George.

This story is short and shortsighted. I envisioned us reaching out to the St. George community with our various healing talents—Wendy as a massage therapist, Judy as an empathic healer (don't ask me what exactly that is) and me as a cranio-sacral therapist and herbalist. But then it got derailed when Jay and Wendy invited a shaman from a Native American tribe in Mexico to perform peyote ceremonies in our home. Wendy and Jay were convinced that he was the "real deal" and everything was legitimate. I was skeptical and convinced we were moving in the *wrong* direction. I was assured by all of them that *I was wrong,* until the weekend of the peyote ceremony.

First of all, the shaman insisted that everyone pay the $150 admission fee up front. We had about ten committed participants and so we sent him a check (from my personal account) for $1,500 just to get him up here. Then his vehicle broke down just outside of the Mexican border, and we were asked to provide money for his car repairs. Yet another $500 from my account. After his arrival, he and his wife insisted that we provide both free room and board while they were staying there. I was still reluctant about the whole event as I felt that the shaman definitely had dark energy around him. But no one would listen to me. I participated in the first nightly vigil of vomiting and chanting songs while everyone got higher than a kite.

The next night, Sunday night, I chose out because I needed to go to work the next day as the office manager for Maaco. It was a good thing someone was sober or they could have burned the house down. They left a sage smudge burning in an abalone shell which melted through my favorite Native American rug and started smoking up the entire house. After the shaman and his wife left, I realized that someone had gone through my jewelry (which I'd kept in the bathroom drawer) and had stolen some valuable items—including my custom-made wedding ring from Kurt. I was devastated by the whole thing especially when I was fired, as a result, from my full-time job. I was the only one in the household "bringing home the bacon" in order to keep the healing center afloat It was soon afterwards that I got "a message from God," that it was time to move on.

Chapter Twelve—Nolan

The next story is one right out of "Harper's Bizarre." You may remember the antagonist in my book, *Heartsong*, better known as Norman—not Bates, but almost. Well, he shows up again in this book as Nolan—with all due respects.

A week or so after the Peyote Event—it definitely was an "event" as it marked the beginning of the end of the first Heartsong Healing Center—Wendy started receiving phone calls from Mary in Salt Lake. Pam had effectively moved Mary out of her own apartment so that she and Joe could live there together. (An assertive pussy carries a lot of power.) So Mary was forced to find another place to live. (Mary is in her sixties, by the way. I thought she would be a great candidate for Jerry.) What was interesting was the fact that whenever Mary would call, the caller ID indicated *Nolan Nebeker*. I thought this was a bit unusual, as Nolan (Norman) was my first love from high school. The last time I'd seen Nolan was at a meeting at Wendy's for the Hidden Valley Healing Center. (You can read all the details concerning *that* meeting in *Heartsong*. Understand, however, that some of the incidents are embellished and consolidated even though the facts are true. I've tried in this book to keep it real.)

My first impulse was that Nolan had tracked me down and was trying to get a hold of me through one of Wendy's and my mutual friends. But then one day Mary contacted me directly in desperation as she'd had enough of Joe and Pam treating her poorly. The caller ID again registered Nolan's name, and I thought it was odd as I listened to her threaten to "do herself in" during a weekend drinking binge. So Judy and I decided it was time to bring out the "big guns." Judy, who was now a self-proclaimed "Shaman *and* Master Herbalist" after her peyote experience (who am I to judge?) brought out the sage and healing totems needed for the journey to Salt Lake to save Mary.

I appointed myself as the "shaman's apprentice" as I had no idea what Judy had in mind. When we arrived in Salt Lake, we called Mary on the phone. We could immediately tell that she was well on her way to drinking herself into oblivion. I told Mary that we were coming right over. She then warned me that there were a few minor details that she hadn't disclosed to me. That after she moved out of Joe's and her apartment, she had mysteriously hooked up and moved into *my old boyfriend, Nolan's house, in Bluffdale.* She claimed she answered an ad in the newspaper for a room for rent. It was all too weird for me! She wasn't sure if Nolan would be okay with us coming over at such short notice.

"Oh, God!" I thought to myself. "What a strange sense of humor *you* must have!" Nevertheless, I assured Mary that Judy and I were both coming over regardless of the complications. We felt she needed our help. I wrote down the address and told her to warn Nolan of our imminent arrival.

Nolan greeted us at the door in his Levi shirt, jeans, and cowboy boots. He seemed happy to see me regardless of the situation. He conveyed his concern for Mary who'd locked herself in her room for the past two days with a few fifths of Vodka. He was glad she was willing to talk to me, as he hadn't been able to get through to her at all.

I knocked on the bedroom door and told Mary that Judy and I had arrived. She opened the door and let me in. I found her in her bathrobe— drunk as a skunk (and smelling like one, too). I told her that we were there to do some spiritual healing and invited her out into the living room where Judy was already burning sage in an abalone shell. I could smell the aroma of burning carpet and I warned Judy beforehand to watch the sage as she had already burned a hole in our carpet down in St. George during the peyote ceremony. I was getting a bit upset from all the burnings as they'd ruined my favorite rug—and now Nolan's expensive carpet was being singed. Nolan, who was in the kitchen, rushed to the rescue—but the damage had already been done. He asked if the healings could happen without all the carpet burnings and was afraid we were going to burn down the house before we were finished!

Judy promptly finished the smudging routine, and doused the smudge-stick. She offered a few prayers—Native American style—and then made a healing circle for Mary and the two of us to sit in. Mary could hardly sit up straight, let alone sit on the floor inside a healing circle, so I offered to sit with her in my arms on the couch as Judy did the ceremony. I sat in attentive silence as Mary rambled on and on through the night. Most of it was drunken nonsense-—something about Pam possessing an evil spirit that was the most powerful evil spirit on the planet. She even had a name for it—something in Hebrew I have no way of remembering—and that we needed to exorcise Pam of her evil spirit. I had come to discount most of these "evil spirit stories" as wild fantasies. They were as real as you *made* them real. But I listened with concern as Mary spilled her guts about Pam and Joe and the evil that the two of them had inflicted upon her.

Now that, to me, was more *real* than the evil-spirit story, and *that one* I could deal with. I told Mary that she needed to put as much distance between her and that relationship as possible. Pam was simply being conniving, and Mary shouldn't put herself in harm's way. I told her of my own experience with Pam at the last "work project" at Joe's cabin and how she had rudely put me in my place. I told Mary the same thing that I'd told myself—Joe simply wasn't worth it.

Mary fell asleep in my arms, and I held her on the couch most of the night. I knew she would be okay by morning. Nolan observed the whole episode from a safe distance, but I could tell he was touched by the tenderness of the scene. Judy had long gone to find an empty bed to collapse in. Her shamanism had exacted a lot of energy from her and she was exhausted. Nolan helped me carry Mary's fragile body to bed and we tucked her in. Then he invited me downstairs to his room and to *his* bed—and yes, you guessed it—we made love. I must say it was nice to connect with him in that way again. He was the first one I'd ever had sex with, and it brought back some precious memories.

And so began our long-distance relationship, Nolan living in Salt Lake, me living in St. George. But after a month or so of one of us driving five hours back and forth on weekends, we felt it was time for me to move in with him. I was definitely ready to leave St. George as the healing center was well on its way to extinction. Mary felt the need to move on to another place, which left an empty room for me to move all of my things into. But I wasn't sure how I felt about moving in with Nolan who had a more than a few problems I didn't know if I could handle.

First and foremost, Nolan was an alcoholic. He would never admit to it, but anyone with a beer in his hand all day long *is* an alcoholic. He'd gotten busted so many times for DUIs that his license had been revoked. So he appointed me his designated chauffeur which I didn't mind so much as his navy blue Jaguar was a lot nicer to drive than my broken-down Subaru. Besides, Nolan's job was mostly doing computer work at home which didn't require a whole lot of driving—except to the bars on weekends. The rest of his health had suffered in the meantime. He had to take medication for his panic-attacks and had a terrible case of bronchitis that often made him vomit during coughing spells. Nolan was a mess, I admit it. So wasn't it my job, as his lover, to fix him? Go figure—I really fixed him good.

The day I was moving my things from St. George, I had a strange premonition that I was going to get into a car accident. It seemed to be all part of the drama I'd created for myself but somehow I knew it would all be for the best. I buckled my seatbelt preparing for the worst. When I arrived in

Salt Lake, I went straight to Nolan's house in Bluffdale to unpack my things. To my disappointment, he wasn't there yet he knew I was moving in that weekend and could really use his help. "That's men, for you," I complained as I hauled in my clothes and other possessions. I then called Nolan's cell phone to track him down. He was at a local bar (no surprise) drinking with his buddies. I was somewhat irritated when he asked me to come pick him up as I was exhausted from driving all day and then unpacking by myself. I, too, wanted to relax—but not at a bar.

Another thing—our sex-life had really gone by the way side as Nolan had a hard time getting it up and keeping it up. He said it was a side effect from the anti-panic attack drugs. So I was interested in attending a yoga class that evening where I'd met a hopeful hunk the weekend before. I was clear with Nolan on my intentions to be in an "open relationship" but I wasn't sure how he'd handle my sexual liaisons with other men. I was sure that in his condition it wouldn't make a heap load of difference.

I struggled with the idea of giving up my yoga experience in exchange for picking up a drunken boyfriend, but my "honoring the relationship" mumbo-jumbo won out and I drove to the bar. Nolan was watching a basketball game when I arrived, and he ordered a Tequiza for me as I sat down at a barstool next to him. I downed the Tequiza and then told him I was going to the nearest restaurant for a bite to eat. I hadn't eaten since breakfast and was famished. Besides, my interest in watching a basketball game on TV lasted a total of five seconds. I asked him to join me, but he said he was in the middle of his ballgame—and that it was more important than food (or me). I ordered a fish dinner at Denny's and dined alone. I regretted my decision already.

An hour or so later, I went back to pick Nolan up at the bar. He then told me he wanted to go to *another* bar as he was tired of *this* bar. I didn't have the energy to argue with him, and so he told his Native American friend who was with him to drive his Jaguar to his house. His friend had picked him up earlier and was ready to go home. So was I.

I sat and watched Nolan down a few more beers as I sipped on a raspberry ice tea at the other bar. I was not a drinker, and I knew I needed the remaining wakefulness to drive home. At 11:30, a half-hour before the bar closed, Nolan decided it was time to leave. We both got into my white Subaru and headed for Bluffdale—the southernmost suburb in the Salt Lake valley. I was tired yet alert, but neglected to fasten my seatbelt—and fastening a seatbelt was not part of Nolan's regular routine. Shortly before midnight, Nolan convinced me to stop at a 7-11 for a case of beer. He didn't want to run out the next day.

After the beer-stop, I was driving in the inner lane as we approached an intersection in Riverton—the closest suburb to Bluffdale. Suddenly, my head hit something rock hard and I was knocked unconscious. That's the last thing I remembered until I opened my eyes to find two paramedics cutting apart my two favorite white sweaters. In my semi-conscious state I begged them to remove the sweaters before they cut into them because *"they are my favorite sweaters and I don't want them ruined!"*

"Look, lady, in your condition, your sweaters are the least of your worries. You've been in a terrible car accident so just try to remain calm. We'll get you to the hospital as soon as we can. Try not to move anything."

The words were pasty and surreal in my ears. I felt a nagging pain in my right leg and arm but somehow I couldn't remember how I'd gotten in that state. An accident—is that what happened when I'd felt my head plow into an inanimate object? I felt blood flowing down my face, and I knew I probably looked like hell. Sure, I could lay still and be calm until I was loaded onto a stretcher and into an ambulance. I felt like an observer just watching another adventure in my Alice in Wonderland life. I just wondered how deep and how dark this rabbit hole went.

Nolan and I were taken to Cottonwood Hospital, the nearest one to the scene of the accident. He was then airlifted to the LDS Hospital, as his injuries were far worse than mine. I learned later on that he'd hit the dashboard going about 50 MPH as a 21-year-old kid pulled a left-hand turn right in front of me. Witnesses on the scene said it was obviously his fault. He confessed later that he thought I was in the turning lane and took his chances that I was turning. It was a bit confusing, I'll admit, as I later returned to the scene and found the road divided into four lanes—one each for right and left turns and two straight lanes. I was in one of the straight lanes. The young driver had made a deadly mistake.

My injuries included a shattered kneecap, a crushed heel, a shattered forearm, and several cracked ribs. Nolan, however, had crushed most of his rib cage and ruptured his aorta when he hit the dashboard. I was hopeful that they had repaired his aorta and that he would be resting comfortably in satisfactory condition, but a severe coughing spell brought on vomiting and he ended up suffocating on it. He rang for the nurse, but one didn't arrive for 15 minutes later and found him with no vital signs. They revived his vitals and put him on life-support, but after a few weeks his family decided to pull the plug as there was no brain-activity detected when they did a spinal tap.

I was recovering and a bit dulled by all the pain meds to the dramatic experience of Nolan's death. Later, I poured out my feelings in a passionate heartsong dedicated to the short time Nolan and I had spent together in this earthly existence. I'll always remember the good times we had and the memories we shared—the first time and the last time we were together.

Last Chance at My Fist Love

You called me princess
The first time we met.
Our high school play,
I'll never forget.
How you melted my heart
With the warmth in your eyes—
All my words of resistance
Turned into sighs.

We were just seventeen,
Too young to know
How or when
Our love would grow.
After twenty-five years
Of lives lived apart.
What we thought had ended
Had a brand-new start.

I got my last chance
At my first love.
Such a perfect design
By the angels above.
The distance between
Time and space transcends—
When you connect at the heart
True love never ends.

Two lonely hearts
Looking for something to share
A second chance for love
And a heart filled with care.
Sometimes miracles happen
In the strangest of ways.
Two hearts became one
For some magical days.

No one can say
Why some things occur.
How it all happened,

It still is a blur—
The flashing lights
The blood all around
"See you later princess,"
Was your last spoken sound.

I got my last chance
At my first love.
Such a perfect design
By the angels above.
The distance between
Time and space transcends—
When you connect at the heart
True love never ends.

Some times at night
I can still feel your touch.
The unspoken words,
"I love you so much."
Our spirits connect
Like our bodies once would.
And we make love like
I never thought we could.

I journey with you
To your heavenly home.
Across starlit skies
Our spirits now roam.
It's like I envisioned Heaven would be—
Though the body is broken
The spirit is free.

I got my last chance
At my first love.
Such a perfect design
By the angels above.
The distance between
Time and space transcends—
When you connect at the heart
True love never ends.

Chapter Thirteen—Kurt

By now, you're probably wondering what had been happening with Kurt and the kids back in Montana. Let me warn you—it's not a pretty story.

After the divorce was signed, it was only a matter of weeks before it was finalized. I was mailed the "uncorrected" legal documents by certified mail. Part of me was remorseful, part of me was hopeful that I would get to spend part of the Christmas holidays with my children. But then came the silence—waiting for Kurt to let me know how and when I could see them.

When Ariel went back with Aubrey and Mike to Montana for Thanksgiving, Kurt insisted that they all stay with him as he went through his so called "emotional break-down." He even had Deserae move back from Smithfield, where Kurt's parents lived, even though she had just begun her senior year at Skyview. I'm sure Ariel, Deserae and Aubrey were all a bit resentful towards me at divorcing their Dad and drawing them all into our melodrama. And, of course, they all felt obligated to rally around Christy in caring for the other kids. Christy now had three of her own—Brendan, Jesse, and Tyler, and Aubrey and Mike had a son—Sean.

That meant that there were now four adults—Kurt, Christy, Mike and Aubrey, two teenagers—Deserae and Ariel, and nine younger children—Jordan, Brendan, Jonathan, Kelsey, Jesse, Jenny, Andrew, Tyler and Sean (in order of age)—a total of fifteen human beings living in a small four-bedroom log cabin with no phone or electricity in the middle of the woods. It's what I call insanity but what Kurt calls "family solidarity." He then effectively enrolled them all in the fight to destroy their own mother—the "wicked whore of the west."

Yes, by that time I was considered a whore. Word had gotten out that I was sleeping around with men. Was this really to anyone's surprise after 23 devoted years to a fanatical polygamist who'd been unfaithful to me several known times and who knows how many unknown times? Sure, I had a few wild oats to sow, but they'd all been sown within the first few months of being single. By January, I was celibate, until I ran into Nolan in March. And it could be argued that I continued being celibate after the first few nights together because Nolan just wasn't very interested in sex. He was inebriated most of the time and mysteriously spent all night at his computer when he thought I was sleeping. He was "hush-hush" about his work, but I figured it had something to do with his connections with "the Beast." (See chapter eight in *Heartsong* for details).

But the "Montana militia" was now rallied together and conspiring to see what it would take to break Mom down so that she would come to her senses, repent, and return home. I suppose that was their benevolent intention for me—although I didn't feel any benevolence from any of them at the time. It was simply violent and excruciatingly painful—especially when Kurt refused to let any of my children visit or even call me in the hospital after my accident. But my oldest son, Jared, was there for me each and every day the entire time. He was a *real* blessing in my life. I don't know what I'd have done without him.

To begin with, the family militia tried the silent treatment. None of my children were allowed to contact me during the entire holiday season—no cards, no letters, no phone calls allowed. Even my oldest son, Jared, who had been living and working in Salt Lake, had been drawn into his father's drama, and refused to speak to me. He was ashamed of my lifestyle and didn't want anything to do with me. That is until after the accident. I sent letter after letter to my children, begging them for a response. I wrote letters each week to Kurt, asking for my rights to visitation and reminding him of his promises to me. Each letter was returned with seething retorts ending with a painful "the children are not available for visitation" slap in the face. It was devastating, and I spent most my nights crying relentlessly at how cruel Kurt, my older children, and my life was.

In March, it had been over four months since I'd seen my children. I was going to a church counselor at Unity in St. George concerning my depression. I couldn't afford a clinical counselor, but I knew I needed to talk to *someone*! I showed the female church counselor my divorce papers, all of my letters and asked her what I should do. She told me to write a letter to Kurt, firmly and clearly stating that I had visitation rights as the mother of my children and that he needed to give them to me. She then told me to let him know a date, time, and place that I would be up to visit them—and that he needed to meet me there with the children. I also offered him a peace offering. I would give him the $200 I owed him for the divorce and the guitar I had taken with me that he claimed was his. It was one of the few things I had taken with me other than my clothes, but he claimed it was his even though he didn't play guitar and I regularly did. But I thought I would give it back as a peace offering. She then convinced one of the other ministers, a hefty, older man, to go with me as protection. Neither of us knew what Kurt was capable of doing at this point.

On Saturday, March 13, 1999, I headed to Montana with Dale (I actually can't remember his name, so I'll just call him Dale) by my side. Our conversation was light and high-spirited, as I felt confident that I would finally get to see my children. I'd wondered, in my mind, how they would have changed. I was sure Andrew, who was only 18 months old when I'd left him, would have changed a lot. I wondered if he would even remember me.

Jenny Pearl and Kelsey May, ages three and five, would have grown a lot since I'd last seen them. They, I'm sure, had suffered the most trauma at not being able to see their mother for so long. And Jordan and Jonathan, now seven and nine, were, I'm sure, stalwart little soldiers in this dramatic battle. I tried to picture their delightful smiles when they were finally able to see their mother again. The tears rolled down my cheeks as the thoughts of embracing all of them passed through my mind. It was bittersweet joy, but at least I wasn't experiencing the depression that had been haunting me for the past few months. At least now, I had hope.

The Montana Mountains are beautiful in the spring—actually they were beautiful any time of year. The snow was melting into small patches along the foothills, and the air was crisp and clean. I rolled down my window, and the fragrant air stimulated memories of not so long ago—of how I would walk with the children along the pastoral creek each day, looking for edible mushrooms, berries to snack on, and herbs for green drinks. I wondered if the stinging nettle or horsetail grass was peeking through the snowdrifts up at Higher Ground, but at that high altitude, I doubted it. I wondered if my white Subaru would even make it up the mile and a half driveway. Oftentimes, we'd been snowed-in at the log cabin, which was a bit nerve-wracking with no way to do laundry or get food. We survived for three weeks one year on stored beans, rice, oatmeal, and powdered hot chocolate. But we were warm and cozy—and I guess that was all that counted. I longed for those "good ol' days" before Christy came into the family and complicated things.

I was a simple, stay-at-home mom, home-schooling my kids, teaching them the things that I thought would be important later on in life—the "Three Rs" but also anatomy, herbology, Latin (root words), spinning, weaving, leatherwork, pottery-making, and cooking from scratch on a wood stove without electricity. I figured these were life skills that all children needed to know to survive in the world—at least in my world of the backwoods. But it was fun and exciting—and we never knew a dull moment. In the early hours of dawn and the hours after bedtime, I would spend my time plucking away on my manual typewriter, writing my latest book or my monthly Higher

Ground Newsletter. This was my lifeline to the outside world, and I thought the only one I needed—until Christy came along. (But that's another story in another book.)

Kurt was poor adult companionship as he would stay in town all day "looking for work" and only come home at night to get his jollies off. I suspected I was a "desperate housewife" but with no TV or computer Internet, How was I to validate it? And so a sister-wife, at the time, seemed like a perfect solution to my desperation. I must admit raising a paschal of children in the deep woods without phone or electricity can be a bit desperate. I was grateful for any help that came along. But let's get on with the story at hand.

In my letter to Kurt, I had agreed to meet him and the children at our favorite park in Missoula on Friday afternoon at 2:00 p.m. I figured this was safe terrain for both of us. I had to leave Salt Lake (which is where we'd stayed the night before) at 5:00 in the morning to make the nine-hour trip. I wasn't too surprised when Kurt didn't show up. Dale and I waited for several hours for him to arrive, but to no avail. We then decided it was too late to drive home and so we got a room at Ruby's Inn. I slept restlessly thinking of my next move.

I was determined to see my children—come hell or high water—after traveling this far. I told Dale I was heading up to Ninemile that morning and asked if he was coming with me. He was reluctant but figured he didn't have a choice. He'd volunteered for the dramatic adventure, and he was willing to see it through. Besides, he figured he was assigned by God to be my protector.

By the time we got to the beginning of the driveway to our log cabin, Dale was getting more than a bit nervous. For the past several miles, traveling up Ninemile Canyon, he became more and more apprehensive at how remote things were beginning to look. He hadn't seen a service station for miles, and the Ninemile dirt road was deeply rutted and slippery in spots from the snowdrifts. As I started up the steep incline, in my front-wheel-drive Subaru, straddling the depressed tire tracks in the melting snow, Dale's courage wavered.

"Stop, Janae, I don't think I can go any further!" he exclaimed.

"Oh, come on, Dale—it's only a little over a mile further, and I know my Subaru can make it. This is nothing compared to what I'm used to in the winter." His pale face froze as the tires started to spin-out on the icy hill.

"No, Janae. You're going to have to stop the car here. I'm a bit too nervous to make it any further. You're either going to have to take me back to town and go at it on your own, or I'll have to wait here in the car while you walk in the rest of the way."

I sighed as I contemplated my options. Missoula was an hour's drive back and the house was only a mile and a half hike, granted, through the snow. It was an easy walk for the kids and me to get to the mailbox, which was another half mile down the county road. I backed down the driveway and parked at the bottom of the hill. I got out of the car, grabbed the guitar in the duffel bag, and handed Dale the keys. "If there's any trouble, just meet me in town at Ruby's. I can handle it alone from here."

I was glad I had worn my moccasin-boots, as the snow was slushy with ice underneath. It made walking difficult, but my determination to see my children again spurred me on. The sun was shining brightly—a good omen, I thought—and soon my parka was off and around my waist. The terrain was all-too-familiar, and I recognized deer and squirrel tracks in the melting snow. These creatures had all been my woodland friends—along with the trees, the flowers, and the herbs. Even the rocks were familiar as I'd called them into my sacred space of life.

Tears began to flow as I realized how much I'd missed my sacred mountain home, and I realized that nothing was any more important than being home. I then resolved in my mind that I would do anything, say anything, be anything, to be home with my children. I would put up with Christy and the polygamy crap, just so I could be back home. Home—what a warm, wonderful word. It melted into the warm wonderful feeling of family.

My tears turned into smiles, and I began to hasten the pace as I neared the gate. Then my heart sank. Kurt had posted personalized "NO TRESPASSING" signs all along the gateposts. They were bold and threatening, saying that if I trespassed, I would certainly be arrested. The facts were that it had been my equity investment from our previous home which had paid the down payment on the land, so I still felt that it was partly mine. Kurt had put the land into a trust that no one could get their hands on—especially me. But he knew I would eventually come for the kids and he'd prepared for my arrival. My fears of being arrested crept into my thoughts—but only for a moment. The joy of seeing my children overrode the feelings of fear, and I pressed past the no trespassing signs. I had committed myself to seeing it through come hell or high water, and it looked like I was in for both.

The pastoral creek was filled with spring run-off as I walked up the road to the house. I knew each curve and bend by heart, and my heart began to beat faster as my pace hastened. The llamas and goats were in their corrals, and I greeted them by name as I passed. Fuscia, our family dog, came running down the path toward me, and I wondered if she would recognize me. Sure enough, after the first sniff, she was wagging her whole body in delight. I loved on her for a moment, and then she walked by my side as a personal guardian angel to the house. I could hear children's voices as I neared the house. My heart leaped with excitement knowing they were my little ones. They were out jumping on the trampoline, and Jordan and Jonathan recognized me and came running over to me and gave me a hug. The others jumped off the trampoline into the snow and joined their older brothers.

"Mom—didn't you see the signs Dad posted! He said he was going to call the cops if you tried to come up here!" Jordan exclaimed. I barely heard him through all the commotion and the emotion that were spilling out. Jonathan was holding baby Andrew and I lifted him into my hungry arms. I didn't care what "Dad" did—it was all worth it for this one moment in time.

Then Christy came out of the house in a blind rage. "Come on kids—you need to come into the house *now*! You know what your dad said if your mom came up. You aren't to see her."

I told them to never mind her that *I was their mother* and here for my visitation—and it better *damn well not be interrupted*. Then Christy came over to me and grabbed Andrew out of my arms. "You better let me have him, Janae, 'cause the cops are already on their way to arrest you. If you make trouble for any of us, we'll not only have you arrested for trespassing but for assault."

I was dumbfounded. Assault—*assault!!* That was the last thing on my mind as I relinquished my hold on Andrew. I WAS JUST UP THERE TO SEE MY CHILDREN FOR GOD'S SAKE! She grabbed Jenny's hand in her free hand and called for the other children to follow her into the house. They obediently but reluctantly followed. I stood and stared blankly as I watched my children file one by one into the house.

I ran to the porch as Kelsey, the slowest child, waved to me as the door slammed in my face. I pounded on the glass-etched door pane, which I'd designed, hoping to break through. "Let me in, LET ME IN!" I screamed in utter agony.

Christy had taken the children upstairs to "safety." She didn't want them to witness their mom's pathetic emotional breakdown. It was more than anyone could bear—or should have to bear. I wept on the stairs for a good ten minutes in total despair. I felt desperate and frustrated but I refused to leave. I then decided to get out the guitar I had strung on my back to play as a distraction to the emotions that had become unbearable.

In the months I had been away I had practiced nearly every day on the guitar the songs I had written years ago. I began singing the words to Even Now in a broken-down voice. It was difficult but it also felt good to sing to my children again—even if they couldn't hear my voice. I continued with Crazy Lady, then Butterfly Love and as I was starting Perhaps Today, I looked in the window and noticed my children standing on the living room couch looking out at me. Emotion swept over me and I began to cry again. Just then a police car with two officers, followed by the Brat (the car my dad had given to me) drove up. Kurt jumped out and started firing accusations at me and then shouted at the cops to arrest me. I could hardly defend myself through the commotion, and when the cops finally calmed Kurt down enough to hear my side of the story, they were stunned. Through tears, I told them how I'd driven clear from St. George to see my children who I hadn't seen for *over four months* and how I'd walked nearly two miles in the slushy snow and that *I wasn't going to move from this spot until I saw them.*

The cops took pity on my circumstances and ordered Kurt to bring the children from the house and let them see me. I gave Kurt his guitar back and told him the $200 I owed him was in the duffel bag. I was allowed ten minutes with my children so I could hug and kiss them and let them know that I was okay. Kelsey wondered why I hadn't written or contacted them. I realized then that Kurt had thrown away the dozens of letters I'd written and had prevented them from any phone calls. They told me that they'd spent Christmas at Grandma King's—a short distance from Salt Lake—and wondered why I hadn't visited them and that they still had my Christmas presents for me. I held back the anger I felt towards Kurt trying to comfort their fears. Yes, I still loved them, and I would do everything in my power so that we could be together again—I promised. After a short time, Kurt interrupted and asked the cops to arrest me for trespassing as I *had* trespassed on *his* property. They then took me to their car and put me into the back seat. The fear of being arrested never had place in my heart, which was now overflowing with joy.

As we headed down the hill, their tires got stuck in the slushy snow. They tried for over a half an hour to get unstuck, and I had to pee BAD! I asked them if I could go somewhere in the woods. I guess they thought I would try to escape, and refused to allow me to pee in private. They said I could just pee next to the car, but I told them that that wouldn't work for me. I got a bit irritated with both of them and they finally threatened to handcuff me if I wouldn't shut up. Before I could complain about their abuse and arrogance, I found myself brutally pulled from the back seat, handcuffed and shoved back in. The cuffs were tight and painful, and with the added discomfort of a full bladder I felt like I was being tortured as they finally started down the hill again. I was definitely paying the price for my supposed insolence.

At the police station I refused to be booked until after I could go pee. I was in serious shape by now, and all I could think about was what inhumane punishment I was being inflicted with simply because I wanted to see my children! The booking officer was a woman, and I asked her if she had children of her own. She said she had two and then I asked her what she would feel like if those children were taken away from her and she couldn't see them for four months! Multiply that by five, and that's what I was going through! She wasn't the least bit sympathetic and had one of the cops throw me into the drunk tank. She said I could pee in there. The concrete walls and floor were cold and harsh. It smelled like urine from the open-gritted sewer running through the floor. This is where I was expected to pee—and so I pulled down my pants and finally relieved myself after hours of discomfort.

I didn't want to be booked and have a police record. I demonstrated my refusal by doing yoga postures on my head and singing all the songs I could think of—on my head. I could tell they weren't happy with my passive resistance. They finally convinced me that if I were booked I could eat dinner and have a clean bed to sleep in that night. I reluctantly agreed as the thought of staying in that stinky cell on a filthy, bare mattress was more than I could bear.

They fingerprinted me, had me undress and gave me an orange jumpsuit to put on. They then served me some unsavory food, a plastic spoon, a toothbrush, toothpaste, and a comb. Now I was destined to meet my six new roommates—women in jail for various reasons. They were all friendly and sympathetic when I told them my story. One, who was there for burning all of her husband's clothing when she caught him cheating with another woman, suggested that I burn down Kurt's house. The thought was appealing for a moment, but then I realized that I was the one who'd paid for the house and helped build it—not to mention it was my children's home, too! After hearing all of their stories, I crawled into a top bunk and cried pathetically the entire night. I simply wanted to die, and the only thing keeping me from it was the memory of my children's smiles.

The next morning, the jailer came in early to get me and told me that I'd been released on bail. I was scheduled for a hearing that morning with the judge. I thought it was Dale who had bailed me out, but when Kurt greeted me at my release, I knew it was him. He'd had a change of heart and had dropped the trespassing charges. He told me I'd actually been arrested for a past warrant on a ticket for driving with studded tires. I recalled the incident and also the agreement Kurt had made that he was going to take care of the ticket. As usual, he never did. Kurt walked with me to the courtroom and sat down next to me as if nothing had happened. The female judge called me to the stand to testify. I could feel Kurt bristle as I told her the entire story. She then dropped all the charges and told me that I had permission to go home and horsewhip my ex-husband for the pain he'd put me through. There was a feeling of relief and satisfaction that I'd finally been listened to.

Kurt told me that he'd drive me to the bus station for a bus ride home as Dale had left already for Salt Lake in *my* Subaru. (I was sure Kurt scared him off with threats, and the drama was probably more than Dale could handle.)

The bus wasn't leaving for several hours, so Kurt agreed to take me to see the children to "make up for things." As we were sitting in the car talking, Kurt tried to make a pass at me, but it was "intercepted." How dare he think he could take such liberties after all that had transpired these past few months? But I knew if I got into it with him that he might not take me to see the kids. So I led him to believe that I was tired and wasn't interested in his romantic advances.

The next hour was spent with my children at Higher Ground. It was a beautiful healing time with Mother Earth as we walked the familiar path by the stream. Kelsey and Jenny showed me their new baby bunnies and goats—and it felt so much like home. I talked with Kurt about trying to resolve our relationship issues, but he told me that Christy wasn't open at all to allowing me back. She now was the ruler of the roost—and the ruler of the rooster and the chicks. The horror movie, *The Hand that Rocks the Cradle,* came to mind and I realized that I really didn't want to get involved in that type of relationship dynamics anyway. But still, I was willing to do *almost* anything to be with my children. But for now, I was enjoying the present moment being with them.

The children were able to give me their Christmas presents they'd made, and I enjoyed reading their cards and letters on the bus ride home. Christy had even included a Christmas present from her—John Denver's last recorded album, *All Aboard.* I was anxious to listen to it when I got home to see if there were any hidden messages in *these* songs. As always—I was *not* disappointed.

Chapter Fourteen—Jenny

"There is something in the heart of every human being that responds to a vision of possibility. A better life, true love, fame and fortune, all await us on the far side of the hill. Whether it is a ship under full sail heading out beyond the distant horizon or a spacecraft lifting off toward some bright and shining star, we can't help imagining, if only for a moment, that we might be on board, leaving the past and all of its pain and suffering behind and giving ourselves to the promise of tomorrow. In the light of that promise, any hardship can be endured, devastating loneliness can be tolerated and dreams can and will come true. For me, all of that was personified in the sight and sound of a slow moving freight train heading west."

John Denver's introduction to All Aboard

I cried. I cried again as the voice from the distant past and beyond spoke the words of my heart that needed so desperately to be expressed. Again, John Denver articulated feelings of hope that no one else could source for me—*even though he was dead!* The first song on Christy's Christmas gift was, *Jenny Dreamed of Trains*:

> When Jenny was a little girl, she only dreamed of trains
> She never played with dolls or lacy kinds of things
> Jenny counted boxcars instead of counting sheep
> She could go anywhere when she went to sleep
>
> All she ever talked about was getting on to ride
> She was living in another time you could see it in her eyes
> And every day after school she'd head down to the track
> Waiting for the train that was never coming back
>
> Jenny dreamed of trains
> When the nighttime came

Nobody knew how she made it come true
Jenny dreamed of trains

The depot's been boarded up, the rails have turned to rust
There hasn't been a train through here since the mill went bust
No one believed her when she said she heard the train
Said she was just a little girl acting kind of strange

Jenny dreamed of trains
When the nighttime came
Nobody knew how she made it come true
Jenny dreamed of trains

Jenny laid a penny on the track one day
In God we trust she walked away
The very next morning all she could find
Was a little piece of copper squashed flatter than a dime

Jenny dreamed of trains
When the nighttime came
Nobody knew how she made it come true
Jenny dreamed of trains

Nobody knew how she made it come true
Jenny dreamed of trains

Oh, God—how I missed my own little Jenny Pearl! Oh, God—how
I missed my kids! Oh, God—how I missed John Denver! The emotions
flowed and flowed and I barely recalled the rest of the album. It was as if all
the emotions I had stored up for a lifetime had reached critical mass and were
now imploding inside me. I didn't know what to do with them except to let
them have their way with me. And so I did. And afterwards I felt purged
and renewed—and once again my heart was open.

I drafted a letter to Kurt telling him of my desire to come up to Montana
again in April to celebrate his and Jenny's birthday, which fell on April 23. I
also told him I was ready to discuss terms of an agreement that we could both
live with that wouldn't cause any more damage to the children. His reply was
another slap in the face. The children would not be available that weekend
as Kurt had made other plans.

So I drafted another letter telling him that I would be up on the weekend
before Jenny's birthday so I could give her her present. I suggested a time and

place to meet—again at our favorite park—and sent it certified mail to make sure he got it. I waited for a confirmation reply from the post office which did come back, but Kurt would not answer either the letter or my phone calls. On the departure date he still had not replied.

This time Judy volunteered to come up with me to assure that I would see my kids—come hell or high water, and again I made the long journey from St. George to Montana. But again I was disappointed as Judy and I sat in the park waiting for Kurt to arrive with the kids. I realized that he was playing his famous control game again, and both Judy and I were outraged. This meant yet another trip to Higher Ground to play out the nasty control drama scene again.

The next morning we set out early. Judy fully supported my decision to visit my kids at Higher Ground. In fact, she wanted to see Kurt and give him a piece of her mind for all the pain he'd put me through. Judy was a true friend, and I felt empowered by her faith and enthusiasm. Perhaps it would turn out differently this time and Kurt would listen to someone else.

We parked the white Subaru at the top of the hill a short distance from the gate and property line. The "NO TRESPASSING" signs were still posted from the previous month, and I warned Judy that she might end up in jail with me. She said she wasn't afraid of what Kurt might do to her because he was just a scared little boy deep inside and was simply acting out. He needed to be taught a lesson.

Judy was amazed by the beauty and remoteness of the place. She couldn't believe I'd lived that far "in the boonies" for so long without electricity or phone. I told her I was a bit insane, but part of me loved the serenity of the woods. I found solace connecting with Mother Earth and the woodland creatures, and my kids had more than fulfilled my life. I had poured every bit of myself into raising them, but now I was at a loss without them.

As we neared the bottom bridge, which accessed the turn-off to a leveled area for future construction, I could see my children walking down the road towards me. I thanked God for blessing me with such good luck. This meant I wouldn't have to go all the way to the house and deal with Kurt and Christy.

When they saw Judy and I walking towards them, they came running down the hill. I embraced them all as tears started to flow. I tried to hide my tears from the kids, but that was impossible. I gave Jenny the birthday present I'd brought for her—a sweet, life-like baby doll with all of the trimmings including extra clothes. Her face beamed with delight as she unwrapped the gift. I gave the other children some healthy snacks and treats so they wouldn't feel left out. The children were raised on a strict diet and, to his credit, Kurt was a stickler about health. It had become a way of life for us—no sugar, no white flour, no preservatives—and I knew my own health had benefited, too. There were definitely some positive aspects to Kurt's fanaticism, but other aspects were completely unreasonable.

As we were all catching up on lost time and memories, I noticed Kurt out of the corner of my eye heading towards us sporting a hunting rifle. My blood turned cold as I motioned to Judy to pay attention. Kurt was livid at our insolence in trespassing on *his* property again. Judy began shouting her accusations concerning Kurt's childish behavior which escalated the tension.

I could tell we were all in for a major hoedown, but I simply wasn't in the mood to dance that dance. I pulled at Judy's sleeve as she unloaded a full load of verbal ammunition on Kurt, trying to convince her that it simply wasn't worth the risk. Kurt was in no mood to listen to anything, and it was best that we be off. As we started to leave, Kurt fired off all the unsavory insults he could muster at me. He'd obviously found out that I was again dating Nolan, my boyfriend previous to him, and he framed it as more evidence of my whorish character. The children certainly didn't need to hear this, so I started walking numbly down the hill. I knew Kurt wanted a fight, and I tried to resist the urge to give in to it. But he continued with the insults, and I finally broke down and cried, "So what Kurt—what would satisfy you? Do you just want me to kill myself so I can get out of yours and everyone's lives?"

"No, Mom, no," the children chorused in tears. "Don't say that—we love you and we just want you to stay with us." It was more than any of us could handle. I grabbed Judy's arm, and we walked away in despair followed by Kurt's menacing threat, "Don't you *ever* show your face here again and upset *my* kids. Next time you'll be thrown in jail for good—and I ain't gonna bail you out."

We walked silently back to the car. Judy was outraged and seething inside. She had not imagined that things could be so outrageous. On the brighter side, I'd delivered my birthday gift to Jenny and had seen my children. What more could I ask for?

During the following month of May, I again wrote Kurt asking for my monthly visitation. Again he replied, "The children will not be available for visitation this month. They will be busy with other things." Again I was crushed and didn't know what to do. I didn't have money to hire a lawyer, and I'd tried every social service organization, including Tapestry for Polygamy, to rally some help. Each had the same answer—Montana was out of their jurisdiction. Besides, Montana was a place where wackos seemed to hide out and make a stand. Kurt was a prime example, and not someone anyone wanted to deal with.

Even Judy had lost the gusto for the fight and wasn't interested in a return trip to deal with *that wacko*. I was desperate, so I wrote Kurt another letter requesting that they all pray for me to return to my Heavenly Home as this life wasn't worth the pain anymore. My birthday was coming up on May 30, and I asked them all to pray for my death as my birthday gift. My life just wasn't worth living without my children. I seriously wanted God to take me home—to "beam me up Scotty"—there was no more recourse for me. I simply couldn't handle it any more.

On Sunday, May 16, 1999 as I was heading up to Salt Lake to move in with Nolan, I felt the urge to plug in the John Denver tape I'd gotten for Christmas from Christy. As I listened in tears to "Jenny's Song," I noticed that the reprise wasn't "Jenny dreamed of trains" but "Jesse dreamed of trains." I played it several times to make sure I wasn't hearing things or losing my mind. Sure enough it was Jesse—the same name that I'd chosen as the character in my book, *Heartsong*. I was overwhelmed by the magical mysticism of it all and knew that John had tapped into the mysterious source that had been guiding and protecting me all along. I cried for my desire to return home…to John. I'd had it with this life, and I was ready to move on. Somehow I knew my prayers would be answered, so all that day I anticipated a car accident in which I'd be killed. I was even looking forward to it to some degree. And around 11:58 p.m. it did happen. But instead of me being killed—Nolan was. How could God be so cruel?

Chapter Fifteen—Ray

I'd always wondered what it would be like to be confined to a wheelchair for the rest of my life. One of those "I just can't imagine living without legs" sort of ponderings. And now I had my chance to experience just that—life without legs. The car accident had crushed my calcaneus, shattered my patella and fractured my tibia in two places requiring extensive surgery. My heel was too crushed to do anything about for the time being so the doctor, who was on call at the time of the accident, stabilized my kneecap with pins, placed a steel plate in my arm, and confined me to a wheelchair until further notice. Thus I was set to find out why ramps on the sides of buildings are such blessings to the wheelchair confined. And automatic doors, low drinking fountains, and friends and family members who have the time and patience to haul you and your wheelchair around. It was life in the slow lane, but I knew I needed time to heal.

Ed, believe it or not, was my knight in shining armor. He hauled me to my doctor's appointments, to see Nolan in the hospital, and to Unity on Sundays. Mary also made herself available for me, although I knew it was a little much to ask of a sixty-year-old woman to lug me around. And my mother, who was an absolute angel through all of it, wasn't capable at seventy to do much but assist me in and out of the bathroom and bring me meals in bed. Everyone's efforts were greatly appreciated and I felt truly loved and attended to.

And then along came Ray. His name suited him—a ray of sunshine in my dark night of the soul. Ed introduced me to Ray a week or so after I was released from the hospital. He was a massage therapist, and heaven knows I needed a massage. Being confined to bed for several weeks makes the body stiff and sore. Add to that no way of getting any exercise, and you realize how important movement is to the body.

When I first looked into Ray's eyes, there was an immediate connection. I hadn't felt this connected to anyone since David and knew it was destiny that Ray had come into my life. My first massage with Ray was a bit of heavenly bliss. His hands felt like rain on a hot August afternoon. They deeply penetrated the soil of my soul, and I was emotionally quenched. Ray had a talent for massage—no doubt—but his talent went far deeper than just bodywork. He was a soul-worker and he knew it. So did I.

Ray lived in Manti—about a two and a half-hour drive from Salt Lake. He came up once a week to work on clients in Salt Lake, which included me after his initial treatment. After our first conversation, I came to realize why I felt so connected to Ray. We had very similar life experiences. He and Trish (his wife) had been involved in a polygamist group in Manti and had experimented with the idea. Sarah, his second wife, had only stayed in the relationship a short while and then moved on. But Ray was convinced of the expansiveness of plural relationships. He said that Trish and he had toyed with several other plural relationships—but none had worked out very well. They were both open and available for the universe to design something that did work. And when I met Trish, I immediately fell in love with her as we had so much in common—even more so than Ray and I.

Ray and Trish offered to take me to Crystal Hot Springs with them and their four children for a camping trip one weekend. My first plunge into the pool and I was in Nirvana. I finally had a way of mobilizing my leg and exercising muscles I hadn't used for months. I experimented as best I could with the water therapy keeping my arm, which was in a cast, dry in a plastic bag. Most of the time I sat on the side stairs and relaxed in the mineral waters. And Ray, Trish and I swapped stories.

By that time Ray and Trish had read my book, *Heartsong,* and had gazillions of questions for me. They both wondered how and where community could ever work given the history and current state of poly-agony. Our discussions were deep and meaningful, and it wasn't long before we got into some real personal space. I expressed that I felt that I had two more children coming, but I knew they would be children of community. Ray expressed that he felt he had two more children also—but Trish didn't want any more children. Ray and Trish had been hopeful that Sarah would have the two children Ray desired, but after two years of trying, they became convinced it wasn't meant to be. Sarah left the relationship realizing that she wasn't up for the polygamist lifestyle.

Granted, Ray and Trish lived a very humble lifestyle—their home in Manti was anything but glamorous. It reminded me a lot of my circumstances in Montana—wall to wall bunk beds and kids. But they seemed to have the same faith that we'd had—that things would get better with time. But I knew with the meager income Ray was making as a massage therapist that the wait would be long and hard. I was glad that I could help Ray by being a regular paying client, and I planned to help out even more when my insurance settlement came in.

I watched from my wheelchair as Ray and Trish pitched the tent for their little girls—Krista and Mary. I played with them in their tent while Ray and Trish finished setting up their tent and the older boys set up theirs. Krista and Mary reminded me so much of my own little girls—Kelsey and Jenny—that I became melancholy. I sang a few camp songs I used to sing for my own children at bedtime to put them to sleep. After they dozed off, Trish and Ray invited me to join them in their tent. Ray lifted and carried me in, and I felt somewhat like a new bride. It was easier than having to stand me up and have me hobble around. Ray lay in the middle between Trish and me, and we talked of how it reminded us of the *menage a trois* energy we'd had in both of our plural relationships.

Such energy was always intoxicatingly erotic, and I guess that's why I seemed to be drawn into such relationships. But in my physical condition I knew that sex was out of the question—especially with my relationship with Ray and Trish just barely developing. When Ray's arm came around me and he started to spoon me, I made it clear I wasn't up for sexual intimacy. He then turned to Trish, and I heard them making love as the moonlight filtered into the tent. It was all highly erotic and very fulfilling regardless of my personal involvement.

In the morning when all three of us awoke, Ray shared with us that he'd dreamed all night of making love to both of us—but he couldn't tell the difference. Trish seemed to go along with all of it, but I wondered if it was bringing up unhealed issues for her. I knew it was bringing up some of mine, because the last thing I wanted to do was recreate an unhealthy triangle like Kurt, Christy and I had had. I couldn't bear the thoughts of putting Trish through the pain I'd gone through and was still coming out of. Immediately my heart became closed to the idea.

But Ray was convinced that the three of us belonged together. On the return trip home, he decided to go on a vision quest to find out from "Spirit" what we should do. He hiked up to the top of a mountain in Manti and meditated for an entire day. The following day Ray came to Salt Lake to share with me his profound experience.

When Ray arrived at Mom's, he carried me into my mother's backyard where we could be alone. As I looked into his eyes—all I could see was love. I knew I was in love with him, and I knew he felt the same way about me. He kissed me passionately until I felt we would both explode. I felt so in love with him and it warmed my heart to be so close to him. Then he shared that Spirit had told him that he was to be the father of my two children and that we needed to come together soon so that this could take place. He'd already told Trish about his vision, and she was perfectly fine with all of it. They both wanted me to move down to Manti to live with them.

It all seemed so perfect, yet part of me was still hesitant to move into another threesome. Ray felt my reluctance and then asked if it would be okay to try it for a weekend to see how it felt. Trish was flying to Oregon to spend time with her grandparents, and had asked me to help Ray with the children. This would give Ray and me a chance to be alone and with the kids so that we could get to know each other better. I told Ray I'd be glad to help as I really missed mothering.

It was a magical weekend for us. The Manti Pageant was playing (it's a large outdoor play that depicts the Book of Mormon story), and we took the kids to it. Afterwards Ray played football with the older boys on the temple lawn as I watched from my wheelchair. After all the children had been tucked into bed, Ray came to where I was sleeping and we gazed into each other's eyes and melted into each other's souls knowing there was a deep connection that went way beyond this lifetime. We had all agreed not to have any sexual encounters—including kissing—until Trish could take part. Although it was difficult at times, Ray and I honored her wishes and just cuddled before going off to our own separate beds.

By July, we were making plans for me to move down permanently. But before that happened, Ray wanted to take Trish on a special trip to Mexico with Scott and Peggy, some friends from Manti. They asked if I'd be willing to take care of the kids and run Peggy's herb shop for the week they were away. I told them I'd be glad to. Ray said that Trish and he would pick me up that weekend and take me down to Manti. I then waited to hear from them.

It was Saturday, July 10, my sister Marsha's birthday. She wanted me to go to a Mormon singles' "lunch in the park" with her at Sugarhouse Park. I told her that being wheelchair bond I was in no condition to meet men and that I was already in a new relationship. I didn't give her the details knowing she would never understand. She begged me to go and, because it was her birthday, I conceded. Besides, Sugarhouse Park was a magical place for me. It was where I'd first synchronistically met Vaughn, so I was up for this little adventure.

Marsha loaded me and my wheelchair into my mother's green Chevy Lumina. I called to see if Ray and Trish had left from Manti. They were just leaving, and I told them that I'd meet them at Sugarhouse Park. By the tone in Ray's voice, I could tell there was something wrong. He didn't want to talk about it and said he'd talk to me at the park.

It was a hot mid-summer day, so we met on a shady terrace. The gathering consisted of the usual attendees of such events—dropouts from society and relationship rejects. Mormon men were unimpressive to me and the women seemed overtly desperate. Marsha introduced me to the ones she knew as part of her dating service. She was on her fifth husband and had become quite a "professional" at meeting men. I wasn't surprised that she had made it her occupation.

She and I had stopped at KFC on our way, and we were enjoying our meals when a good-looking guy with his three children showed up carrying a volleyball net. He was definitely my type—a John Denver look-a-like—and I asked Marsha if she knew him. She said she'd never noticed him before at the singles' ward and wondered if he was recently divorced. She urged me to introduce myself to him, as she knew instinctively that he was my type. I resisted her urgings and sat in my wheelchair watching the volleyball game.

After an hour or so, I wondered what time it was, as it seemed like Ray and Trish should have been there by then. I mustered the courage to ask "the John Denver look-a-like" the time as I'd noticed he was wearing a watch. It was just past three, and I was a bit discouraged that Ray and Trish hadn't arrived. I then asked him his name. It was Brad.

Something about him seemed safe and familiar, and we soon got into a conversation concerning my recent accident and our opinions about meeting people at Mormon singles' functions. He said he had just recently divorced and was already tired of the dating scene. There were so many desperate women out there, and he just wanted friendship for now.

I told him that I wasn't Mormon anymore; that I'd come to the park with my sister because it was her birthday and that some friends would be arriving any minute. Brad and I talked for over an hour until Marsha announced that it was time for us to leave. Brad then asked me my phone number and what I was doing the following day. At that point I'd given up on Ray and Trish showing up and told Brad that I normally went to Unity Church on Sunday morning. He asked if it would be okay to pick me up and join me at the service, and I replied it would be fine.

Chapter Sixteen—Brad

Ray called on Sunday morning and apologized for not meeting me at the park. Trish had had a sudden change of heart and had asked Sarah to baby-sit for the week. I felt that Trish's issues were starting to surface, and I knew I needed to give the two of them some space. Perhaps after their week alone together, she would feel differently.

Brad was a bit late picking me up, and by the time he put my wheelchair into his monstrous green Ford truck and drove the short distance, the meeting had already started. I felt a bit conspicuous as Brad wheeled me down the aisle to find a seat. It was crowded and people seemed a bit annoyed by the disturbance. But soon we'd located a seat near the front, and Brad helped me out of my wheelchair and sat me down next to him. The musical part of the service was just beginning.

I always enjoyed the upbeat band complete with electric guitars, synthesizers and drums. It was a far cry from the whiny organ music at a Mormon Church. The songs were popular with a nostalgic flavor. As the band began playing Kermitt the Frog's *Rainbow Connection*, I couldn't help but feel sentimental. These days everything felt that way, as my heart was raw from my recent near-death experience. But I still felt brilliantly alive, as God had given me a new lease on life. I could feel the transformation in me and in those around me—and I never wanted this fresh zest for life to leave.

Brad gently took my hand as he noticed tears running down my cheeks. I bet he never thought he'd see anyone cry over *Rainbow Connection*. But Unity was all new to him, and as we moved into the guided meditation delivered by Mike—Unity's beloved pastor—I could sense Brad's resistance. I squeezed his hand in reassurance as we both closed our eyes. Mike's meditations and messages were always inspiring and right on target. He spoke straight from the heart—and to the heart. I was hoping Brad was getting it, but I wasn't sure whether anything was penetrating. Afterward, he seemed vague and dismissive of the whole experience, and I assumed that it was just because it was new. I remembered my first time at Unity—it was different, but

I'd absolutely loved it! It was like coming home. But from Brad's blunt observations—it was far from coming home for him.

After the service, we passed on the coffee-break gathering, and Brad drove me straight home. He said he had weekend visitation with his three kids and needed to spend the time with them. He said they might go swimming in the pool at his condo later that evening, and asked if I was interested in joining them. This piqued my interest as I remembered the water therapy at Crystal Hot Springs. By now I'd gotten the cast off my arm and was looking forward to some movement in the water with it.

That evening, Brad helped me into the water from my wheelchair just as the sun was starting to set in the western skies. He said he loved watching the sunset from the swimming pool, and we sat in his favorite spot watching the sky turn pink and then brilliant red. It was magnificent. His children were charming—Jonathan, his teenaged son, Holly and Brooke, his two little girls. I so enjoyed the feelings of family again and we all played Marco-Polo in the pool until it was too dark to see. Brad then delivered me home in his new truck. It was an expensive vehicle, and I wondered what Brad did for a living to be able to afford the deluxe condo and a new truck. When he told me he worked as a floor-covering salesman, I was a bit disappointed. What a terribly boring job, I thought. Not much to start an absorbing conversation about. Should I ask, "How's the carpet business these days?" or "Do you sell very much oak flooring?" These weren't items of interest even in my most obscure reality. Floors are what people walked on—not something they paid attention to. But Brad was charming, and I figured that somewhere, somehow we'd find ways to relate to each other.

And it wasn't long before we were doing just that. We discovered that we were the same age and had gone to rival high schools—he went to Olympus and I went to Highland. We'd probably unknowingly crossed paths at one of our school's athletic events before. He knew a couple of my cousins and friends that went to Olympus although he didn't really know anyone from Highland. He said he was kind of shy when he was in high school, and I could tell he hadn't changed much.

But soon he was picking me up each evening for "pool-therapy." I could tell Brad loved playing the "knight in shining armor" for me the "helpless maiden." And I was loving it too. I soon met his roommate, Neal, a jolly old soul who loved to cook. Some of his meal combinations were a bit bizarre, but I must admit they were tasty. He loved the idea that Brad had a steady girlfriend and that he could tease him about. He would kid about the first time Brad carried me up the stairs to his bedroom loft and said Brad finally met a woman who couldn't run away from him. And maybe there was some truth to that, but I was twitterpated and willing to see where things would lead.

One of our first dates was at the same Oriental restaurant that Ed had taken me to. The fortune in the fortune cookie had read, "You will be married within a year." I laughed out loud and shared it with Brad. I said that marriage was the last thing on my mind. I didn't even believe in it any more and joked that it was precisely the cause of all divorce. But fate had its way with me and on December 12, 1999, only six months after we'd met, Brad and I were married. Pastor Mike from Unity performed the ceremony as he was the only one who would marry us in an "open marriage." But I don't really think Brad *got* what an *open marriage* was because we have regularly debated its meaning throughout our entire marriage. I even wrote a poem early on in our relationship describing it quite graphically.

The Ballad of the Thorne-Birds

Her heart was pierced by cupid's arrow,
His prick was big, his mind was narrow.
But sometimes narrow minds run deep,
Into his arms, she took the leap—
And landed on a bed of nails,
With gnashing teeth and weeping wails,
She crucified herself on his...
Excruciatingly erect penis.

Her life was filled with melodrama,
Twenty children called her "mamma."
Half her own, half were step
She loved them all, she was adept
At keeping everyone from guessing
How she kept her mind from messing
Up and down she rode the current,
She needed help, her call was urgent!

The Bird of Destiny released her crap,
And landed squarely in her lap.
She brushed it off—it stuck like glue,
I guess her karmic debt was due
She stabbed him with her prickly thorn,
But greater pains they both had born.
And so they stuck it out, no doubt
Fate had chosen them this route

"They'll never make it!" was everyone's voice.
"It doesn't matter, we have no choice!
For God had chosen us to be
His predecessors throughout eternity."
They struggle against tremendous odds,
Knowing someday they could be gods!
For only Destiny's voice is heard,
And to the rest—they flip the bird.

Most of the men I'd been in relationship with were astonished by my decision to marry Brad. Ray was crushed and begged me not to marry Brad as he felt I'd be miserable for the rest of my life. He was probably more right than he realized, but what was I to do? By now David and Ray, the two men I *had* fallen in love with, were more or less happily married and Ed had already moved on to a new relationship. Joe was in a committed relationship with Pam and Jerry was still committed to Judy. And Nolan was dead. All I wanted was a slice of the "happily ever after" pie I felt I deserved. I thought Brad was my best chance at obtaining that. But was I ever *wrong*. I didn't realize it at the time, but I had managed to magnetize my exact polar opposite who owned every single one of my trigger points. He would teach me every hard lesson I needed to learn about myself.

We spent the next seven years of our lives arguing over points of view, doctrines of faith, relationship dynamics, child-care strategies—annoying the hell out of each other and everyone around us. If Pam was the drama queen, then Brad was the drama king. I apologize to all of you whom Brad and I offended because of the control dramas we played out with each other. You know who you are, so I won't mention any names. I'm sure that there are dozens of you, and I'm deeply sorry for the trauma we've caused in your lives.

You should also know, however, that Brad has his good points. He was there for me during my entire rehabilitation from the car accident. He literally and figuratively was my personal "crutch." I hated crutches as they hurt under my arms, so Brad became my "crutch" for several months until my kneecap was completely healed. The doctors wanted to do surgery on my foot and put a metal plate in my ankle, but I didn't want that permanently inside my body. I opted instead for holistic medical treatments and went to Dr. Gary, my chiropractor friend, for acupuncture. I also continued seeing Ray for massage therapy until Brad went to war with him and kicked him out of *his* apartment and out of *my* life. Regardless of all the personal drama, my foot healed completely, and I was able to run a marathon six months later just as I'd promised the surgeon who told me I'd never walk normally again without his surgery. It just goes to show you the power of mind over matter—and holistic healing.

During all of my rehab, Brad was as patient as Job and also taught me the lesson of patience. He was late for everything (including Ariel's wedding), so I renamed myself "the lady in waiting" and him "Johnny come lately" or the shorter version "Pokeyman." Besides frustrating the hell out of me, he began to domesticate my wild, adventurous spirit. I grew to appreciate Brad's simple ways and learned not to resist his resistance. Believe me, Brad was resistant to every new experience I drew into our lives. And I always got into my shit by resisting his every resistance. I felt like I was dragging a stubborn mule with me every where I went. And it got really old after awhile until I figured out that I could go places without him and actually have more fun. That's when his resistance melted as he realized that I was going to parties and dances without him. And he felt he needed to be there to monitor my experiences or else I'd certainly get into trouble.

Sometimes I felt that Brad was the most oblivious person to his surroundings I'd ever met, but sometimes he'd speak such profound statements that I'd wondered if he'd channeled a higher source. He was always full of surprises and unexpected delights. On any given day, half of me wanted to leave him and half wanted to stay. I stayed for the sweetness I saw in him and the hope that someday he might wake up and "get it." Or maybe I'd wake up and "get it." But I believe that after seven years it was really a little of both of us waking up and getting what relationship is all about in the first place—to learn more about ourselves and having someone else show us our blind spots. Of course, at one point we knew that there was a higher source that brought us "back together" for what turned out to be the third time in our lives.

The first time we realized that we'd known each other before was early in our relationship. It was when he'd read my book, *Heartsong* and realized that I'd been a ballet dancer. He then shared that he had taken ballet for a couple of years when he was about ten because his mother had forced him to do it. She told him if he was to be a good football player—that he needed to take ballet for grace and balance. The story sounded all too familiar and we soon realized that he was one of the two boys in my ballet class. We both reminisced about the wobbly winding staircase we climbed to get up to the ballet room and the strict teacher who thumped out the beat with her wooden dowel. We both remembered our conversations with each other, as I was one of the few girls in class friendly enough to talk to the "shy boy on the back row." We were surprised to discover that those two children had been him and me.

But the next incident came as an unbelievable surprise to both of us. One day, after four years into our marriage, we were driving down the road near

53rd south and 9th east and passed an old restaurant called the Italian Village. Almost simultaneously we both remarked that we had gone on a date there in high school. We pulled a U-turn and went back there for dinner—for old time's sake. We were both drawn to a window booth and sat down at the same booth we remembered sitting on our date. Then things started to get really weird. We both started having a real sensation of *de-ja-vu* as we started to recall our dates. It was my first date—a Seminary Computer Date—and if I remembered correctly—he was from, oh, my, God—Olympus High School. Brad then started to reminisce his date—a Seminary Computer Date from—yes, Highland High. Could it be? No it was impossible—but all the details started coming out over dinner. *We suddenly realized that we had been each other's first date and didn't know it until four years after we were married!*

This was just too incredible! But as we described what each of us had worn, what our double dates looked like and what Brad drove—his dad's two-toned station wagon—we both realized that God had indeed played a perfect cosmic joke on us. We had programmed our perfect mates through a seminary computer dating service—and had dreamed up each other over twenty years before. I then remember staring into Brad's big blue eyes for the first time and falling in love with him then. I asked him why it had taken so long to call me back for a second date. Of course, I knew he was slow and always late—but this was ridiculous!

He then recalled one thing about the date that had really derailed him—that I had asked to say a prayer, out loud, over the food right there in the restaurant. That would be me as I was trained from childhood to say a blessing on the food at *every* meal. It was my first date and I thought I couldn't eat unless the food was blessed. He thought it a bit strange as was the way I preached to him all night from the scriptures. He believed I was a bit square and wasn't interested in suffering through a second overly spiritual date. At that time in his life he was interested in fast, easy chicks—and wow had I'd ever changed since then. I was still preaching, but my doctrines had taken a 180 degree turn.

We both wondered what our lives would have been like if Brad had asked me for a second date—all the pain and heartache we could have avoided from our previous marriages. But then we realized that sometimes God knows best and answers prayers in their own due time. I remembered praying for a week after our date that Brad would call me back, so I suppose all prayers are answered in one way or another. It had taken us years to heal from the damage of our previous marriages. Brad, too, had been in an abusive marriage. His ex had a violent streak, and both of us reacted negatively to any type of control drama that surfaced. Unfortunately, those reactions usually ended up as control dramas themselves, but we stayed with the conversation, which is really the saving grace in any relationship.

Brad also had the "need to fix everything" personality type—perhaps a diversion from fixing himself. Most of the time this was a good thing as he helped me out of a lot of sticky situations like the one in which an inept lawyer almost lost the settlement for my car accident. If it wasn't for Brad taking the initiative to find out that my attorney hadn't filed the paperwork, I would have lost $50,000. I was very grateful to him for that. After paying off all of the medical expenses I was left with money to hire another lawyer to go after Kurt for custody of my kids. Even after the car accident, Kurt remained a total jerk by not allowing me regular visitation.

On the first visitation after the accident, Brad came up as my protector. Kurt insisted on having visitation in a small out-of-the-way park in Lewiston, Idaho. He also insisted that he supervise the visitation himself. Brad stayed near the car as I hobbled on crutches to meet the children. Kurt held Andrew and refused to let me touch him. The other children were glad to see me after several months of wondering what had happened but were afraid to show me any affection with their father in view.

About ten minutes into the visit, Kurt noticed Brad standing near the car and told him that he needed to leave. Brad refused, and that sent Kurt into a violent rage. He went after Brad and threatened to kill him with his bare hands. Brad got into the car and I joined him, leaving the kids upset and crying. I told him to drive away as this type of violent behavior wasn't worth it. Brad had a gun in the car and had a concealed weapons permit, and I was afraid he might use it if Kurt got too threatening. Kurt smashed at the car windows with his bare hands, and Brad pulled the gun warning Kurt to get out of the way or he'd use it. We then drove to the nearest police station and filed an assault report on Kurt. It was ugly and it got even uglier after we got home.

About a week later, Brad received a phone call from an FBI agent who told him to watch his back for the next few days as someone had come in and testified that Kurt had tried to contract a murder on Brad. The guy told the FBI that Kurt had asked him to "take care of Brad." He had refused but wasn't sure if Kurt had tried to hire someone else. It was one of Kurt's ex-con friends who just wanted to make sure that we were aware of Kurt's extremely violent intentions towards Brad. Brad was stunned and when he told me about the call, I was also stunned. I was hoping that the FBI would arrest Kurt for aggravated assault and attempted conspiracy to commit murder, but as the weeks went by, we realized that even the FBI didn't want to risk stirring up a hornet's nest. They were hoping it would all blow over, and they said they didn't have enough evidence to arrest Kurt and charge him. In the meantime we were told to stay at someone else's place for safety, so we stayed at one of Brad's friends. Kurt's friend who had turned him in later refused to allow his testimony to be used, so there was really no hard evidence except for the police report we'd filed.

Then I hired a lawyer (Brad's divorce attorney) to fight for custody of my kids. We thought we had a good case for custody until Kurt pulled a fast one. He had the older children sign a written statement that they thought their younger siblings would be better off in their father's and Christy's custody. He also had neighbors and friends write similar letters supporting his position. My lawyer said we would be in for a long, ugly, expensive battle against Kurt that may do more damage to the children than good.

We finally settled out of court for custody of Ariel—if I agreed to pay my share of the orthodontic bills amounting to over $3,000. We also got the supervised visitation dropped and regular scheduled visitations ordered. Kurt was also ordered to have the children available for phone visitation each Sunday, but he only honored that the first week after the order. He never was concerned about the children or my feelings but only about his need to be in complete control. And I was always at a loss to know what to do about it. I'd already spent thousands of dollars on lawyers, and I felt beaten down at every crossroad. It was an extremely discouraging and frustrating situation with Kurt, and I hoped things would change over time. It was a slow process, but eventually things did become more bearable.

Brad was loving and supportive throughout the entire battle with Kurt, and we felt overjoyed that Ariel finally got to move in with us. Brad had also gotten custody of his son, Jonathan, and so we began to build a home with our two teenaged children. It was challenging at times, as they were both in the same grade and yet complete opposites in personality. They both had been raised by one "abusive-controlling" parent and one "try-to-get-along-at-all-costs" parent, and they were confused by the different disciplinary tactics Brad and I tried. I attempted to make Ariel toe the line, while Jonathan was always trying to push the limits with Brad. It was hard for the two of us to come together on a united front.

Ariel constantly complained that she got punished for the exact same things that Jonathan got away with. I tried to remind her that she was my child and Jonathan was Brad's—but that didn't hold much water for her. But her and my close relationship and the open communication I encouraged among all of us got us through the challenging teenage years. In the end, Ariel graduated from high school and went on to graduate from college with honors. Jonathan, however, dropped out of high school during his final semester and went to work for my son, Jared, in construction. Again, there are no right or wrong choices—just choices and consequences.

Another thing Brad encouraged me to do was to get *Heartsong* published. He found me an excellent editor that he knew—Lavina Fielding Anderson—and I paid her with some of my insurance settlement. I appreciated much of what she did, but some suggestions came from an ex-Mormon perspective (Lavina had recently been excommunicated from the Church along with several other prominent LDS scholars), and I felt some bitterness coming from her every time I dealt with Mormon issues. She also tried to edit out a lot of the sexual content that was probably overwhelming to her. This book is being edited for only stylistic changes and linguistic continuity. The content, however, is the naked truth as far as I can see it.

Brad and I sent several dozen copies of *Heartsong* to publishers we thought might be interested. After several months of receiving gracious "Thanks, but no thanks" letters (some were impressed with the book but didn't quite know where to place it—fiction or non-fiction.) I gave up trying to publish it and proceeded to give out manuscripts to people who asked for a copy. That let me be in control of who read it and to be able to directly get their response. As you have witnessed from some of the responses to my book, I wasn't very responsible. I let things get a bit carried away.

I insisted that Brad read *Heartsong* before we were married so he would have full disclosure about who I was and what I wanted to create in my life. I made it *very clear* to him that I was polyamorous which is defined as "many loves" or "expanded relationships"—just like in my book. But that didn't affect his monogamous attitude towards our marriage. We were always in conflict about this one single issue and it seemed like we spent more than half of our time arguing about it. I must admit after looking back over it all, I'd probably chosen differently as I'm not sure *any* relationship is worth *that much conflict and drama.*

Chapter Seventeen—Kerry

After Ariel and Jonathan moved out on their own, Brad and I needed a change of scenery from the Sandy condo. Neal had moved out right before Brad and I got married, but I never considered the condo as part of my creation. I had simply moved in with Brad because it was convenient.

In the meantime, I'd helped develop Brad's floor covering business into a thriving manufacturers' rep agency called NUMAD—Natural Unique Materials for Architectural Design. I also attended night school at the Utah College of Massage Therapy and received my massage therapy license. After graduating, I began an out-call business called Massage Connection, supplying massages to guests at Salt Lake City's high-end hotels like the Marriotts and Little America. But after a year or so of hauling my massage table up staircases and down hallways of hotels, I decided I wanted to set up a practice from a home base. Then the opportunity of a lifetime presented itself.

Joe and Ed (my two former lovers) were working on a tile-floor project out in Draper for a man named Kerry who was a retired mortgage broker interested in setting up a rehabilitation center for drug addicts. He was using some high tech alternative therapy procedures like rapid eye therapy, subliminal hypnosis, and neuro-net brain stimulation, and he wanted a licensed massage therapist on board to help with the detoxification process. Detox and health transformation were my specialties having had a strong background in holistic healing and herbs in addition to massage. I'd also studied Lypossage—a massage technique to eliminate toxic waste which creates cellulite. I was ready to put a protocol together for renewing the body calling it the Nu Yu Total Body Renewal System.

Kerry's large facility was on a beautiful seven-acre lot—a former fourteen-bedroom polygamist home which Kerry had turned into a healing retreat/rehab center. He also had a large five-bedroom modular home on the property that he said Brad and I could move into for the price of fixing the damaged plumbing and electrical system. I was also offered my own therapy rooms—three in all—if I'd put in the time and expense to fix them up. It seemed like a great opportunity for us. The doors were being opened, so we walked through them.

We expended a lot of time, money and effort into what was now called— Higher Ground Healing Center. Brad and Kerry decided on that name. I thought it was terribly unoriginal naming it after our place in Montana. But maybe the energy of Higher Ground was there as business started to build as I brought in clients for the Nu Yu Total Body Renewal System, and they were experiencing tremendous, measurable results. As part of our promotional efforts, each month we hosted an open house for local health product vendors, offering free demonstrations and information to the public. The open houses grew more and more successful, and clients for my Nu Yu program and memberships to the Higher Ground Healing Center flooded in.

As Brad and I became confident of Higher Ground's success, we started sinking all our money into developing the seven acres. We decided to move our Togenberg goats to the site since we'd been keeping them on some land that was part of my inheritance in Draper, which my mom's family was getting ready to sell. The goats required that we put in hundreds of feet of fence, and Brad, Jared and Jonathan built a large chicken coop and sheds along with the fencing. Brad in his enthusiasm purchased a variety of hundreds of chickens, ducks, geese, llamas and also some Cherro sheep (a rare endangered Navaho variety). Kerry brought over his horse and we began to feel like we were in the midst of Old McDonald's Farm. All we needed was a pig, and we'd be in business. Instead, Kerry and Brad opted for buffalo—not because of my spiritual connection to them but for the meat.

Now you've got to understand Brad's resistance to anything mystical. He thought my White Buffalo Woman story was cute and imaginative but highly irrational. In fact, he often mocked my belief in animal totems, Native American Shamans, and in Kundalini energies. He even tried one morning to vacuum up Patrick's spirit when I was attempting to connect with him spiritually because of Brad's fear of the unknown. I had a good laugh (and I'm sure Patrick did, too) when Brad completely ruined the brand-new Hoover vacuum cleaner, which couldn't be repaired.

Brad thought these were all figments of a deranged imagination—until one day I got sick of his mockery. I told him that *that* day he would discover his *own* animal totem in a very convincing way.

We were headed up to Logan to visit some of Brad's floor-covering dealers. On the way up north, Brad kept spotting dead birds on the roadside and was compelled to stop each time to collect them for their feathers. Mysteriously, I didn't see any of them anywhere on the road, but sure enough every few miles Brad stopped and threw another—what we discovered to be owls—into the back of the truck. By the time we got back home there were 13 in all! I

felt that that was a significant and superstitious enough number to overcome
Brad's doubts about animal totems! But he still contends that it was merely
a "strange coincidence," and so I decided to give him the Indian name of
"Wise Guy." The name he gave himself is "Man who sees through bullshit."
(Except for his own.)

But then came a trip to Montana to look for some buffalo to bring down
to Higher Ground. I thought that this was an insane idea—to fence in wild
buffalo in a Salt Lake suburb. But Brad and Kerry were insistent that they
wanted to raise buffalo at Higher Ground. Still unconvinced, I told Brad
that there were several herds of buffalo near Missoula if he wanted to get the
low-down on what it would take to raise buffalo in a fenced area in a semi-
crowded neighborhood. I promised him on my next visitation with the kids,
we would go look for the herds.

As fate would have it, on my next visit to Montana, Kurt was acting out
his control dramas again and wouldn't let me see my children for part of the
weekend. I knew it was bullshit that they'd made "previous plans," but he
continues to do this just to get my goat and to convince me who's in charge of
the universe—*his* universe. To me, it's just another confirmation of my need
to get as far away as possible from his out-of-control male ego.

But this gave Brad and me an opportunity to look for buffalo. Brad called
a place near Dillon, which was over a hundred miles from Missoula. I really
wasn't looking forward to the long drive after driving the entire previous day,
yet Brad was determined and so we started out early that morning for the long
drive. About 30 miles east of Missoula, I spotted a small herd of buffalo in a
pasture by the side of the road. Surprised that I hadn't noticed them before,
we decided to stop and ask at the house next to the herd how to get in touch
with the herd's owner.

A sweet, country gal told us that this particular herd was just a small
portion of a larger one up Gold's Canyon—several miles up the road. She
gave us directions and a phone number. We called and the owner agreed to
meet us. We followed the directions to his office and met him there. We were
amazed by the hundreds of acres of buffalo-filled pastures. Buffalo are such
awesome creatures to me—in spite *and* because of my personal fascination
with the White Buffalo Woman legend. They represent one of the truly wild,
undomesticated breeds of animals still left in North America. I feel they
could never be truly tamed—just like me.

As Brad was in the office negotiating for the purchase of a few head, I
was drawn to a young buffalo in a fenced pasture across the road. The owner
had said that "Daisy" had been bottle fed from a calf and was somewhat of
a "pet." Sometimes she was a real nuisance following people around to be
petted. She didn't realize her own strength, however, when she nudged them

with her horns for attention. I ventured over and petted Daisy's head as she nudged the fence. This was the closest I'd ever been to a buffalo, and her magnificent beauty amazed me. The owner then suggested that we take a drive out to the north pasture to see the "white buffalo." My heart skipped a beat at the suggestion that *they actually had a white buffalo nearby.*

"Yea, a lot of Indian chiefs made a big to-do about it when she was born. They all came out and blessed her and did a ceremony. They even ran an article on it in the local newspaper. I'm not really sure what it's all about. Something about it being a sign of the return of the White Buffalo Woman." My mouth dropped. I didn't know whether or not to spill the beans all over the floor to this roughneck cowboy about the significance of the white buffalo—and me. I finally just asked, "Can we see her?"

"Sure, I don't see why not? Just go through the gate and around that hill and you'll find her herd in the next pasture. Just be sure you close the gate on the way in and out. We don't want any of 'em gettin' away."

Brad made the purchase of six, two-year-olds—four cows and two bulls—for $1,000 (part of the purchase price was a tax-exempt donation to Higher Ground) and made arrangements for their delivery after we fenced the property later that summer. Buffalo require a special tensile strength wire and double-fencing to prevent on-lookers from potential injury. I had my doubts if the six buffalo would ever be delivered to Higher Ground, but I figured it was a good investment in the white buffalo herd.

After the purchase we headed towards the north pasture. There were a few white yaks in with the herd and Brad thought that white buffalo might not be so rare because he thought the yaks were buffalo. I told him that the long horns on the yaks were a dead giveaway. Buffalo had short horns curling forward with a hump on their backs. (Sometimes Brad is rather dense in such matters. He claims he couldn't see the horns from that distance.) As we rounded another hill, I noticed the white buffalo in the herd. She was standing apart from the others, quite regally as if she were perfectly aware of her contrast to them. The other animals even gave her space as they headed around her and towards the bales of hay, which had recently been delivered. I wished I'd brought my camera as we were able to get several hundred yards close to her to get some excellent pictures. But then I thought, no—picture taking seemed like such a touristy thing to do—kind of an insult to the sacredness of oracles. I recalled how I abhor anyone taking pictures of me, which always registers in any of my photos.

We sat for about fifteen minutes observing the white buffalo, and as I looked into her eyes, there was such a mystical connection between us—as if we were one in spirit. I could have stayed there all day merging with her soul, but I felt Brad was getting a bit spooked by it all and wanted to leave. I was amazed by the coincidences that had brought my animal totem and me together. The next day we brought the kids out to see her—and they truly appreciated the significance of her presence there. And they all enjoyed petting Daisy, too.

Soon afterwards it became quite clear that Draper's Higher Ground was headed for trouble. Kerry kept bringing in more and more drug addicts to be rehabilitated which created a lot of chaotic energy for everyone involved. When Kerry met a gal from Manti and started spending weekends with her, leaving the healing center vulnerable, the proverbial shit hit fan. One addict stole a Massage Connection check and began duplicating our account number and making checks of his own. Over $3,000 was stolen from our business account before we finally figured out what was happening.

The bank reimbursed us, but Kerry begged us not to file formal police charges as he was at risk for harboring known drug-addicts. And Kerry was having problems of his own keeping the druggies from hot-wiring his cars and taking them on joyrides on the weekends he was away. And then some valuable art objects from the center ended up missing, and we realized Kerry was into some deep shit.

We didn't realize how deep the manure was until we found a five-day eviction due to foreclosure notice stuck to Kerry's front door one morning. I'd felt that something was up by how suspicious he'd been acting. He'd been consulting a Native American Chief to see if he could transfer the entire estate into his so-called "tax-exempt" reservation. It turned out that the Chief was the same Sioux who had taken David G to South Dakota to the Pipekeepers. (Remember the story when David G came into the Native American store wanting to buy White Buffalo Woman Christmas cards? Interesting coincidence.)

Unfortunately Kerry, this whole time, hadn't paid a dime on the mortgage payments and was doing some squirrelly legal process called "redemption." I wasn't privy to the details, but it became quite obvious that the whole thing was illegal when Paul, one of Kerry's roommates and confidantes, was arrested for fraud and sent to prison. And now Kerry had been served an eviction notice, which included *us* having to vacate the premises in just *five* days!

Brad and I were pretty upset about the whole thing and demanded to know the entire story. Kerry then revealed how he had bankrupted the entire estate in a last attempt to save it from foreclosure. But instead of saving it, a land-developer named Dave had bought it out of bankruptcy and was now the new owner of the entire property. Legally, it was a done deal. Ethically, well that was anyone's guess. Regardless, Brad and I were in the cross-fire of legal indiscretions and we were now scrambling to find a new home for us, our animals and our belongings.

Chapter Eighteen—Patricia

The next experience is another one fit for *Ripley's Believe It or Not!* By now you've probably noticed that my life runs along the lines of uncanny synchronicity. What can I say? Believe it or not!

The first time I met Patricia was at a Christmas party the first year I'd come down from the "Wild Montana Skies." Ed took me to the party as he thought I'd enjoy meeting another "family of friends" he'd connected with. My first impression of them was that they were the "high society" type, and I felt a bit awkward in my jeans, leather vest and moccasin-boots while everyone else wore evening attire. It was at Patricia's home, an elegantly decorated antique "cottage" in the midst of Cottonwood Heights—an exclusive suburb of Salt Lake.

Patricia, an ex-movie star with all the trappings, greeted us cordially at the door. A beautiful ivory grand piano graced the living room and everyone sat on antique chairs surrounding it for the evening's Christmas performance. And what an impressive performance it was! Steve, the pianist, played for the Utah Symphony and Patricia, Lois and Lorraine, all professional singers who attended Unity Church, performed Christmas music extraordinaire. Gary (another John Denver look-alike who actually played the guitar) delighted us with a perfectly memorized rendition of "The Grinch Who Stole Christmas," and I immediately fell in love with him. Robert, who was later introduced as Patricia's partner, was the talented chiropractic physician of the group, and I also fell in love with him later on in the story.

I was amazed by the exceptional talent this group had to offer, but it was fairly obvious that few of them were impressed by my unconventional back-woods ways. I hadn't cut my hair, shaved my legs or worn make-up for at least fifteen years, and my talent for music amounted to singing lullabies, camp songs and a few of my own songs on the guitar.

Sheri was about the only one who I could identify with. She was dressed more casual with a new baby in her arms. We had a genuine heart to heart conversation about her polyamorous relationship with her two Steves (the pianist was the baby's father and her husband was a lawyer named Steve). I shared with her how I'd just left a polygamous marriage in Montana and was anxious to meet some friends with similar beliefs. I really felt a connection with Sheri and also with a guy named Stewart who'd traveled up from St. George for the party.

Ed had connected with an attractive, available woman and suggested I find a ride home. Stewart politely offered to take me home, but instead we ended up at a friend's apartment. Stewart's unique sense of humor and boyish looks were attractive to me, but it wasn't long before I found out that he was one of David T's best friends. And it wasn't too long afterward that I learned that Patricia was the ex-movie star that David had lived with in Cottonwood Heights!

Out of respect for David and respect for myself (I never screw a man on the first date), I asked Stewart to take me home after we enjoyed a steamy make-out session. But I did promise to spend New Year's Eve with him in Las Vegas and overnight at Lake Mead. This adventure ended in a spurious trip to Sedona, the details of which I won't go into (for David's sake) as *that was truly an unbelievable story* with more of David T's friends. Suffice it to say I was too much for Stewart to handle as he had a reputation to keep in the Mormon Singles Ward in St. George. But I must admit Stewart was one of the reasons I moved down to St. George in the first place. But let's get on with Patricia's story.

By the time I'd gotten married and had moved to Draper, Patricia had also moved into a log home in Draper a few blocks away. She was still having her cottage meetings, which consisted of the same group of people meeting each week to study the *Course in Miracles*. I was familiar with the course (and with miracles), and soon Brad and I were attending some of her weekly meetings—rubbing elbows with the aristocratic elite. I was having a *de-ja-vu* of my former "arms length" relationship with Rose (Andie McDowell) which wasn't very fulfilling but a bit superficial and contrived. Brad really started feeling uncomfortable when it was rumored that certain members of this new group were "experimenting with E" at some of their parties. Here we were trying to rehabilitate drug-addicts at Higher Ground Healing Center, and they were in the process of creating them!

That's when my relationship with Patricia became strained—at best. We heard a rumor that Patricia was in danger of losing her home because she couldn't make the mortgage payments or taxes. Joe then turned Patricia on to Paul (Kerry's friend) who convinced her to go through the same "redemption" process Kerry was doing. Well, as far as I was concerned, they all needed "redemption" but not in the way they were talking about. Karma was taking its toll and it seemed like Brad and I were caught in the middle.

Patricia caught wind that Brad and I needed a place to land until we could figure out what to do with ourselves. We'd rented a storage unit for our stuff and the animals were being boarded by a local horse trainer. Patricia "generously" offered us a room at her cottage for $600 a month. She was already renting a room to her friend, Stacy and a therapy room to Amy, a massage therapist. We figured this was how Patricia was supposedly paying her mortgage.

We declined her offer because Kerry offered us the use of his travel trailer as a good will gesture. Patricia came over and helped me clean out the travel trailer and then offered us a parking spot in her driveway for $200 a month. Brad told her sarcastically that "it was real neighborly of her" but instead offered her a trade for one of the dishwashers from the healing center for the first month's rent. At this point we were desperate, and began selling anything that wasn't literally "nailed down."

That weekend we had a gigantic yard sell and sold everything we couldn't fit into the storage unit. I sold all of the "stuff" that Kerry told me was junk left in the travel trailer which Patricia and I had cleaned out. But we found out later that it all belonged to his niece. She came over the day before we were evicted to claim her "stuff," and we all got a Scotch blessing for selling it at the yard sale. I offered her $50, which was a lot more than I'd sold all it for, but she flatly declined. Kerry caught the brunt of her anger, which he then passed along to me. This gave me the perfect opportunity to unload all of the pent-up feelings that had been festering inside of me and—I must admit—*it felt good.*

One of the most bittersweet moments was regarding the beautiful raised-bed garden Brad and I had created that spring. It had taken us over a month to build a terraced, semicircular garden, using broken-up concrete and terracotta from a neighbor's demolished driveway. I must admit, it was one of my finest gardening creations. I saw tears in some of our friends' eyes when I offered for them to take any and all of the plentiful produce that was just coming on. I'd planted lettuce, spinach, peas, carrots, broccoli, cauliflower, tomatoes, peppers, squash, cucumbers, and more, and the plants had just reached the peak of their production. I couldn't figure out why I'd felt so compelled to put so much effort into creating this garden only to see it all go to waste. I concluded that it must be some leftover karma from some of my past indiscretions. Little did I know that this was one of our "saving graces"—a scene which touched Dave's (the new land-developer's) heart and produced a miracle.

After Kerry and his menagerie of druggies and friends had moved out of the big house and Brad and I were safely tucked away in Kerry's travel trailer at Patricia's—a fascinating series of events occurred. First off, the police came to repossess the travel trailer which they claimed didn't belong to Kerry but was a stolen vehicle. We figured things couldn't get much worse as we moved our few belongings into Patricia's garage and put a couple of foam pads on her patio terrace to sleep on. After a few nights under the stars, I felt at home again—camping out at the mercy of God hands—a very safe place to be.

Brad, on the other hand, was at his wit's end. He was traumatized by all the recent events, scrambling to find answers to what he saw as dilemmas. A few days later, Dave called and asked Brad to come down to his office. He wanted to explain his side of the situation. That same afternoon, Patricia was served a *three-day eviction notice for foreclosure on her house*! Obviously the "redemption process" wasn't working for her either and we were *all* in the same boat—up the creek without a paddle. Patricia was devastated—wondering how and where she would move her house full of priceless antique furniture to in just *three days*.

Then Brad came home with the news. After talking with Dave (who felt compassion towards Brad's and my situation) he offered us a deal of a lifetime. He needed a caretaker for the big house and someone to clean up Kerry's huge mess. (Kerry had indeed left the house a disaster.) Dave generously offered us $3,000 to clean up the home and a place to stay—*for free*—until he decided what to do with it. We could move all of our belongings into the big house as soon as it was clean. And then Brad related the rest of the story which Dave had revealed to him. Kerry had cheated the previous landowner (a polygamist named Jeffs—I believe Warren Jeffs' brother) out of the estate. As a mortgage broker, Kerry had offered to catch up Jeffs' mortgage payments in exchange for Jeffs' putting the place into Kerry's land trust. As soon as Jeffs was back on his feet (he had suffered a heart attack and was out of work), Kerry was to allow him and his family back into the home and to catch up on their back mortgage payments. An option would be for Kerry to sell the place and give Jeffs his equity. Instead, Kerry took advantage of the whole situation and simply moved in.

Sandy, a real estate agent from Richfield, had apprised Dave of the situation as she was acquainted with the Jeffs' and Kerry's former "business dealings." Brad brought home an inch stack of copies of Kerry's previous illegal transactions—including the Jeffs' deal. We were simply one of the many victims of Kerry's scams. And as victims, both Sandy and Dave felt sorry for us and arranged an act of benevolence.

I could hardly believe my ears as Brad related the entire story to me. Then it was Brad's turn to be amazed as I related how Patricia had just been evicted from her house—again because of one of Kerry's scams. I then asked Brad to call Dave and see if Patricia and Stacy (her tenant) could also move into the big house with us as Kerry had also scammed them. Dave consented to allow Patricia to move in with all of her furniture—including the ivory grand piano and large Jacuzzi. Stacy moved her bedroom furniture into one of the large bedrooms, and Amy (the massage therapist) moved her equipment into one of the therapy rooms. Robert and Gary also joined us a few months later, and we all lived in community for nearly eight months until Dave decided to tear down the house. The property was worth more than the building so it had to go—along with its occupants. In February we all got the word that we needed to find another place to call home.

In the meantime, I'd received part of my inheritance money from the Draper farm and ended up purchasing the pink modular home from Sandy (which was her commission for arranging the deal for Dave). I figured she'd helped us out through all of it, and I felt I owed it to her. After moving the house to three various locations (all weird stories I won't trouble you with), we finally plopped it on some property near Indianola where Joe's cabin was located.

I then felt inspired to move to Las Vegas for the rest of the winter to look for a job as a massage therapist at one of the large casinos. One of Brad's floor-covering manufacturers was also considering moving its headquarters there, so Brad and I took the proverbial "gamble." In the meantime, Patricia, Stacy, Amy, Robert and Gary were on their own. We thought we'd found a suitable home for all of us out in Herriman, but that deal fell through (another of the too weird stories), so I figured it would be a while before community would develop again. But as I look back on it all, there were some real sweet memories from Higher Ground in Draper.

Patricia continued with her *Course in Miracles* classes and we got better acquainted with her family of friends which was loosely named "The Cottage Crowd." One friend, for whom I really gained an appreciation, was Brian. He was the networker of the group and organized the entire move of Patricia's furniture—accomplished in just one day including the huge Jacuzzi. It was a real testimony to the power of community. Brian was in an open relationship with his wife, Michelle, and outwardly it seemed like they had the knack for making it work. The rest of us seemed to struggle with open relationships (especially Brad and me) until we finally gave up. Robert also gave up and left Patricia to marry Carol, a former acquaintance of mine from a David Daida Tantra Workshop. And Robert's other partner, Jolynn ended up in relationship with Brian and Michelle. Gary moved back in with Sheri (along with one of the Steves) and continues to struggle with that relationship. I know this all seems very complicated which expanded relationships are. Go figure!

During the holiday season, Patricia, Robert, Gary and Carol performed a fabulous Christmas rendering of the "Frog Prince" which Patricia had rewritten herself. It was delightful and was followed by a fabulous formal dinner party, which is one of Patricia's fortes. Another of Patricia's talents was teaching drama classes one of which Brad and I attended for several months. I wrote and performed several comedy monologues, but one of my dreams was to perform a dramatic reading of my White Buffalo Woman poem, *Gift of the Sacred Pipe* in a costume made from white leathers. In January, this was realized and was followed by a sacred pipe ceremony conducted by Amy's partner, Mike, a pipe-carrier and Sundancer. It served as the final tribute to the Higher Ground community.

Chapter Nineteen—The Bellagio

If the worst fear in life is to be abandoned by your loved-ones, kicked out into the snow and left under a viaduct to die a cold, harsh death, then it was time Brad and I faced our fears and moved past them. Actually it was Brad's fear—the fear of having no place to live—that compelled us to move to Vegas and live in my dad's old Jayco pop-up trailer.

Ah, the sweet surrender of unfettered simplicity. It was the call of serendipity moving through us, and I was loving it! It reminded me of the good ol' days when we (Kurt, the kids and I) lived in a teepee in the wilds of Montana. I never felt so connected to Mother Earth and free from the burdens of managing a household of…stuff. I wanted to be free of things and all the time and energy they consumed. I wanted to be free to explore new environments, new realities, new people, places and…definitely *not* things. Relationships. I wanted to explore new relationships. I was tired of the old set pattern of friends and how I was relating to them and them to me. We had already formed our opinions of who we were and how we should act. And so we acted out those realities for each other in the boxes we had created for ourselves—and I wanted out of those boxes! The only viable option was to do something radically different—to change realities—so Brad and I did.

The Oasis was just as the word described—a virtual paradise in the desert. It was also the name of the trailer court we ended up in. But this was no tacky trailer-court—this was prime-time mobile-home heaven. It had an eighteen-hole miniature golf course surrounding the perimeter, two massive swimming pools (one for adults and one for children), a large Jacuzzi, a workout area, a convenience store, a movie theater, and all the amenities you could imagine for seniors.

Yes, it wasn't until after you turned 65 that you truly *got* what life was *really* about…living…and enjoying it! Of course, by then the government starts to help with the bills, or your IRAs or retirement funds become available. But why is it that by the time you can *really* afford to live life the way you *really* want to—you're too old to *really* enjoy it! This was a wake-up call for Brad and me when, at the tender age of 47, we started mingling with the re-tired trailer-elite.

But since we didn't have any Social Security checks coming in, IRAs or retirement funds, we both went to work. I landed a job almost immediately as a classroom manager for the Nevada College of Massage Therapy (a branch of UCMT), and Brad started representing some of our NUMAD products in Las Vegas, concentrating on a new "Rock Carpet" line.

After a few months of classroom managing, I found out why the college had a hard time retaining classroom managers. The entire job description was "student retention." That meant you had to do everything up to and including hog-tying students to their chairs to keep them in class. By the first quarter I was in the "red-zone" because I was down .05% of the allowable classroom retention. I had to come in for an extra hour each week (on my dime) to be counseled by my supervisor about what I was or wasn't doing right to keep students in class. It was all bullshit, and by the time summer had arrived in Vegas (early May) I was ready for a new job relationship. Besides pop-up trailers, we were told, are terribly hot in the summer without air-conditioning.

The day I put in my letter of resignation describing my frustrations of class-room managing was the day the Bellagio called me for an interview. Of course Brad answered my cell phone and automatically said "yes" as it was more his dream than mine that I work at the Bellagio. But I suppose all the filling out of applications for a "real" job in Vegas finally panned out, and I started the ladder climb to obtain a massage therapy position for "the largest and finest spa in the world." At least that was their claim to fame, and who was I to argue? If I had to work somewhere, it might as well be for the best!

That summer we moved back to Salt Lake to get out of the Vegas heat and to wade through all the red-tape, rings of fire, and horse-pookey I had to go through to obtain a work-card, health-card and finally an employee-card for the Bellagio. I was feeling ready to escape the system and head for the mountains again, but Brad convinced me (again) that it was all for my own good and was such a great learning opportunity. I guess I was still on the "Learn Your Lessons the Hard Way" track and figured that I might as well enjoy the ride while I'm still on board the train. I must admit, however, that it was an excellent opportunity to perfect my massage skills and to meet some incredibly interesting people.

Some of the first I met were the other massage therapists who'd been hired for the grand opening of the new spa in December. I found out that I was the first of about 50 therapists they'd hired so I was on top of the totem pole—so to speak. Linda, a former actress from LA, was one of the first therapist I connected with who was near my age and a real fireball. Her dramatic effects keep everyone entertained and on their toes. I also connected with Cindy and Maggie, a couple (in every sense of the word) who'd also moved down from Salt Lake. They were both former teachers at UCMT and also taught at Nevada College of Massage Therapy after I'd left. The four of us were in the first group that began training in October, which is when Brad and I moved back down to Las Vegas into a two-bedroom apartment.

But the co-worker I connected with most intimately was Mariamma. She was hired a while later and ended up being one of my partners during the Bellagio hot stone therapy training. We felt an immediate connection with each other and, as we started sharing stories, I immediately recognized why. Mariamma had moved from Boulder, Colorado to join her polyamorous partners, Chas and Saundra, along with her two teen-aged daughters, Simyra and Asia. She had met Chas and Saundra at a Lifestyles party in Boulder, and they had all fallen in love. Chas, of African American descent, and Saundra, a Latina, both had degrees in social work along with Chas being an ordained minister. They had moved to Las Vegas to pursue their careers and also make their fortune in real estate which was really happening down there at the time.

I was fascinated by their relationship dynamics and how they were making things work. Threesomes, I have found, are difficult relationships to maintain as the sexual energy is by nature imbalanced but constantly seeks to become balanced. At least that was my experience with Kurt, Christy and me. When Sandy joined the mix, it really created an imbalance of sexual energy, which tipped over the apple cart so to speak.

I was wondering how long it would be before Mariamma's apple cart would start to topple, but unlike my relationship with Kurt, Chas was open to Saundra and Mariamma exploring relationships with other men besides him. In fact, he encouraged it. They frequented "swingers' bars" (we joined them one night at the Red Rooster and quickly got our fill of that porn scene), where they allowed the energies of the present moment to manifest itself wherever, however, and—whatever. I was fascinated with some of Mariamma's experiences at the swingers' bars and felt somewhat jealous of the freedom her relationship offered. Brad was in *no way* to the point of allowing me my sexual freedom. His jealousies were obvious and uncontrollable, and so I gave up on any ideas of pursuing an open relationship with him.

But we both grew to love Mariamma and her two teenaged daughters—from a safe distance. And I also grew to love and appreciate Chas in spite of my initial Mormon prejudice against blacks. I rarely connected with Saundra who had four young children at home. But by the time I was ready to quit my job at the Bellagio, a whirlwind of upheaval had struck their relationship, and it all fell apart. Issues which had been suppressed for years finally surfaced and caused a major fall-out. I won't go into the details here for privacy's sake, but Mariamma remains one of my dearest friends. It's rare in life to find someone to whom you can spill your uncensored guts to and not be judged in any way.

I could write volumes about the experiences I had with clients at the Bellagio. Doing an average of 32 massages a week, I connected with a lot of different people and often felt like a temple worker working in a beautiful marble temple—endowing people with health and vitality—assisting them to open up all of their chakras (energy centers). People from all over the world showed up on my massage table to be caressed by my loving hands. Many would say, "You must be the best massage therapist here as I asked for the very best." That gave me a sense of pride in my work, and I always strove to do my best, regardless of how exhausted I became. As I worked on people from all different nationalities and ethnic groups, I began to relate them to different chakra energies and created the following list:

Chakra One—Tribal Energy—African—Red
Chakra Two—Sexual Energy—Latin/Hispanic—Orange
Chakra Three—Power Energy—Asian—Yellow
Chakra Four—Heart Energy—Australian—Green
Chakra Five—Creative Energy—European—Blue
Chakra Six—Intellectual Energy—Russian—Purple
Chakra Seven—Integrated Energy—American—White

I also realized that we are all part of a rainbow of humanity and each of us has his or her own unique color, energy or culture to share. I explored the idea of honoring and enjoying each individual's diversity and what each culture had to offer. I fell in love with the African tribal energy and admired how they stuck together in a sort of soulistic brotherhood. I enjoyed the sexual energy of the Hispanics and the pride they had in their family solidarity. The Asian women were powerful in their grace and innocence. The Asian men were powerful in their economic prowess although I felt there was a definite imbalance between the two sexes. The Australians I massaged were the most openhearted and friendly of all the nationalities and always provided a tonic for my soul. The Europeans thrilled me with their creative expressions about my massage being "brilliant" or "fabulous." They were delightfully open conversationalists. The Russians, on the other hand, were generally quiet and intense—except for the ones who engaged me in intellectual conversation—which I enjoyed immensely. The Americans, who were the majority of people I massaged, were all over the spectrum—an amalgamation of all the colors of the rainbow.

But by March, I was ready for a change. I had been working ten-hour days, four days a week and my body was starting to feel the impact. In March, I was invited to attend a two-week training for Watsu water massage at Harbin Hot Springs in California so that I could get off of my feet and into the water.

But in June my body suffered a breakdown of thoracic-outlet syndrome. It felt like I was having a heart attack. Robert (my chiropractor and friend) examined me and said that my "Vagus nerve" (no joke) was being impinged from all the massages I was giving and that I needed to take a break. At his advice, I took a three-month leave-of-absence for the summer and worked along side Brad in our NUMAD business—traveling the entire Western United States. It was a good break and it allowed my body to heal.

In October, I was ready to go back to work again after two-weeks of advanced training in Watsu at Harbin. Poneeh, the spa manager, shifted my schedule to two-days in spa and two-days in Watsu. I loved Watsu and realized that I'd finally found my therapeutic niche. But Bellagio wasn't selling Watsu nearly enough to make it profitable. And when I discovered that Harbin was teaching Waterdance in April, I knew I wanted to go there again for a month to learn Waterdance.

Also, our 18-month lease on our apartment was up in April, and I didn't want to renew it as the new property owners had let the complex go to the dogs. Brad tried to convince me to stay at the Bellagio as they'd offered to pay for my Waterdance training, and I was still making good money. But my body and spirit were both screaming that I needed to leave Las Vegas and go back to Utah to turn my healing retreat dream into a reality. All of my Togenberg goats had died that winter because of roving coyotes, and I still had the obligation of caring for my six Cherro sheep on our 15 acres in Indianola. Plus I truly did miss my "family of friends" back in Utah—not to mention my mom and immediate family.

Regardless of Brad's desire to stay, fate had her way with me again. After an embarrassing incident in the break room (I accidentally bled on one of the chairs after being called in for a bogus Watsu session—and then got reprimanded for it!), I put in a letter of resignation. There is only so much bullshit one can suffer through before it becomes too deep and suffocating. It had finally reached critical mass because of a myriad of unresolved issues concerning stolen cash tips, incompetent assistant managers, and bogus scheduling. Then there was all of the valuable time I wasted waiting to book Watsu sessions, which management was charging me taxes on and not paying me for.

So after another trip to Harbin for four weeks of Waterdance training, Brad and I packed up all of our "things" and moved back to Utah. Jared, my oldest son, had just purchased a four-bedroom home with plenty of room to store our things. And my mom, who was then 83, appreciated the idea of having Brad and me move into her large home on Dallin Street to help her. With no rent or utilities to pay (we offered to help Mom out each month with money, but she refused) we could put all of our funds towards building the healing retreat in Indianola.

Chapter Twenty—Harbin

I had the most fascinating lucid dream about six months before I'd moved to Vegas to work at the Bellagio. I believe it came as a response to a question I'd posed to the Universe or God—"What is the most effective therapy to activate Kundalini energies?" And so one night, while I was asleep in my bed in Draper, I had an incredible dream.

I was invited to visit an intentional community somewhere. My guide (I thought he was a spirit-guide) took me to this garden paradise where each evening around sunset, the members of the community stepped into a beautiful large pool to perform some kind of ceremony with each other. I couldn't tell exactly what the ceremony entailed, but it was like they were dancing with each other in the water. The dance somehow activated their Kundalini energies to where they felt open enough with each other to gather in a grassy area surrounded by flowers and engage in group sex.

I know this sounds pretty wild (and it certainly was!), but when I awoke I felt the most erotic, ecstatic energies moving through me that I'd ever experienced. Even though the guide, who ended up being my sexual partner in my dream, was *not* Brad (he reminded me of another friend, Dean from Reno) I immediately woke up Brad to make love to him before the energy subsided. I didn't dare share the dream with him, considering Brad's typical reaction to things like group orgies and other men was not positive.

As I started my Watsu One class at Harbin, I couldn't help being drawn to Kevin, one of the guys in my class. He was definitely of the tall, dark and handsome type—but I just couldn't put my finger on why I was so drawn to him. One night after class, a group of us (including Brad and Kevin) were in the lower pool practicing the Watsu moves we'd learned that day. We were all nude (which is something Brad and I are pretty comfortable with having joined a naturist group several years earlier) and Kevin had me in his arms showing me some advanced, leg-over moves he'd learned in Watsu Two. I'd learned that Watsu puts the receiver in a type of dream-state. And so when

Kevin was stretching my legs apart to put one over his shoulder, I immediately started to recall the dream I'd had months earlier. As I opened my eyes to look into Kevin's face I immediately recognized that *he was the man in my dream!*

I was so astonished that I immediately described the dream to Kevin not anticipating what his or Brad's response might be. Kevin, I could tell, was genuinely flattered. Brad, however, was outraged and immediately pulled me from Kevin's arms and marched me back to the dressing room. *He was not happy with me sharing my erotic dream with Kevin!*

Throughout the entire Watsu One class, Brad was on his guard for any other "inappropriate" advances towards Kevin. But neither Kevin nor I could deny the energy that was pulling us toward one other. Kevin was also in a "committed" relationship with a wife who was about as understanding as Brad regarding such things. And so we kept our physical distance for our partners' sake—but our spirits danced the dance of intimacy nevertheless. By the time the class ended, Kevin had nothing to worry about because Brad's jealousy was redirected toward someone else—our teacher, Harold.

Harold Dull had invented Watsu about twenty years prior. He was a Zen Shiatsu Master who had moved to Harbin to help develop a clothing-optional spiritual retreat. He was also a sort of Sausalito counter-culture poet who had never grown up. Harold also reminded me of how Dr. Seuss might look and act—full of grandfatherly kindness with an unmistakable look of mischief in his eyes. And one could never be sure what Harold was up to for he was a true mystic. I enjoyed his class demeanor of teaching all the techniques and information needed to perform Watsu, but still leaving students with the question—what is this *really* all about, Harold? I really *got* what Watsu was about when I read this poem in Harold's Watsu manual.

If you happen to find your way into the warm pool at Harbin Hot Springs
and an old man with a white beard drifts up to your side
and, casually mentioning he comes up every weekend to teach the Shiatsu
     classes,
asks if you would like some in the water—"Watsu" he calls it "something I
     developed in the pool here…I like to practice it every chance I get…"
accept
and you will find yourself being floated
your neck in the crook of his arm your sacrum in his hand
as he rocks you back and forth…back and around…back into a world
     without
     sound…back into the waters of the womb
as he swirls and sways you the way dolphins play
as he stretches leg and arm and back every way water allows

or drapes your legs over his shoulders and lifts you clear of it
the way an old man plays with the daughters of creation
and sets you down astraddle his held out leg
so that the chakra in your perineum is held from below by his thigh
and your hara by one hand
and your lower back by the other
so that the energy locked in that bowl is free to rise all the way up your spine
and join that old man's
two intertwining dragons spiraling heavenward...

Or
refuse.
Maybe he is just another lecherous old man
coming on
to all the pretty girls in the pool
"Thank you
I just want to be by myself..."
He
will find another
and another
and another
The sky is filled with dragons

The profound images created by his poem brought tears to my eyes. At the end of class I gave Harold a huge hug and told him how much I appreciated his efforts in creating a therapy to open up Kundalini energies. I then asked him for a personal, professional session the next morning.

The first Watsu session I'd ever experienced was actually a Waterdance session with Rutherford (who was God's gift to women—and knew it), a teaching assistant for our Watsu class. That first time when I relaxed into Rutherford's masculine arms and we went waterdancing underwater, I knew I'd found heaven...and Disneyland...and Wonderland...or all three put together. *It was absolutely magical!* I was hooked and I knew then that Waterdance is what I wanted to spend the rest of my professional life doing. (And, of course, I immediately fell in love with Rutherford. Surprised?) But then came my Watsu session with Harold.

The air in the teepee pool was thick with steam as Harold and I entered the warm water. We were required to receive ten professional Watsu sessions from certified practitioners in order to become Watsu certified. I felt incredibly privileged to receive a session from the creator of this modality. As I stood with my back against the wall, Harold asked me what my intention was for this particular session. The first thing that came to mind was, "I really want to know what Watsu is about—no holding back." He smiled his mischievous "Cat in the Hat" smile and nodded acknowledgement and brought me to the center of the pool. As I melted into the crook of Harold's arm with his other hand lifting my sacrum to the top of the water, my eyes closed to enter into his mystical water world. Instinctively, my body relaxed completely, and I knew I was in for the experience of a lifetime.

Harold started slowly unwinding the resistance my body had developed through years of old energetic holding patterns—my holding onto physical or emotional past wounds. I knew I'd held onto major male issues as all of the physical injuries from the car accident were on my right side—my male side. And Brad hovering over me like a hawk ready to strike was enough to compress those emotions into a virtual volcano. But I knew my body was ready to release, and I knew that I was in the hands of a Master.

As Harold did a perineum stretch where he put my feet together and collapsed my legs against the wall, I felt my body erupt into a full Kundalini explosion as he released them. I hadn't felt this type of energy release since I'd had spiritual oneness with Patrick. I knew I'd suppressed that energy to maintain the relationship with Brad, but I didn't realize how much my body wanted to release it. Body waves or krias (as Watsu practitioners call them) snaked through me like spiritual orgasms—opening up my chakras one by one. I could feel the energy spiraling up my spine the way it had done when Patrick had opened up my chakras for the first time. And then I could feel Harold's energy join mine as we both laughed out loud together at the explicit joy we were experiencing together. As our energies joined in spiritual orgasms, the energy shot out of my crown chakra into pure, breath-taking brilliant light. It was like an explosion of light had gone off inside my head and catapulted me into a different dimension. I could tell that Harold was experiencing it too as he held me tenderly against his body. We were both like children quietly enjoying the rapture of *Nirvana*—so quiet and peaceful… and *so deliciously real. I truly never wanted it to end!*

But even Nirvana must come to an end, and Harold took me back to the wall and set me on my feet. As I opened my eyes, he smiled an acknowledging smile—his face aglow. I fell in love with him in that moment, and again we embraced. We both knew it was time to let others use the pool for their Watsu sessions. But I knew that I'd truly discovered what Watsu truly was about—to its fullest extent.

After showering and dressing, Brad met me on the way to the dining room for breakfast. "How was your session with Harold?" he asked, noticing the glow on my face. "Incredible," I replied. "I experienced a full Kundalini awakening with him and it was…indescribable."

Brad's face went stone cold. I could feel the jealousies over what I'd experienced with Harold erupt inside of him the same way they had erupted inside of Kurt when I'd told him about Patrick. Why were the men I married always so jealous of my Kundalini experiences? I could sense the rage arising in Brad, but I knew it came from his ignorance about what had happened. He'd also discounted my experiences with Patrick, calling them "figments of my deranged imagination." But now he had *real* evidence surrounding him everywhere at Harbin that these intimate spiritual connections were possible. But since I'd experienced them directly with Harold instead of Brad, he wanted to lash out at Harold with the same vehemence that Kurt had lashed out at Patrick. And I was concerned for Harold.

"Don't do anything stupid," I told Brad as he headed for the dressing room to find Harold. I continued to the dining room for breakfast.

After breakfast I walked up the circular stairway to the classroom dome. (The Watsu center was a unique architectural creation of several large white domes set on pedestals that looked like large mushrooms—another "Dr. Seuss" feature.) The class had started to gather for our closing celebration. Harold had not yet arrived, and I took a seat next to Kevin. He knew something was up, and I told him about my experience that morning with Harold and how I knew that Brad had gotten into it with him. Kevin smiled a knowing smile and gave me a hug. "Don't worry," he said. "I'm sure Harold will know how to handle Brad."

Harold arrived late as the entire class waited for him. Brad was behind him, and I could see his angry face through the window of the door as Harold closed it. He remained there during the entire closing celebration—glaring at us as if we were mischievous children. And perhaps we were guilty of mischief—of indulging in the mystical wonders of Watsu.

The next time I went to Harbin for a Watsu Three and Aquaternatives class, Brad tagged along again—just to keep Harold and me in line. Harold taught Watsu Three with Teri Thomas as his teaching assistant, and Teri taught Aquaternatives by herself. I grew to love Teri's professionalism and her open conversations concerning energetic boundaries. I felt that some of these subjects weren't covered adequately in Watsu One and Two and needed discussion in more detail in the advanced Watsu classes. She agreed. But Harold was reluctant to breach the subjects of Kundalini energies and spiritual oneness—he felt it was delving too much into the "unexplainable."

Harold argued that each person experiences energy releases differently and we need to honor each individual's experience by not labeling it. Otherwise we assume (making an "ass" out of "u" and "me") that everyone's spiritual experiences and paths are the same—which they aren't. As Watsu therapists, we simply need to be aware of the expression of energy releasing without attaching ourselves to the form. Of course he knew and I knew—that that was all bullshit. Harold knew exactly what he was doing in his Watsu sessions—and why—but he didn't want his students to be privy to it.

During that two-week class period, Brad got involved with a work-study student named Tai. Shit hit the fan when he agreed to do a two and a half-hour massage on her in the dome where I was trying to sleep—the session lasted until well past midnight. I knew I was PMSing and also feeling like Brad was doing some payback for what he considered my previous indiscretions with Kevin and Harold. So in my feedback form to the administration, I wrote a seething, scolding letter about the violations of relationship boundaries that were so prevalent at Harbin. I knew Brad and I had got sucked into a payback war, and we still have issues concerning Kundalini energy that I'm not sure will ever be resolved. But pushing his limits is not the answer—nor is living a life of suppression.

And so it was with these unresolved issues that I began Waterdance classes in April with Richard and Shantam. Richard Bach was one of my favorite authors (*Jonathan Livingston Seagull, One, Bridge Across Forever*) so I figured someone with that same name (although my teacher spelled his Bock) would be someone I'd immediately connect with. I was right! Richard, who also taught Quantum Light Breath and Divine Ravishment classes, was a master teacher, healer and shaman. According to the description of his teaching style in the school guide—"it is warm, personal, and a direct extension of his being—a combination of childlike joy and deep, passionate connection." That perfectly described Richard.

Shantam, a woman about my age who is absolutely gorgeous inside and out, was Richard's teaching partner. She is also a Master Hypnotherapist with an extensive background in Watsu and Waterdance. According to her instructor's description—"With a gentle, compassionate presence and an innate, intuitive ability to communicate from the heart, Shantam offers enthusiastic support, insight and a wealth of personal experience to anyone wishing to learn more about this work in the water and about themselves."

With Richard and Shantam at the teaching helm—it was full steam ahead. I was mysteriously tossed into the waves of Waterdance, anticipating the magic this class would create...and I wasn't disappointed.

The first day we simply worked on breath connection—an essential ingredient to Waterdance as breath connection is paramount to taking someone underwater. We learned to synchronize with each other's breath and about the various breathing patterns in individuals. Some are deep, slow breathers, while others breathe quickly and shallowly. It's important to attune to each person's breath pattern before taking them under.

During the rest of the class we learned the techniques for taking people underwater, utilizing different moves and stretches, and these took the mystery out of Waterdance. After several days' practice, I was convinced I could be an expert Waterdance therapist—my dream since my first Waterdance with Rutherford. By the way, Rutherford was the teaching assistant for Waterdance—which was okay by me. Brad was definitely having his issues with it as Rutherford and I continued to connect in very profound ways. I knew he had advanced to higher levels of understanding of Kundalini energy, which I got to experience in my final Waterdance session with him despite Brad's protests.

My personal session with Richard was literally out-of-this-world. I went to places I'd never been to before, and I knew Richard wanted to go there with me—but he maintained his professional boundaries, which Brad truly appreciated. Again I experienced *Nirvana—a space where nothing exists but the breath and the present moment—and pure love.* It was absolute perfection!

I then did a session with Shantam where we "danced with the dolphins" as dolphin energy arose as part of my intention to "heal the planet." I felt we'd experienced lifetimes together, which were now culminating in the present moment. It was a profound experience for both of us. She also told me that she felt I was an ancient healer or shaman. She also said that on her way to class that morning she was stopped by a pure white cow that stood right in the middle of the road and wouldn't move. I then showed her the birthmark on my left foot and told her a little bit about the White Buffalo Woman legend. She was fascinated, and I told her I would send her a copy of my book, *Heartsong.* (Instead, I gave a copy to Davida, a teaching assistant who'd asked for a copy, and I told her to share it with Shantam when she finished reading it. I hope she did.)

As the class came to its final closing ceremony, I felt impressed to share a tape recording of two of John Denver's songs, which came to mind in the Waterdance sessions. I offered the first song in honor of Shantam:

Dolphin Song

Two days before the moon was round
You felt the urge of sun's light beams
The muffled world of dolphin sounds
Slipped down and back
Into your dreams…

For nine full months that passed before
You learned of all of life's ancient rhymes
And mother sensed a farther shore

And brought you forth
Into these times…

So taste the air of your new world
And gently guide us to your mind
It knows the wind, its sails unfurled
And holds to heart the dolphin kind

Welcome precious earthmade child
We met you first in your father's songs
And mother smiled, and waters wild
It's in this place…
You now belong.

I know you know of all these things
And feel the faith of the dolphin's sigh
For you were born on silver wings
To taste the highblown crystal skies

So sing one day to all of us
The songs you learned in dolphin lair
Giving hope for life with all we must
And teach us how their grace to share

The second song was in honor of Richard who is truly a gift to mankind.

The Gift You Are

Imagine a month of Sundays
Each one a cloudy day
Imagine the moment the sun came shining through
Imagine that ray of sunshine as you

Remember your darkest hour
With dawn still far away
Remember the way that you longed for morning's light
Think of yourself as a candle in the night

Make believe this is the first day
Everything all brand new
Make believe that the sun is your own lucky star

Then understand the kind of gift you are

The gift you are…
Like the very first breath of spring
The gift you are…
All the joy that love can bring
The gift you are…
All of our dreams come true
The gift you are…
The gift of you.

You are the promise of all the ages
You are the prodigal son
You are the vision of prophets and sages
You are the only one

Dream of a bright tomorrow
Know that your dream will come true
Carry the dream in a sparkling crystal jar
Then you will know the kind of gift you are

The gift you are…
Like the very first breath of spring
The gift you are…
All the joy that love can bring
The gift you are…
All of our dreams come true
The gift you are…
The gift of you.

The gift you are…
Like the very first breath of springtime
The gift you are…
All the joy that love can bring
The gift you are…
All of our dreams come true…yes they do
The gift you are…
The gift of you.

The gift you are…
The gift of you…

I couldn't contain the tears that streamed down my face as I realized that Harbin had experienced a month full of rainy weather—until the day I'd arrived. Then the entire week had miraculously turned sunny...like the very first breath of spring.

Chapter Twenty-one—High School Reunion

Re-union. What a fabulous word to dissect—returning to union. So what exactly does that mean—returning to union? Was there a time and place in which we all experienced a type of oneness? Do you remember (now there's a good word too, re-member—returning members) that time of oneness? Is life really about remembering the reunions? We were...and still are...one big human family. So why is it so difficult to remember this union and the return to unity that brings us so much joy and pleasure similar to what even a simple high school reunion brings? Is that perhaps what heaven is like?

It was my thirty-year high school reunion, and I wouldn't have missed it for the world. I had missed my twenty-year reunion (Kurt wouldn't agree to take care of the children while I journeyed to Salt Lake), and I'd regretted it. But this time there would be no regrets. No mis-takes—missed opportunities.

Carol, my dear friend from high school who lives only a block from my mother, called me in Las Vegas to tell me about it. She said she was definitely going and wanted to make sure I knew about it as she was anxious to reconnect with me and some of our old friends who had told her they'd be there. I was excited to see them again—especially my best friend Shirlene (who was the character Charlene in my book, *Heartsong*).

I drove to Salt Lake on Thursday as I had Thursday, Friday and Saturdays off at work. I'd also traded another therapist for Sunday off so I could be back to work fresh on Monday. This was an important event for me, and I wanted to be prepared. Vegas was hot that time of year, and I figured Salt Lake would be, too, so I packed a few spaghetti-strapped tops and skimpy skirts, which I normally wore on my days off in Vegas. But Salt Lake turned cool that weekend, so I dug deep into my old wardrobe I'd left at Mom's and pulled out an orangey sweater and mid-calf skirt and vest I'd sewn years earlier. Not exactly what I'd had in mind to make a dazzling impression on my classmates, but it would have to do. I accented the outfit with some funky jewelry my eighteen year-old daughter, Destiny, had given me for my birthday. Brad dressed down, as usual, and, despite his usual resistance about attending such events, we both showed up, and, believe it or not, we were on time.

We were greeted by a woman in her late forties whom I never would have recognized had she not told me her name. She'd gained so much weight that I never would have guessed it was her. Her friend, Launa, I hardly recognized either as she had lost so much weight since high school—and was really looking good. Both of them recognized me immediately and were surprised at how little I'd changed.

"If they only knew," I thought to myself as I moseyed over to the refreshment table to see if there was anything "good" to drink. Only the usual "Mormon punch"—with nothing added. I grabbed some just as my old next door neighbor, Carolyn (whom I hardly recognized) grabbed me by the arm.

"Is that Janae Thorne?" she exclaimed as I spun around to greet her. "Carolyn—is that you?" I could tell that she and her friend, Suzanne, had been drinking as they were in a spirited mood. "Hey, where'd you get the good stuff?" I asked. Suzanne pulled a flask of vodka from her boot and replied, "We had to bring it with us—what do you think?" I laughed and asked Carolyn about how her mom and brothers were doing. She had three older brothers who were as wild as monkeys and were always getting into trouble. She said they had all three settled into good paying jobs and were doing quite well. Her mom had sold the house next to ours on Oneida Street years ago and had moved into a small condo closer to town. Carolyn was divorced and freewheeling it, having the time of her life (and I must say I was a bit jealous).

Just then my best friend, Shirlene, showed up. It was Carolyn's excuse to exit as Shirlene and Carolyn were polar opposites.

"Janae!" she exclaimed as we both embraced each other warmly. "It is *so good* to see you! I was hoping you would come." We talked for a brief moment and then Shirlene pointed to the table her husband was sitting at. "Why don't you and…Brad (I filled in the blank for her) grab a bite to eat and come sit with Randy and me. Then we can sit and catch up on everything."

I had brought a few copies of *Heartsong* and had left them out in the car. I was anxious to share my story with her, as she was one of the characters in my book. As we caught up on our life's journeys and where they had taken us—I showed her a picture of Kurt, me and our ten children and other more recent photos of them. She showed me pictures of her, Randy and their three children. They looked like the typical happy Mormon family (and I must say I was slightly jealous). Actually, the truth of the matter is—I wasn't really jealous of either Carolyn or Shirlene's lives. Mine was rich, full, and exciting and I was squeezing all the joy I could out of every ounce of it—and it showed.

Everyone I met commented about how young and vibrant I looked and wondered what I was doing *right*. Most of my classmates seemed so old and tired, talking about dull jobs, church positions and what college their children were going too. Boring. Nobody could believe that I had mothered ten children, let alone survived a polygamous relationship.

Many had read my recent article in the Salt Lake Tribune about my journey into and out of polygamy and wanted to know all the details. I was more than willing to share. I also shared the story about how Brad and I had met—for the third time—and how we didn't realize we were each other's seminary computer dates until four years into our marriage. They were all amazed by *that* story, and also the story about Nolan and my "fatal attraction." Some had heard about the car accident and Nolan's death, but of course everyone wanted to know those details, too. They commented that I needed to write a book about my life's experiences—that it would make a best seller—and I told them I'd already written one and promised I'd e-mail everyone as soon as it was published. But I realized, even then, that there was a sequel in the making that might be even more interesting than the first book.

One old friend, who shared my first name, came up to me and asked what part of Montana I'd lived in when I'd had my polygamous experience. I told her up Ninemile Road near Missoula. She said it may seem like a strange coincidence (was I surprised?) but she and her husband had gone hunting up in that vicinity a few years prior and had happened onto what she thought was a polygamous compound. There was a passel of children jumping on a trampoline outside a log home. As she described the location and description of the house, we both couldn't believe that, yes, this was my home at Higher Ground! It was an amazing coincidence that Janae shared with me, and she gave me her e-mail address and phone number and told me to be sure and call her when my book became available. I promised I would.

As I sat and visited with several other of my old friends including Carol from Mom's ward and Lori with whom I'd raised ducks. But then I felt drawn to a certain table at which was seated "my very first love." Okay, I'm really going out on a limb with this one (kind a like I did with Kevin at Harbin), but Ron has always been my "first love." I grew up with him in Parley's Sixth Ward. His dad was the bishop—mine was the door-greeter—so we just didn't start out on equal footing. I must admit that I'd always, for as long as I can remember, had a crush on Ron. But we were like ships passing in the night and never quite got connected in real life. But in my dreams...

that's a different story! To this day, I dream about Ron almost once a month. He shows up as a knight in shining armor to rescue me from all my life's perils. He's the one I can pour my heart out to, and I know he will always understand and accept me. He never judges me for anything but is always there to comfort and support me. He's always been my "dream-lover" and *there he was sitting right across from me at my class reunion.* He was with his own beautiful wife, of course, as Brad and I sat across from them and visited for a while.

Ron had all the characteristics of the perfect husband. He was good-looking, talented (we had sung in choir together), and successful. I wonder, even to this day, if he truly was the "soul-mate" that I was supposed to marry, but things had gone terribly *wrong.* The last I'd heard concerning Ron was from my brother, Bruce, who had just gotten off of his mission to Australia. Ron, who was two years younger than my brother, arrived in Australia just as Bruce was leaving. Bruce told me that Ron asked about me and how I was doing. It was at about that time that I'd gotten into a relationship with Kurt. Ron told Bruce that he had always liked me and that I should wait for him to get off his mission and not marry Kurt who Bruce had disliked from the beginning. Perhaps that would have been my perfect destiny, but I blew it when I married Kurt.

Life seems to take its own charted course and perhaps relation-ships (vessels that we relate in) sometimes get steered off course only to re-unite at a different time and place. As Ron gave me a warm hug and slipped me his business card (he was an insurance salesman), he told me to call him. I put it in my purse along with the rest of the cards I'd collected from other friends. But I'm still hopeful that someday there will be a *real* reunion of souls—just like in my dreams, Now *that*, to me, would definitely be heaven on earth!

Chapter Twenty-two—Windstar Reunion

Okay, okay, you've got to admit that I've been pretty good about *not* including *too* many John Denver's songs in this book. (I'm told my other book was a bit over the top with the John Denver songs. Oh, well, it is what it is.) But this next story *is* a bit over the top with the John Denver songs.

The night after my high school reunion, I had a "Vagus nerve episode"— it felt like a heart attack. There was no pain, just numbness in my right arm and a sense of panic like I wasn't getting any energy to my heart. I tried to calmly meditate and breathe through it, as I didn't want to disturb Brad or call an ambulance. But by early morning I was convinced that I needed to see Robert right away.

Robert had moved in with Carol in a house a short distance from Mom's where I stayed each time I came to Salt Lake. He and Carol had secured an office space just walking distance from their home, so Robert was glad to meet me at his office that morning. As he checked my muscle reflexes using kinesiology, he remarked that my Vagus nerve had suffered an impingement that caused me to feel like I was having a heart attack. My heart was fine, but the *thoracic outlet syndrome* I was experiencing definitely needed to be addressed. It was caused by the excessive number of massages I was performing at the Bellagio. He did some spinal adjustments that relieved the compression and then recommended a break from work for a while as it would never heal at the pace I was going.

When I got back to Vegas that Monday morning, I told Pooneh that, according to my doctor's orders, I needed to take a three-month leave-of-absence for the summer. I gave her a few weeks to adjust the schedule and make arrangements for my leave, and then Brad and I left for new and uncharted adventures "on the road and hanging by a song." Actually, being on the road gave me a lot of time to write new song lyrics. One of my favorites, which I dedicate to my dad, who was also a traveling salesman, is called "Crossroads to Heaven."

Headin' home on a sunny day
Down highway ninety-three,
Flowers bloomin', breezes blowin'
Someone's callin' me.

And I wonder why as I pass by
Just who put them there,
Those little white crosses and bloomin' wreaths
Markin' crossroads to heaven.

My mind goes back when I was a kid
Livin' in Salt Lake City,
My daddy was a travelin' man
Sometimes we'd all go with him.

Headin' north on a wintry morn'
Mom, Dad, Jimmy and me,
Playin' with Jimmy in the back of the car
The semi we never did see.

And we wondered why as we passed by
Just who put them there,
Those little white crosses and bloomin' wreaths
Markin' crossroads to heaven.

Now Momma's gone, and Jimmy too
And Daddy's no longer travelin',
And every time that I pass by
I see three crosses on the road to heaven.

The years went by and now I'm grown
Doin' what daddy used to,
They say I'm nothin' but a travelin' soul
But I guess it's what I'm used to

Headin' home on a sunny day
Someone's callin' me,
The bumper sticker says, "Pray for me,
I'm drivin down ninety-three."

And I wonder why as I pass by
Just who'll put it there,
That little white cross or that bloomin' wreath
Markin' my crossroad to heaven.

I know it's a sad song, but what can I say? Being on the road isn't all *that* sad, but it does tend to get rather boring. So to liven up things, I insisted that we camp at every clothing optional retreat that was convenient. Sometimes we'd stay for several days in an area (like at Mountain Air Ranch—MAR— near Denver), and I'd hang around by the pool while Brad set up dealerships for Rock Carpet (a natural rock and epoxy floor covering). I told Brad it was my way of making all the traveling worthwhile, as I was interested in learning how clothing optional retreats were designed and managed. I think my fascination with nudity came from a spiritual revelation while reading the Gnostic Gospel of Thomas:

His disciples said, "When will you appear to us and when shall we see you?"
Jesus said, "When you strip off your clothes without being ashamed and you take your clothes and put them under your feet like little children and trample them, then (you) will see the son of the living one and you will not be afraid."

I truly resonated with the idea of being *au naturel,* and we brushed shoulders (and other parts of our bodies) with a lot of naturists who enjoyed life in the raw. We were enjoying "the bare necessities of life" as we baked in the sun (with no tan lines), swam and soaked in the pools, played billiards, and had wild, crazy parties on the weekends. We had a few "near sexual encounters" with couples we met, but at the last minute either Brad or I would always bail out. It was fun and exciting, nonetheless.

While we were heading towards California in September, my friend Dean from Reno called. Now you've got to understand the relationship Brad has with Dean—*he absolutely hates his guts!* He's one of the many men Brad has "gone to war with," but in Dean's case, it was nuclear.

It all started back when we were in Draper living at Higher Ground. Dean was an old friend of Patricia's who'd been helping her with her "redemption" process as he was also doing it with some property in Reno that his partner, Junelle, owned. His intention was to put in a healing retreat on the land—free and clear. (You guessed it—it didn't happen.) When he came out to Draper to meet with Patricia, he also came to visit Brad and me at our healing center—just to see what we'd put together. Dean was impressed with what we'd developed, and I immediately felt a connection with him probably because he was one of the few people who could truly speak my language. He was a professional tarot card reader, which really didn't score any points in Brad's book. He figured Dean was simply a professional philanderer (not philanthropist) and made it a point to take issue with everything about Dean—Brad's habit with every guy I connect with.

Well, I did the *wrong thing* (according to Brad) by giving Dean a copy of my book, *Heartsong*. He deeply connected with what I'd written and actually *got* my experiences with John Denver and his songs. I finally found someone with whom I could talk intimately about John Denver's songs and, yes, I couldn't help but fall in love with Dean. We soon discovered that we'd followed similar paths (he knew some of the same people I knew in Logan and in Manti) and our relationship started blossoming in spite of (or because of) all the shit Brad threw at it.

But Dean was also in a constraining relationship with his own partner, Junelle (who he claimed was his soul-mate—sound familiar?). So we kept at a safe distance (like I did with his look-alike, Kevin, at Harbin), but we enjoyed deep conversations on the phone and when he visited his son in Salt Lake, we got together for a tarot card reading (to Brad's chagrin).

Well, Dean called to invite Brad and me to join him at a Rocky Mountain High Festival at Lake Tahoe sponsored by the California Windstar Connection Group. He knew I couldn't resist such an offer, especially since we were headed that way to enjoy our annual *Nudestock* event in Sacramento the following weekend. (Picture *Woodstock* in the nude and you've got *Nudestock.)* And then I made the *big* mistake of inviting Dean to join us at *Nudestock*. Brad was furious! The last thing he wanted was to meet Dean in the nude and end up in a menage a trois, as he figured this was what was being set up since Dean had recently broken up with Junelle.

But to make a long story short, Dean and Brad were in an all-out war at Lake Tahoe and again at *Nudestock*. (Don't you hate the sound of cocks fighting?) I tried to avoid the turbulence by avoiding them both. In the meantime, I enjoyed the John Denver imitators during the day and singing songs around the campfire at night. But even I can admit after a weekend of hearing *only John Denver songs,* I was ready to throw tomatoes at the next person who sang "Rocky Mountain High." But then we were invited to attend the Windstar Symposium in Aspen, Colorado which John Denver's brother, Ron, had started up again—with Tom Crum as one of the guest presenters. So after *Nudestock* we went back to Colorado for the symposium, which was followed by a weeklong tribute to John Denver.

Wow! Was I ever in John Denver heaven. There were John Denver look-alikes and imitators everywhere singing *nothing but John Denver songs.* (And, yes, after the first day, I again got my fill.) But before all of that was the magic of Windstar—and this next story was *truly magical!*

The first day of the Windstar Symposium, Brad had to set up a Rock Carpet dealership in Glenwood Springs, so he drove me into Aspen early, and I listened to Jane Goodall speak on her experiences with chimps in the wilds of Gombe, Africa. I purchased a couple of her books for reference on my next book, *Becoming One* (it's actually a rewrite), and then I went to lunch with Tom Crum who'd been sitting in the row behind me. He couldn't believe how much I'd changed since I'd last seen him and was excited about my adventures at the Bellagio and Harbin. I caught him up on Kurt and the kids—and how I'd liberated myself from *that* marriage. He was still with his wife, Cathy, who was going to be there the following day when he did his Aikido demonstration. I was anxious to see her again, too.

No matter how I pushed and prodded Brad to be on time, we were late to Tom's presentation. I was somewhat disappointed, more for Brad than for myself, as I'd wished that he could "get" what Tom was talking about—peaceful conflict resolution—especially after the recent dramas with Dean. Despite missing part of the presentation, Brad was intrigued by what Tom had to say and bought copies of his two books, *The Magic of Conflict* and *Return to Center*, which he graciously autographed. Cathy was selling books with Tom, and I introduced them both to Brad. Cathy promised that she would stop at the Bellagio the next time she was in Vegas visiting Edith, John Denver's mom.

This was not news to me—that John Denver's mother spent her winters in Las Vegas. A massage therapist friend, Caitlin, lived in the same condominium complex as Edith. I'd given Caitlin a copy of *Heartsong* and then asked her to pass it along to Edith, but Caitlin never got back to me about it. I'd brought several copies of *Heartsong*, in case I met up with her or John Denver's brother, Ron, at the Windstar Symposium   I'd felt that giving them both copies was the next step in getting *Heartsong* published.

That night was the musical part of the Windstar Symposium. One of the John Denver imitators we'd met had mentioned that he was going to be performing with Cassandra—John Denver's former wife. This sparked some interest in both Brad and me, and so after a lousy Mexican dinner and some time relaxing at Glenwood Springs, we returned to Aspen for the concert.

We arrived early this time (the scolding I'd given Brad for being late that morning seemed to have paid off). We secured seats on the front row to the left of the stage. As the first act—the John Denver imitator—was starting into "Rocky Mountain High," a group of noisy punkers came in and found seats right behind and to the left us. One teen-aged girl, with long dark hair and an olive complexion, sat down right next to Brad. We could tell right a way that they were high, and one of the guys offered us a drink from a bottle he'd brought with him. It was wine, so Brad and I graciously accepted his offer. Now we felt part of their group.

As Cassandra came on stage for her act, the entire rowdy group exploded in cheers and applause. The teenager sitting next to Brad jumped to her feet and exclaimed, "Go Mom!" We then realized that Brad had been *sitting right next to John Denver's daughter this whole time.* We found out her name was Jesse when Cassandra acknowledged her presence.

Cassandra was hot—and *she knew it.* She looked delicious in her chocolate leather tank top and frayed miniskirt, her hips gyrating to the sounds of her Brazilian maracas. Brad couldn't keep his eyes off of her—and neither could I. She had to be my age or older, and yet she looked as young as her teen-aged daughter, Jesse.

As Cassandra sang the ballads of her life with John, the story became clear (to those with ears to hear anyway) that she'd been unfaithful to John (go figure) and that was the cause of their separation and divorce. Brad and I became convinced that Jesse was *not* John Denver's *real* daughter—given her complexion and all—and Cassandra's songs alluded to that fact. But still, who could deny John's fascination with such a sex-goddess. She was incredible.

After the concert, Cassandra was reunited with her daughter and her friends. Brad and I were among them and shook her hand and congratulated her. Then an astonishing thing happened. Cassandra got a strange look on her face when she saw Brad and reached out and gave him a big hug and a full-blown kiss. "You remind me of someone," she said as Brad's face blushed with a mixture of excitement and embarrassment. After their mystical encounter, I shared with her that I'd written a book called *Heartsong,* which was about the song I'd received from John the morning following his death. She then said, "Can you play it for me?"

I froze. "You mean right here and right now?"

"Absolutely," she said, grabbing a guitar from the stage before the stagehands could pack it up.

"Well, I haven't played for a long time—being a massage therapist at the Bellagio for the past year—but I guess I could wing it." Then a strange feeling came over me, flooding me with confidence. "Yes, I think John would like that," I said as I sat down on the stage and played "Heartsong" the best I could.

Heaven wouldn't be heaven without you
No, it just wouldn't be the same,
Not to see you, to touch you, to love you
No, I just couldn't handle the pain,

So I sit and I sing you my heartsong
Hoping someday you'll find ears to hear,
And I wait, and I watch, and I wonder
Hoping someday I will hold you near.

It's my heartsong I sing in the morning
It's my heartsong I sing every night,
It's the song of two lovers together
Two hearts beating as one…beating as one…take flight.

Life isn't worth living without you
Your love makes everything worthwhile,
To touch you, to hold you, to love you
To see you break out in a smile,

So I listen to hear your heartsong
It plays a tune in my heart,
And I still have the faith and the wonder
That someday we'll never be apart.

I hear your heartsong in the morning
I hear your heartsong every night,
It's the song of two lovers together
Two hearts beating as one…beating as one…take flight.

Cassandra's eyes filled with tears, which ran down her beautiful tanned cheeks. I knew she'd been deeply touched by the words of the song—if not by the melody. I set the guitar down and embraced her, telling her I was glad I could share it with her. I felt a deep connection between us as we hugged for an extended time. I fell in love with her—as I knew John had—for her spirited beauty and goddess empowerment. I envied her—not because she'd been married to John but because she had the courage to get on stage and tell the truth—the real story about her and John. I knew someday I'd find the power to tell the truth the way Cassandra had.

She wrote her address on a piece of paper and told me she wanted a copy of the song. I told her I'd do one better—I'd send her a copy of my book,

Heartsong. She said she looked forward to receiving it and then said goodbye to Brad and me as she rushed out of the door with her daughter and friends. We looked at each other dumbfounded and smiled. We'd been set-up by the angels, and we both knew it.

The next week, during the John Denver tribute, I was able to give both Ron and Edith copies of my book. I also gave them bouquets of flowers, which Ariel had been flooded with from her new husband, also a Brad, whose family business was flowers. She'd given me a few bouquets when we were passing through St. George. I told Edith that I'd love to give her a massage when she came to Vegas that winter, and I told her we had a mutual friend, Caitlin, who lived in her condo complex and worked with me. She said that would be nice and gave me her address and phone number to call her.

But life happens and even though my intentions were to reconnect with Cassandra and Edith (and Ron), it hasn't happened—*yet*. Of course I'm excited to see what next year's Windstar Symposium will bring. By the way, Brad grew out his hair and styled it like John's, found some round wire-rimmed glasses, and began practicing the guitar daily—just in case Cassandra shows up again.

Chapter Twenty-three—The Da Vinci Code

Dan Brown—you're the man! Every author (including myself) wishes they could write as brilliantly as you. Plus the plots you weave are masterful and enticing, inviting us all to investigate the labyrinth that leads us to our own Holy Grail.

And so it was that I entered the labyrinth of my own mind and began the investigation into my own spiritual path which led to my own Holy Grail. I began with my roots—where my spiritual belief systems began—in Mormonism.

I purchased dozens of books, which were in the recommended reading list in Dan Brown's *Da Vinci Code*—books on Freemasonry, the Nag Hammadi, goddess worship, Mary Magdalene legends, the Knights Templar legends, etc. I read them all, and made a connection back to Mormonism. It's an incredible journey, so buckle your seatbelts. You're in for a ride!

First, I'll start with the basics—where Mormonism came from in the first place. According to Mormon history, Joseph Smith (its founder) was praying to God after reading in the Bible, James 1:5:

"If any of you lack wisdom, let him ask of God, that giveth to all men liberally, and upbraideth not; and it shall be given you."

What a great promise from God! Joseph decided to ask God *directly* which church he should join after doing a thorough investigation of the many Christian churches in his community in upstate New York, and he did receive a *direct answer from God!* According to the story (which I'd been taught since childhood), two heavenly personages appeared to Joseph, one introducing himself as God, the Father, who then introduced the other as His son, Jesus Christ. Jesus then told Joseph Smith not to join *any* of the churches as they've all fallen away from the truth. In other words—they've all been corrupted throughout the centuries by the dictates of designing men. Sound surprising?

Now I'm not here to proselytize for Mormonism (I was excommunicated years ago because of my polygamist affiliations—without a church hearing, mind you!), but I want to share some fascinating insights I've recently had. According to my research into some of the teachings of the Primitive Church (the first century Christian "heretic" Church), Mormonism is the closest religion to reflect those teachings. Of course, all Mormon children are taught this concept when we attend Primary. It's one of thirteen basic "Articles of Faith."

"We believe in the same organization that existed in the Primitive Church, namely, apostles, prophets, pastors, teachers, evangelists, etc." (Article Six)

But what I've found goes way beyond just the "organization of the Primitive Church." Take for example, the first principles and ordinances of the Gospel as stated in the Fourth Article of Faith:

"We believe that the first principles and ordinances of the Gospel are: first, Faith in the Lord Jesus Christ, second, Repentance: third, Baptism by immersion for the remission of sins: fourth, Laying on of hands for the gift of the Holy Ghost."

So let's look at the first principle of the Gospel—"Faith in the Lord Jesus Christ." It doesn't say or mean faith in *any* man or religious dogma—it simply means *faith in the Lord Jesus Christ.* So if we're to have faith in the Lord Jesus Christ, what exactly did he teach? We know through modern discoveries or rediscoveries of hidden manuscripts like the Apocrypha, the Dead Sea Scrolls, the Nag Hammadi Scrolls, and the Essene Gospels, that there's an underlying "hidden" gospel that never was included in the "canonized" scriptures. The common scriptures were simply voted upon by a group of men (believe it or not, there was not *one woman* present) at the gathering at Nicaea in 325 CE, later known as the "Nicene Council." It's from both the canonized scriptures and these hidden scriptures that I've uncovered some interesting insights into *true* Christianity or, in other words, the teachings of the Lord Jesus Christ. We'll get into some further discussion regarding these later, but first let's go back to the first principles and ordinances of the Gospel.

The second, "Repentance" is somewhat ambiguous since it doesn't get into much explanation of *what* we're to repent of. I'll assume that if we're to repent (literally meaning to feel regret about a sin or past action and change your ways or habits) or, in other words, we are to turn from that which is false to that which is the true. Repentance also means to turn from our sins (separations within) that keep us from the at-one-ment or oneness with God. (Please excuse the word extractions but it helps clarify my "come from".) And this leads to the third principle (or ordinance) of the Gospel which is "Baptism by immersion for the remission of sins." This is one I'd like to look at in a bit more detail. What exactly does Christ teach about baptism? I've included a few scriptural references:

"And Jesus, when he was baptized, went up straightway out of the water: and, lo, the heavens were opened unto him, and he saw the Spirit of God descending like a dove, and lighting upon him: And lo a voice from heaven saying, This is my beloved Son, in whom I am well pleased." (Matt. 3:16, 17)

"And Jesus came and spake unto them, saying, All power is given unto me in heaven and in earth. Go ye therefore, and teach all nations, baptizing them in the name of the Father, and of the Son, and of the Holy Ghost." (Matt. 28:18, 19)

"John did baptize in the wilderness, and preach the baptism of repentance for the remission of sins." (Mark 1:4)

"Jesus answered, Verily, verily, I say unto thee, Except a man be born of water and of the Spirit, he cannot enter into the kingdom of God." (John 3:5)

But where exactly did baptism come from? Obviously, it was something that John the Baptist had introduced to his own followers even before Jesus came on the scene. The Essenes (a group which some believe John and Jesus were part of) practiced these water rituals as stated in *The Essene Gospel of Peace,* translated by Edmond Bordeaux Szekely.

> After the angel of air, seek the angel of water. Put off your shoes and your clothing and suffer the angel of water to embrace all your body. Cast yourselves wholly into his enfolding arms, and as often as you move the air with your breath, move with your body the water also. I tell you truly, the angel of water shall cast out of your body all uncleannesses which defiled it without and within. And all unclean and evil-smelling things shall flow out of you, even

as the uncleannesses of garments washed in water flow away are lost in the stream of the river. I tell you truly, holy is the angel of water who cleanses all that is unclean and makes all evil-smelling things of a sweet odor. No man may come before the face of God whom the angel of water lets not pass. In very truth, all must be born again of water and of truth, for your body bathes in the river of earthly life, and your spirit bathes in the river of life everlasting. For you receive your blood from our Earthly Mother and the truth from our Heavenly Father.

I thought this was pretty interesting regarding water ritual. But even more interesting to me still is the information I uncovered in the book, *The Templar Revelation* by Lynn Picknett and Clive Prince concerning the history of baptism.

Where did John the Baptist get the ritual of baptism from? Further delving revealed that it had absolutely no precedent in Judaism although references to ritual washing—repeated immersions symbolizing purification—are found in the Dead Sea Scrolls. However, it is inaccurate to describe these rites as 'baptisms': what John advocated was a single, life-changing act of initiation that was preceded by confession and repentance of sins. The fact that this ritual was without Jewish precedent is indicated by his title or nickname—John *the* Baptist—the only one, not one of many. Indeed, it has often been taken as an innovation of his, although there are, in fact, many precedents and exact parallels *outside* the Jewish world.

Baptism as the outward and visible symbol of an inward spiritual renewal was a feature of many of the mystery cults that existed throughout the Hellenistic world at the time. It had a particularly long tradition in the ancient Egyptian mystery cult of Isis and, significantly, baptism in her temples on the banks of the Nile was preceded by public repentance and confession of sins to the priest.

Being a Watsu and Waterdance practitioner, I understand firsthand the power of water rituals or water therapies. They can serve to unlock and unleash the powers of spiritual enlightenment like no others I've witnessed.

It's through this fluid medium that I've seen the true powers of God manifest in the form of *kundalini* energy. There is a sacred, mystical connection here that I'm just beginning to understand. If it's truth, then it will be verified in many different ways and by many witnesses. It's then that we can understand it to be a correct principle and align with it to guide our lives. I believe this is one way that we receive the gift of the Holy Spirit and experience what the Primitive Church called "Gnosis" or "to know God for oneself." It's by this means that we can gain a direct connection with God and become "sourcers." This leads us into the fourth principle or ordinance of the Gospel, "Laying on of hands for the gift of the Holy Ghost."

Okay, this will probably seem rather weird since I'm a massage therapist but, I've witnessed first-hand some incredible healing and spiritual awakenings during my "laying on of hands" therapy sessions. Is that really what this gospel principle is all about? Let's take a look at some other references concerning the concept of "laying on of hands." First, from the canonized scriptures let's see what Jesus' own experiences were:

"While he spake these things unto them, behold, there came a certain ruler, and worshipped him, saying, My daughter is even now dead: but come and lay hands upon her, and she shall live.

"And when Jesus came into the ruler's house, and saw the minstrels and the people making a noise, He said unto them, Give place: for the maid is not dead, but sleepeth. And they laughed him to scorn.

"But when the people were put forth, he went in, and took her by the hand, and the maid arose. And the fame hereof went abroad into all that land." (Matt. 9:18, 23-26)

"And these signs shall follow them that believe; In my name shall they cast out devils; they shall speak with new tongues; they shall take up serpents; and if they drink any deadly thing, it shall not hurt them: they shall lay hands on the sick, and they shall recover." (Luke 16:17, 18)

"Therefore, leaving the principles of the doctrine of Christ, let us go on unto perfection; not laying again the foundation of repentance from dead works, and of faith toward God, or the doctrine of baptisms, and laying on of hands, and of resurrection of the dead, and of eternal judgment.

"For this will we do, if God permit. For it is impossible for those who were once enlightened, and have tasted of the heavenly gift, and were made partakers of the Holy Ghost, and have tasted the good word of God, and the powers of the world to come, if they shall fall away, to renew them again unto repentance; seeing they crucify to themselves the Son of God afresh, and put him to an open shame." (Hebrews 6:1-6)

So is there a more significant side to the whole "laying on of hands" story that we are missing here? In Mormonism there are several laying on of hands rituals performed for the sake of initiation, healing and endowment. The first is done when children are eight years old immediately after their baptism. This is the "laying on of hands for the gift of the Holy Ghost." Also, the Elders of the Church are available to lay on hands for the sake of healing the sick. This power is given to them by a laying on of hands Priesthood ordinance reserved only for *male* members. Female members can only perform blessings of faith with no Priesthood power available to them and the Church even frowns upon that if it involves the laying on of hands. (Is this because women already have "Priestess power" innately available in them which perhaps men in authority are afraid of?) But what intrigues me most is the initiatory work in the temple which involves a washing and anointing of the entire body in preparation for receiving the Holy Endowment. Could this laying on of hands ceremony be similar to the laying on of hands Mary Magdalene performed on Jesus? In Margaret Starbird's book, *The Woman with the Alabaster Jar,* we find the following:

> The story of the anointing of Jesus by the woman in Bethany is one of the most important events recorded in the New Testament Gospels. It must be extremely significant, for it is a rare event indeed that is reported in all four canonical Gospels. The story of the anointing is easily the most intimate expression of Eros/relatedness in the recorded events of Jesus' life, and for that reason alone it deserves careful scrutiny. Yet it has rarely received the recognition it deserves. What was the meaning of the action of this woman at Bethany? And isn't it likely that the woman who anointed Jesus at the banquet at Bethany was the same woman who encountered him in the garden near the tomb at dawn on Easter morning?
>
> One evening, according to Mark 14:3, "while Jesus was in Bethany, reclining at the table...a woman came with an alabaster jar." The action of the woman at Bethany can be understood as a prophetic recognition of Jesus as the Messiah, the Anointed One, an action construed as politically dangerous because it proclaimed the kingship of Jesus.

In ancient Israel, kings, priests, and prophets were anointed with oil to receive their authority as those "chosen" to represent Yahweh. The sacred olive oil was carefully prepared by the priests in the Temple and mixed according to a prescribed recipe with other spices: cinnamon, myrrh, sweet calamus, and cassia. Its secular use was prohibited on pain of excommunication. But the woman of Bethany did not use the sacred oil of the Temple priests. She opened "...an alabaster jar of very expensive perfume made of pure nard. She broke the jar and poured it on his head."

Along the same lines of what we discussed earlier about the priestess' rights and rites, Margaret Starbird goes on to explain:

> The anointing performed by the woman at Bethany was similar to the familiar ritual practice of a sacred priestess or temple "prostitute" in the Goddess cults of the Roman Empire. Even the term *prostitute* is a misnomer. This term, chosen by modern translators, is applied to the *hierodulae,* or "sacred women" of the temple of the Goddess, who played an important part in the everyday life of the classical world. As priestesses of the Goddess, their importance dates back through the centuries to the Neolithic period (7000-3500 BC), back to the time when God was honored and cherished as *feminine* throughout the lands that are now known as the Middle East and Europe.

> In the ancient world, sexuality was considered sacred, a special gift from the goddess of love, and the priestesses who officiated at the temples of the love goddesses in the Middle East were considered holy by the citizens of the Greek and Roman empires. Known as "consecrated women," they were held in high esteem as invokers of the love, ecstasy, and fertility of the Goddess. At some periods of Jewish history, they were even a part of the ritual worship in the Temple of Jerusalem although some of the prophets of Yahweh deplored the influence of the Great Goddess locally called "Ashera."

> In the Gospel context, the woman with the alabaster jar of unguent may have been one of these priestesses. But curiously, Jesus does not seem to have been at all affronted by her action when she anointed him.

This is captivating stuff to someone who was raised on the idea that the only acceptable marriage is a "temple marriage." I was, in fact, married in a Mormon temple, and to this day parts of the sacred endowment ceremony fascinate me, but blood-oath promises of secrecy keep my mouth shut about these sacred (or secret) ceremonies. (Actually you can read the entire temple ceremony online, if you wish.) But what intrigues me most, thanks to Dan Brown's *The Da Vinci Code*, is the history of temples and temple rites. That's where the truly fascinating research begins.

Going back to some of Margaret Starbird's points, temple rituals were performed thousands of years ago. Most Judeo/Christians believe they started with King Solomon in the famous "King Solomon's Temple." According to my research, these temple rites were actually based on the *Kabbalah*, the inner and mystical aspect of Judaism that's been handed down over the centuries by a discreet tradition that has periodically changed and corrupted it.

Some of its corrupted forms have been found in the traditions of Freemasonry. Most Mormons will find it interesting that Joseph Smith joined the Freemasons for the express purpose of "borrowing" from their ceremonies to include them as part of the Mormon temple ceremony. That's why there are so many similarities between the ceremonies of Masonry and Mormonism. Even the symbols on the sacred temple garments are found in Masonry—the compass and the square—which, when overlaid, form the points of the Star of David. (See *Mormonism, Magic and Masonry* by Jerald and Sandra Tanner.)

"So what does all this mean?" you might ask. Well, to put it in a nutshell or "bottom-line it," the temple ceremonies yesterday and today were for the purpose of what is called *Hieros Gamos*. Google it when you're online for some interesting information. I've found opinions of what exactly this Greek term means, but the most informed I've found is from Margaret Starbird's, *The Woman with the Alabaster Jar*.

> We have already mentioned that in the Near Eastern religions of the Sumer, Babylon, and Canaan, anointing the head of the king with oil was a ritual performed by the heiress or royal priestess who represented the Goddess. In Greek, this rite was called the *heiros gamos* or "Sacred Marriage." The anointing of the head had erotic significance, the head being symbolic of the phallus 'anointed' by the woman for penetration during the physical consummation of marriage. The chosen bridegroom was anointed by the royal priestess, the surrogate of the Goddess. Songs of love, praise, and thanksgiving accompanied the couple, and following the

consummation of their union, a lavish wedding banquet
was celebrated in the whole city amid general rejoicing of the
citizens. The feast sometimes lasted for days. The blessing of
the royal union would be reflected in the continued fertility
of crops and herds and the well-being of the community.

We, as Mormons, are informed at an early age about the blessings we'll
receive if we are "married in the temple." It is the *only* marriage that will
last throughout the eternities, we are told, for it's an everlasting marriage
contract between us and God. But let's stop right here. Okay, that sounds
very romantic and enticing—but then insert "celestial *plural* marriage" and
what have you got? *Confusion!* (Con=not, fusion=together) How does all of
this come into the picture, anyway? Well, it all started with King Solomon.
How many wives did he have? One for every day of the year? I guess if his
wives were indeed temple prostitutes then it really all made sense. (At least it
was more equitable as far as the sex was concerned.)

So the question of plural wives was a valid one that Joseph Smith posed
to God one day when he had been reading in the Bible about Solomon's
many wives and concubines. And God's answer is found in Doctrine and
Covenants 132. I won't quote it here, as it is a *very long* answer. You can read
it yourself, but the debate goes on, both inside and outside of the church, as
to whether or not the "new and everlasting covenant of marriage" *is* "celestial
plural marriage." That's where Mormon Fundamentalists come into the
picture and argue that the two are the same. And then the issue over "keys,
keys, who holds the keys" comes into play. It can become very confusing for
any student of Mormonism. So let's go back to the scriptures—the canonized
and uncanonized versions—for answers.

It seems obvious to me and anyone well read in the scriptures (or even
slightly read) that practically all the prophets and kings who ever talked with
God were polygamists. You name them—Abraham, Isaac, Jacob, Moses,
Solomon, David—the list goes on and on. Well, this is all fine and dandy if
you are *male!* (Is that why there are no females recorded in the Bible as having
spoken to God? They weren't living the laws of plural marriage!)

But the real question here, for me as a Christian, is—how did Jesus live?
Wouldn't he be our greatest example? Well, we know already that there's been
a big cover-up regarding these issues, but a lot has recently been uncovered
concerning Jesus being married. The best book I've found on the subject
was written by an ex-Mormon Fundamentalist named Ogden Kraut entitled
Jesus was Married. (Now there's a positive affirmation.) He did a thorough
investigation and came up with evidence and conclusion that Jesus was not
only married to Mary Magdalene, but he also had other wives he was so-called

"married to" such as the two sisters, Mary and Martha of Bethany, the woman at the well who received "the living waters" (curious what that might be) and others who were known among his female followers.

One curious episode concerns the "woman taken in adultery." (John 8:2-11) This story actually took place *inside* the temple. Was Mary Magdalene perhaps this woman who was actually a "temple priestess" performing temple rites? Why was she brought before Jesus if he wasn't intimately connected to her as a "husband" as it was the husband's responsibility to stone his own wife if she was guilty of adultery? Why then did Jesus *not* condemn her if she was indeed committing adultery? Interesting.

Another curious story is the one concerning the Samaritan woman at Jacob's well. (John 4:5-30) If she was committing adultery by having five husbands and not being married to the man she was then living with, it would have been a great opportunity for Jesus to condemn her. But instead, he gave her the "living waters, which shall spring up into everlasting life"—a precious blessing rather than a cursing because perhaps she was "doing the works of Abraham." Something to think about.

But really what exactly does Jesus say concerning marriage in general if he's the expert on the subject. Well, one of his best known discourses on marriage is found in Matthew 22:23-30 and also recorded in Mark 12:18-25:

> Then come unto him the Sadducees, which say there is no resurrection; and they asked him, saying, Master, Moses wrote unto us, If a man's brother die, and leave his wife behind him, and leave no children, that his brother should take his wife, and raise up seed unto his brother. Now there were seven brethren: and the first took a wife, and dying left no seed. And the second took her, and died, neither left he any seed: and the third likewise. And the seven had her, and left no seed: last of all the woman died also. In the resurrection therefore, when they shall rise, whose wife shall she be of them: for the seven had her to wife. And Jesus answering said unto them, Do ye not therefore err, because ye know not the scriptures, neither the power of God? For when they shall rise from the dead, they neither marry, nor are given in marriage; but are as the angels which are in heaven.

So is Jesus telling us that there is no marriage in heaven? But if it is so that it is "on earth as it is in heaven" then why get married in the first place? Again we go to the words of Jesus found again in Matthew and Mark.

"The Pharisees also came unto him, tempting him, and saying unto him, Is it lawful for a man to put away his wife for every cause? And he answered and said unto them, Have ye not read, that he which made them at the beginning made them male and female, and said, For this cause shall a man leave father and mother, and shall cleave to his wife: and they twain shall be one flesh? Wherefore they are no more twain, but one flesh. What therefore God hath joined together, let not man put asunder." (Matt. 19:3-6)

Now here's a big clue to the mystery of eternal marriage. "What therefore *God* hath joined together, let not man put asunder." This could be the missing clue to the first marriage question of whether or not these brothers were eternally married to the one wife. Perhaps it wasn't God who brought them together by the Holy Spirit of love, but merely by convenience. Oh, I forgot to finish the quotation. Jesus goes on to say in Mark 12:26, 27:

"And as touching the dead, that they rise: have ye not read in the book of Moses, how in the bush God spake unto him, saying, I am the God of Abraham, and the God of Isaac, and the God of Jacob? He is not the God of the dead, but the God of the living: ye therefore do greatly err."

Hum, does this mean that God is only acknowledging known polygamists as being "the God of the living?" In other words—is plural marriage (for both men and women) the gateway to heaven? This is curious until you relate it to some of the Gnostic scriptures found at the Nag Hammadi describing Jesus' relationship to Mary. In the Gospel of Philip we read:

"…the companion of the (Saviour is) Mary Magdalene. (But Christ loved) her more than (all) the disciples and used to kiss her (often) on her (mouth). The rest of (the disciples were offended by it…). They said to him, 'Why do you love her more than all of us?' The Saviour answered and said to them, 'Why do I not love you as (I love) her?'" (Note: the parenthesis are "fill-in-the-blanks" estimations by the translators as many of the scrolls were badly damaged.)

The book, *The Second Messiah,* by Christopher Knight and Robert Lomas, explains:

> The Gospel of Mary tells us that she was favoured with visions and insight that far surpassed Peter's. Another document, the *Dialogue of the Saviour,* describes her as the

apostle who excels all the rest... "a woman who knew the All". Gospels that refer to the equality of women were rejected by the Roman Church under the catch-all accusation of being Gnostic, but in these versions it is clear that there was a power struggle between Peter and Mary Magdalene. In a document called "Pistis Sophia", Peter complains that Mary is dominating the conversation with Jesus and displacing the rightful priority of Peter and the other male apostles. Peter asks Jesus to silence her, but he is quickly rebuked. Mary Magdalene later admits to Jesus that she hardly dares speak to Peter because: "Peter makes me hesitate; I am afraid of him, because he hates the female race." Jesus replies that whoever the Spirit inspires is divinely ordained to speak, whether man or woman.

And then in the Gospel of Thomas we read:

"Simon Peter said to them, 'Make Mary leave us, for females are not worthy of life.'
Jesus said, 'Look, I shall guide her to make her male, so that she too may become a living spirit resembling you males. For every female who makes herself male will enter the Kingdom of Heaven.'"

Wow! Now that's powerful stuff when you put it all together. You mean all I have to do is become like a male (and become a polygamist like Abraham, Isaac and Jacob) in order to become a "living spirit?" Or do I just need to be married to Jesus? Perhaps they are one and the same as that truly could be the "Bridal Chamber" or *heiros gamos* Jesus talked about that is only available to those who have oil in their lamps or have obtained the "Holy Spirit" for themselves. This is a Gnostic Christian concept, by the way, and is also supported by many Mormon prophets including Joseph Smith. "I would that we could all be prophets!"

Now I know I'm really getting into some deep water here, but please indulge me for a moment. (I am a woman, ya know.) What exactly is the gathering of Israel talked about in the scriptures? Or the United Order talked about by Joseph Smith. Or better yet, here's a great quote from the book, *On the Kabbalah and Its Symbolism* by Gershom Scholem describing the *Shekhinah*.

The mystical organism of the Torah, which embodies the name of God, is thus correlated with the mystical body of the Community of Israel, which the Kabbalists regarded not only as the historical organism of the Jewish people, but also as an esoteric symbol for the *Shekhinah*, its members being, as it were, the members of the *Shekhinah*…

The mythical nature of these conceptions is most clearly exemplified by the distinction between the masculine and feminine, begetting and receiving potencies in God. This mythical element recurs, with rising intensity, in several pairs of *sefiroth,* and is expressed most forcefully in the symbolism of the last two. The ninth *sefirah, yesod,* is the male potency, described with clearly phallic symbolism, the "foundation" of all life, which guarantees and consummates the *hieros gamos,* the holy union of male and female powers.

The notion of feminine potencies in God, which attain their fullest expression in the tenth and last sefirah, represents of course a repristination of myth that seems utterly incongruous in Jewish thinking. Consequently it seems necessary to say a few words about this idea, that is, about the Kabbalistic conception of *Shekhinah,* which is a radical departure from the old Rabbinical conception…

In Talmudic literature and non-Kabbalistic Rabbinical Judaism, the *Shekhinah*—literally in-dwelling, namely of God in the world—is taken to mean simply God himself in His omnipresence and activity in the world and especially in Israel. God's presence, what in the Bible is called "His face", is in Rabbinical usage His *Shekhinah.*

The shekhinah, the author goes onto explain, is the feminine manifestation of God…the Holy Spirit perhaps. In the theology of Judaism it meant God's presence in and throughout the world or in Gnostic terms "Sophia" or wisdom. In modern-day Christian terms it could mean the third member of the Godhead or the Holy Spirit.

Well, that may sound a bit mystical or mythical (according to the usage of the word) but I think if you saw the movie or read the book, *The Da Vinci Code* it would all make sense. The symbolism in the movie is radical. In the end it's the Jewish "Star of David" or the signs of the male and female coming together in unity that breaks the code. It is also the sign of the cup and the sword coming together which are the symbols of the female and male genitals uniting if you've read Riane Eisler book, *The Chalice & the Blade.* But the best information I've found regarding this symbolism is again found in Margaret Starbird's *The Woman with the Alabaster Jar.*

> "Is there anyone who remembers the former glory of this house?" asks the Hebrew prophet Haggai. The date is 520 BC, and the Temple of Solomon on Mount Sion lies in ruins. The Jews have returned to Israel after their seventy years of exile in Babylon, the city equated with pagan sun worship. The Word of God to Haggai is that the Temple is to be rebuilt and that blessing will begin to flow again when the foundation of the Temple has been laid—not after the Temple is finished, but when it is begun. When we understand the blueprint of the true Temple—the sacred, life-giving balance of male and female energies inherent in the cosmos itself and the symbolism that portrays the composite wisdom of antiquity—blessings will begin to flow like a gentle river into the parched lands of Earth. As found in the promise of Isaiah, the desert shall bloom. Universal peace and well-being can be restored when the blueprint for the Temple is embraced in our consciousness. The blueprint is (the Star of David).

There's also some interesting stuff found in *The Temple and the Lodge* by Michael Baigent and Richard Leigh.

> God, in both Judaism and Islam, was One. God was a unity. God was everything. The forms of the phenomenal world, on the other hand, were numerous, manifold, multifarious and diverse. Such forms bore witness not to the divine unity, but to the fragmentation of the temporal world. If God was to be discerned in the creation at all, it was not in the multiplicity of forms, but in the unifying principles running through those forms and underlying them. In other words, ultimately by the degrees in an angle—and by number. It was through shape and number, not by representation of diverse forms, that God's glory was held to be manifest. And it was in edifices based on shape and number, rather than on representational embellishment, that the divine presence was to be housed.

This concept, by the way, is the entire history of Masonry. Masons were compelled to build structures in which God's presence could dwell. This is also the emphasis for Mormon temple building—to create sacred space for sacred ceremony. Interestingly enough, archeologists have found that in the architectural ruins of Solomon's temple there remains the Star of David in its foundation—just like in the Rosslyn chapel. Could this be the *real* treasure that the Priory of Sion and the Knight's Templar were trying to protect? Not surprising, this is the same blueprint for my own Rainbow Light Centers that God has inspired me to build.

But let's go back to the concept of God being a "Oneness" or a unity. This concept is pervasive in all mystical religions including Mormonism. One of my favorite scriptures in Mormonism comes from the Doctrine and Covenants:

"I say unto you, be one: and if ye are not one ye are not mine." (D & C 38:27)

So where did this concept of oneness originate? Obviously it was a principle of Judaism recognized as the "Gathering of Israel" or the *Shekhinah*. But let's go to some of my favorite scriptures in the canonized New Testament regarding "the oneness."

"And the multitude of them that believed were of one heart and of one soul: neither said any of them that out of the things which he possessed was his own; but they had *all things common*." (Acts 4:32)

So what does this term "all things common" truly mean? Does it mean all things common *except* for our bodies and our sexuality? I believe Jesus would have made this distinction if this was the order of things on earth as it is in heaven. Perhaps this is the lifestyle that the Gnostic Christian "heretics" lived that got them into so much trouble. Constantine felt the need to organize a whole army of Christian Crusaders to wipe them all out. Is the fear of sexuality in common or "orgies" really the fear here? Is that why pagan sexual rituals have been outlawed throughout Christendom? Does this powerful ritual cause a real threat to the powers that be? Obviously, or it wouldn't have been suppressed for so many years. When Joseph Smith tried to introduce these ceremonies in the temples as "The Holy Order" ordinance, he was persecuted, prosecuted and run out of town—and eventually killed. Here's a little tidbit I found on www.goddess.org regarding orgies:

Nowadays the word *orgy* connotes something depraved and degenerate. That was not the original meaning for the word. The word "orgy" comes from the Greek word "orgia" meaning "secret (or sacred) worship." Since most secret worship involved sexual rituals and Christians were opposed to anything sexual, the word orgy came to have the debased meaning it has today, rather than the noble spiritual meaning of the original word.

Okay, I know that's really going out on a limb for most of you, but if you simply look at the concept of "all things common" rationally and mathematically it makes sense in terms of empowerment. If two people become intimately unified then we get the equation—one plus one equals two. Don't we then have more power in the power of two? That's the power of marriage or the oneness. But what if this power is increased exponentially rather than additionally? That if two people are intimately unified on correct principles, then the power is increased by 2 to the power of 2—which is 4. Now if you can take this concept into a community sense—where people are intimately unified on correct principle—I believe you now have the power to shift the planet into a new age of love, peace and enlightenment. Challenging, yes. Impossible, no.

I know there are many individuals out there who "get" this concept and who are already "one in spirit" with other people. But the *real* challenge is taking it one step further and becoming "one in flesh." But isn't that what life's all about anyway—creating Heaven on Earth? It is for me. If we could catch the vision of what this type of loving community could be like—nothing could stop us from creating it. Just read my book, *Heartsong,* if you want to catch a glimpse of this vision.

But then, if you're like me, you say it's already challenging enough just to become one with my current partner. (Remember Brad's my polar opposite, so if we can do it anyone can.) But after seeing the movie, *The Davinci Code,* we both got a huge epiphany. Our two last names—Thorne and Bird—when symbolized together form the sacred Star of David. But that isn't all. When you reverse two of the letters in both of our names, and add an "e" to the end they become— Bride/Throne—Bride on the Throne. I know that's a bit of a stretch for some people but you've got to admit by now—God has a strange sense of humor!

Chapter Twenty-four—Angels and Demons

If you think I went "out on a limb" already—this chapter should convince you that I'm *way out there*. So move over, Shirley MacLaine, 'cause at least you've got a limb to stand on. And again, Dan Brown, my hat's off to you for inspiring my next adventure down the rabbit hole.

It all started, of course, when I read Dan Brown's *Angels and Demons*. I ate it up just like I did the *Da Vinci Code*. But this book was almost scary in how close it was to home. I had been spoon-fed at an early age the "Great Conspiracy" by my mom who was a devoted follower of Ezra Taft Bensen and Cleon Skousen (they were popular expositors of the "vast international conspiracy" and lived in our ward when I was growing up). The term "Illuminati" was a household word in our home. It was the catchall word for every evil conspiracy that ever existed—its goal—to overthrow Christianity and start a New World Order. At least that's what I was taught as a kid, but as an adult I learned to question everything I was taught.

But then there was the shocking incident with Patrick who named the Illuminati as being responsible for the death of his comrades and perhaps ultimately responsible for his own murder. He stated in his tapes that is was an Illuminatus disguised as a Catholic Priest who was following them as they were uncovering ancient petroglyphs in Mayan Temples. (A little too close to the whole Dan Brown epic, don't you think?) I suppose it was partly this fear that kept me quiet about some of my own spiritual illuminations. But no more. I really wanted to get to the bottom of this whole Illuminati thing, so I sent it out to God to give me some insights concerning it. That is when I received the following letter in the mail out of nowhere (actually it was from Grove City, Ohio).

Dear Janae,

This is a personal letter just to you. Notice: this is not a mass mailing; this letter came to you by first-class mail, not by third-class bulk mail. This is not a solicitation for money. In fact, you will get something of immense value from us <u>absolutely free</u> with no strings attached. So, read every word very carefully because you will never get another letter from us again.

Janae, please keep what I tell you secret, because this information is confidential. These words are meant for you only.

There has existed for many years an exclusive association, a secret society, of the world's most famous and powerful people. These include renowned actors and musicians, leading scientists and intellectuals, self-made entrepreneurs and artists, millionaires, professional gamblers, Casanovas, statesmen. Many of these people you would instantly recognize. Before I go on, let me state that everything you read here is absolutely and verifiably true.

This association has uncovered some shockingly powerful secrets. And they share these secrets only amongst themselves. In fact, these secrets are the reason these well-known individuals have achieved great prosperity.

Janae, I have some incredibly exciting news to share with you. Members of this association have analyzed your profile (you'd be unbelievably flattered if you knew who these individuals were). Please forgive them, but they've discovered something special about you.

It seems you, Janae, possess several rare traits they are searching for. Because of these traits, which we'll talk about later, they have chosen you to become part of their exclusive club and to share their secrets, too, **absolutely free!** By the way, as you read this, you may be saying to yourself that this is all a bunch of hooey. But I swear on the Bible this is all true! You see, every seven years this association picks a handful of individuals from around the world possessing your unique traits to share in their secrets—in fact, they are going to reveal to you absolutely free, the Greatest Kept Secret of All Time for Money, Power, Romantic-Love! In your case, your hidden talents must be phenomenal for the members to select you!

How did these gifted people find you? For now, that must remain a mystery.

But I can shed light on how they found you by first telling you my own story: Seven years ago I was like you. Out of the blue, I received an invitation from this society. Just like you, they said I possessed special traits. I was flattered, excited, yet skeptical. But, when they sent their secrets to me personally a few days later **for free**, just as they said they would, my luck changed so completely I thought God must be guiding me, giving me special powers!

Like me, the day you receive this secret package, for free, Janae, will be the luckiest day of your life! It will be the most important event that will ever happen to you. For, by the time you finish reading that package, you'll know exactly what to do to make $5,000, $10,000, even $100,000 cash… IN THE NEXT FEW WEEKS!

Plus… prosper in every area of your life: emotionally, personally, physically, romantically and financially.

You'll even learn how to control anyone and make any man or woman like you, admire you, or love you!

All the money, power and romantic love you've ever wanted can come to you easily, effortlessly and automatically. All you have to do is learn the simple, secret system a renowned Du Pont scientist spent his entire life uncovering.

Janae, are you skeptical like I was? Well, just as this elite group did for me, we're going to send these very secrets to you, personally, for free! Why? Because we believe that you are a rare find. We want you to join us. Remember, these are the very same secrets that the world's most successful celebrities, entrepreneurs, scientists, professional gamblers, investors and Casanovas possess…But you must return the enclosed free-invitation form by this Friday, August 12, 2005.

Now here is the story as told by a TV celebrity and copywriter who personally used this discovery to go from broke to a famous multi-millionaire in less than a year:

(Note: the next page and a half of the letter described, what I believe was Kevin Trudeau's story as told in his book, *Natural Cures "They" Don't Want*

You to Know About. But I won't bore you with those details—I just wanted to know *who the heck had written me that letter.* It was finally revealed on page 5.)

> Although the above famous Nouveau Tech man had more to tell, I interrupted here because right now you may be asking, "Why am I receiving this invitation?" Janae, have been selected to be sent the Nouveau Tech secrets—Nouveau Tech secrets that have laid hidden from ordinary eyes for 2300 years—for free—because members of our elite group, of our Secret Society, have discovered that you possess rare potentials that few others have…. And you'd be amazed to know just who these particular world-renown members were who chose you! But, alas, it's a secret society and although everything I say here is true, their identities must remain anonymous. Those who chose you, though, do realize your special qualities YOU'VE GOT IT! You just have not fully realized your special qualities yet…

Well, the bullshit just kept getting piled higher and deeper as I read on and on about my so-called "special qualities." I knew I was being set up for a scam—but I was curious who these scammers were.

Thank God for modern-day technology and the Internet. I googled Nouveau Tech and guess what I pulled up? The ILLUMINATI! Nouveau Tech was a front name for today's Illuminati! I logged onto a chat-room where letter after letter appeared about how individuals had been scammed by this organization. The book that they were finally convinced to order by Dr. Frank R. Wallace is *not absolutely free* but costs $139.95. (A small price to pay for wealth and power beyond your wildest dreams!)

The reviews I found were anywhere from discordant disappointment to seething accusations of a book being written by the Anti-Christ for the purpose of overthrowing the Christian society. I was curious as to what was in this book that would get these God-fearing folks so up in arms, but I certainly wasn't going to pay $139.95 to order it.

When Brad came home, I showed him the letter and told him what I'd discovered on the Internet. He nonchalantly read the first few paragraphs and replied, "Oh, I got a letter like this years ago and ended up ordering the damn book. It was a real waste of time and money."

"You mean you have a copy of this Nouveau Tech book somewhere that I can read?" I asked excitedly.

"I believe I still have it, but it's probably in storage in Salt Lake. But I think the title was different, something like 'Neo-tech,' but I'm sure the author was the same—Frank Wallace."

The next time we were in Salt Lake, I made Brad take me to the storage unit to locate the infamous book, and we somehow found it. It was a black inch-thick paperback with the title *NEO-TECH DISCOVERY by Frank R. Wallace—Prosperity and Happiness through Personal Affairs and Relationships, Business, Finance and Investing, Art and Pleasures*. I was sure it was the same book talked about on the Internet as being the Nouveau Tech book. I turned to the inside cover, which sported a picture of San Francisco Bay with its impressive bridges and buildings with the subtitle "Nature Conquered" in bold letters.

"A bit arrogant, aren't they?" I said to myself as I began reading the book in the car on our trip back to Las Vegas.

"Listen to this bullshit," I told Brad as we drove. "This is the whole underlying premise for the book."

"Neo-Tech is a noun or adjective meaning fully integrated honesty. Neo-Tech allows the guiltless creation of earned power, prosperity, and romantic love."

"That doesn't sound like bullshit to me—that actually sounds right on target," Brad commented.

"Just wait a minute—let me go on."

Neo-Tech is a collection of 'new techniques' or 'new technology' that lets one know exactly what is happening and what to do for gaining maximum advantages in all situations. That technology is needed to be competent—to guiltlessly and honestly obtain the wealth and happiness available to everyone but achieved by so few. Neo-Tech provides the power to profit in every situation by nullifying neocheating and all other forms of mysticism, not only in others but within one's own self. Indeed, Neo-Tech eliminates mysticism—eliminates the harm of all mystics, false authorities, neocheaters, and their infinite array of deceptions. Neo-Tech lets a person gather all power unto one's own self while rendering mystics and neocheaters impotent.... Neo-Tech is the process of converting outmoded bicameral mind (the automatic, split mind as described in

Neo-Tech III) guided by mysticism and external "authorities" to a new, independent mind guided by guiltless, rational advantages.

"Well, who can argue with that—I've always told you I have a problem with mysticism." Brad commented.

"Do you even know what the word 'mysticism' means?" I replied.

We then jumped back into our running debate over mysticism, which is a subject that gets gnawed-on, chewed-up, spit-out but never digested. I argued that most people didn't understand the true meaning of the word, "mysticism." They thought it was something mysterious, incomprehensible and evil. But if you looked it up in the dictionary, the meaning implies "the process of obtaining a direct connection with God." This was the path of the proverbial "mystic"—to obtain direct contact with God or Gnosis.

The book, *Neo-tech*, indeed discounted mystics and, by the same token, discounted the reality of God. This had always been the roadblock in Brad and my relationship—that he discounted my "mystical" experiences as psychotic episodes that were impossible to prove. I could tell that he'd bought into this Neo-tech thing, hook, line, and sinker, years before I'd even met him. Now we'd finally gotten down to the root of our problems. I was a believer in mysticism—he was not.

I scanned the pages to discover Neo-tech's definition of mysticism.

Mysticism is defined as: 1. Any mental, psychological, or physical-force attempt to recreate or alter reality through dishonesty, rationalizations, non-sequitur, emotions, deceptions, or force. 2. Any attempt to evade reality or contradict life.

Mysticism is a disease—an epistemological disease that progressively undermines one's capacity to think, to identify reality, to live competently. Mysticism is also a collective disease that affects everyone who looks toward others, or the group, or the leader for solutions to his or her problems and responsibilities. The symptoms of mysticism are dishonest communication, out-of-context assertions or attacks, use of non-sequiturs, jumbled or non-integrated thinking. Those symptoms are most commonly exhibited by neocheating politicians, clergyman, union leaders, media commentators, university professors, entertainment personalities. Such public neocheaters are the Typhoid-Mary spreaders of mysticism. In fact, through the ages, the most virulent spreaders of mysticism have been those neocheaters who wangle respect and values from legions of life-fearing, dependent people populating this world. Mysticism is a disease. But it is also the tool that neocheaters use to justify or rationalize the use of force, fraud, or dishonesty to usurp values from the producers. For example, mysticism is used to create illusionary standards and false guilt designed to beguile individuals into surrendering their earned values and happiness.

Mysticism is also the leaving the mind open to irrational ideas as well as trying to impose irrational ideas onto others. Mysticism is the fertilizer of deception.

Mysticism is a rebellion against life, effort, values, and the conscious mind. Mysticism brands people with government faces and is the neocheater's tool for controlling others and plundering producers.

Mysticism is based on a false and evil idea: the primacy of emotions. Mysticism is the opposite of Neo-Tech.

Mysticism is the only disease of the conscious mind. But as with drugs and alcohol, mysticism is seductive—seemingly comfortable, like a warm, old friend…until the destructive consequences and hangovers manifest themselves.

Neocheating is defined as: Any intentional use of mysticism designed to create false 'realities' or illusions in order to extract values from others…Neocheating is the technique for expropriating unearned money or power by using mysticism to manipulate thinking defaults in others. Neocheating is the means by which politicians, clergymen, union leaders, many journalists and the academe usurp power and values.

I finished reading to Brad the book's definition of mysticism. "Okay, I did agree with one thing—that there are a lot of mystics out there trying to usurp other people's power by becoming mediums or go-betweens to God. But someone who is truly a mystic and receives direct communication from God would *never* try to interfere but would encourage each individual to find a direct link to God. But to deny that there is such a thing as authentic mysticism and authentic mystics does not demonstrate…what is it they called Neo-tech?…'fully integrated honesty'."

I knew I'd opened up the proverbial "can of worms," but I thought I'd give it one more shot with Brad.

He responded, "Well, you've yet to *prove* to me anything about your own so-called mystical experiences or direct communication with God. All I have to go by is your own purported experiences with Patrick and your Kundalini experiences at Harbin. I've never experienced anything like that myself so maybe they only exist in your *own* mind."

"So what about Harold and Richard and Shantam? Are we all experiencing a group hallucination of mysticism? Or what about other mystics who have experienced altered states of consciousness like Jesus or Buddha or Muhammad…or even Joseph Smith? Are we all products of delusional experiences? Just because we can't *prove* our experiences to non-believers doesn't mean they don't exist. It's like telling a person who is color-blind that colors exist. It may be beyond his scope of reality to comprehend them—but to others who have eyes to see—there is a verdant rainbow of color that defines our reality. You can't define your reality by someone else's. It's all relative to the individual's perception or belief system concerning life. I love Brian's tagline statement in his e-mails: We don't see things as they are—we see things as *we* are."

"Are you saying that there's something 'special' about you so-called mystics? That your world is any more *real* than ours? Or that you live on a 'higher consciousness' level than we do? Now that to me is elitist bullshit and is exactly what that book there is telling you is an epidemic in our society. Elitist bullshit! And I'm all for fighting this disease myself as it's the thing that's caused the most damage to our society…and our relationship!"

I knew the conversation had deteriorated, as usual, to the level of emotional warfare. I'd learned not to engage any more at that point having had seven years' history of no-win debates that always escalated into a lot of hurt feelings. There was no more convincing Brad of the validity of mysticism than there was of him convincing me that it was an illusion. I could no longer deny my own experiences with Patrick and Harold…and God…than to deny that there was a God. It was no longer a matter of faith. It was a matter of knowledge. And this was something each individual has to obtain for her or himself. It requires that they truly desire it and be willing to take the necessary steps to obtain it. It is not easy to come by—but it isn't impossible.

The rest of the drive home was silent as I scanned the rest of the Neo-tech book and realized it wasn't something I wanted to waste any more time on. I concluded that Neo-Tech—along with the Illuminati—was the rational mind, the male ego mind, completely out of balance. It wasn't the conspiracy I thought it was but simply societal schizophrenia—the left brain and the right brain in a state of alienation and separation. I wondered as I glanced at Brad scowling at the road ahead if the separated parts of his mind would ever be united.

During the next week or so, I received similar letters from a myriad of psychics saying almost the exact same thing the Nouveau Tech letter had said—that if I bought into their program I'd soon become rich and famous beyond my wildest dreams. I purchased a few of the psychics' readings (hey, I was curious and they included free talismans with interesting symbols), but I was severely disappointed by the generic psychic readings I was offered. I lost interest after a few months but, to this day I receive one or two letters from psychics every week—even after I moved to Salt Lake and changed addresses. I figure I'd gotten on some "Outer Limits" mailing list and was doomed to receive junk mail from the far side forever. Oh well, I guess that's life in the stupid lane. And I finally agreed with Brad that an imbalance or over-reliance on mysticism can be another way to get you way off track.

I wasn't satisfied, however that I'd uncovered all that I needed to know about the Illuminati. I still felt there was further research to do to make this chapter in my life complete. So I did the only thing a sincere researcher does—I went to the library to study the Illuminati.

At the local library I typed "Illuminati" into the computer card catalog and only came up with two references—a book, and a DVD titled "Revelations of the Mother Goddess" by David Icke. I checked out both and left the library somewhat disappointed. I crossed the street to where my car was parked. Next door there was a little herb shop with a sign that read "Ephedra—Now Available". I was curious about the whole ephedra scare and was tempted to stop and talk to the storeowner about it, but my time was running short for other errands. But as I walked past the store, I was literally stopped in my tracks and told by the spirit that I needed to go in. I resisted knowing I could easily spend an hour talking about herbs and health. Nevertheless, I surrendered to the prompting, walked in and immediately was drawn to the book display.

On one of the shelves in plain view was a book that caught my eye (it was bright blue—my favorite color—and had an impressive photo of Earth from outer space). The title also caught my interest: *Blue Blood, True Blood— Conflict &Creation: A Personal Story* by Stewart A. Swerdlow. I picked up the book and thumbed through it noticing that it was about aliens and the Illuminati. Curious, I thought—a bit far-fetched but what the heck, it may be interesting to research. When I saw the price of $39.95, I cringed and set it back down knowing that Brad would crucify me if I ever spent that much money on a book. We were on a tight budget since leaving Vegas.

The store manager came up to me at that point, and we started an interesting conversation about the book and the whole Illuminati conspiracy theory. I told him about what I'd discovered about the Nouveau-Tech Society—what I now considered the modern-day Illuminati. He then told me about some different authors and radio talk-show interviewers who had some interesting takes on the whole Illuminati conspiracy. I told him about my experience with Patrick and how I believed that the Illuminati were responsible for his death after he'd appeared on the Art Bell Show. I showed him the materials I'd gotten at the library and he told me that David Icke was a good reference as he'd written several books concerning the Illuminati, and he'd also heard an interview on a talk radio show with him.

I was anxious to get home and watch the video and research the book, so I cut my conversation short (it had only lasted a half-hour or so). I quickly ran my other errands and got home in the early afternoon to spend my time researching. The book from the library was random and fragmented and left me with little to go on. I decided to plug in the *Revelations of a Mother Goddess* DVD and view it before Brad got home from work. (He by then had a regular job at a regular floor-covering store with regular hours. I guess Brad's just a regular guy married to an irregular partner who has lots of curiosity.)

In the video, David Icke, a British broadcaster, led me on a wild journey through London and into the annals of the Illuminati underground. (It was most fascinating *and* entertaining.) His claims were that the Illuminati controlled all of the world's economics, politics, royal families, militaries, governments, media, etc. through a process of mass mind control. Sure, I could buy that—just look at the propaganda in news reporting and TV commercials—it's all about scare-tactics and controlling people's choices. But then it got very bizarre. He was about to disclose the "Biggest Secret" (he'd also written a book by that title) and was about to reveal it in an interview with one of the Illuminati's programmed "Mother Goddesses" named Arizona Wilder. (She'd been deprogrammed and went by a different name for her own protection.)

Arizona Wilder disclosed that she'd been in many secret Illuminati blood rituals involving many world leaders including—George Bush, Henry Kissinger, Gerald Ford, Ronald Reagan, Hillary Clinton, the Queen of England, Prince Charles—the list went on and on. But that's not the most shocking part. At the height of the frenzy of the blood ceremony involving human sacrifices, all of the so-called dignitaries *shape-shifted into reptilians!* At that point in the video, Brad came home and had a great time poking fun at the rest of it—including me for buying into it.

Well, I'm not sure I was buying into *any* of it (I mean, come on—this goes beyond even my wildest imagination), but it was interesting that I had been led to a book in an herb store that had similar information in it. I knew I was on a dragon hunt and couldn't be stopped until I'd uncovered the dragon… but at a safe distance, thank-you!

The next week I returned the materials to the library and purchased the blue book at the herb store. (And yes, I caught hell from Brad for it!) I read the entire thing in two days and wrote the following synopsis. First, here's a quote from the author's preface:

> As far as the history of this planet is concerned, you can consider that everything you ever learned is a complete lie. All history and science books are rewritten to accommodate the agenda of the controllers of this planet. These books are just as false as the New Age material spewing forth from such places as Sedona and Santa Fe, to name a couple of Illuminati meccas. Disinformation is rampant everywhere.
>
> My information comes from my Montauk Project indoctrinations, experiences, conversations with scientists involved in Illuminati programs, communications with alien and interdimensional beings whom I met at various government projects, and through the probing of my own Oversoul.

The book then goes into a lengthy history of planet Earth—of how it's basically a refugee camp for aliens who survived a "great galactic war." The war was between the Lyraens—peaceable blonde-haired, blue-eyed humans from a star system known as Lyrae and the Draconians—a warmongering reptilian race from the constellation Draco. The author then describes the subsequent lineage history of the descendants of these two warring groups and where they ended up according to the strands of DNA recorded in each race.

But the bottom-line is this: the Draconians implanted their DNA into some of the Lyraens who were descendants of Mary Magdalene race and created a hybrid half reptilian/half human strain that can shape-shift at will. These are "The Bluebloods" or the ruling class of Illuminati controllers. These hybrid Reptilians are in control of Earth and perform blood rituals and ceremonies using humans as the source of food and hormones which sustain their existence. The Reptilians are androgynous but can reproduce themselves by implanting fertilized eggs into what they term the chosen "Mother Goddess." (Remember the DVD *Revelations of the Mother Goddess*? Well, she was one of them.)

The leader of the Earth's Illuminati is called the "Pindar" and is a member of the 13 ruling Illuminati families and always male. The title, Pindar, is an abbreviation of "Pinnacle of the Draco" and is also known as the "Penis of the Dragon." Symbolically, this represents the top of power, control, creation, penetration, expansion, invasion, and fear. The holder of this rank reports to the purebred Reptilian leader in the inner Earth.

Okay, now I know this is all sounding a bit far-fetched (it was to me), but then it started reminding me of one of my favorite scriptural passages in Revelations. I got out the Bible and read:

> And there was war in heaven: Michael and his angels fought against the dragon: and the dragon fought and his angels,
>
> And prevailed not: neither was their place found any more in heaven.
>
> And the great dragon was cast out, that old serpent, called the Devil, and Satan, which deceiveth the whole world: he was cast out into the earth, and his angels were cast out with him.
>
> And I heard a loud voice saying in heaven, Now is come salvation, and strength and the kingdom of our God, and the power of his Christ: for the accuser of our brethren is cast down, which accused them before our God day and night.
>
> And they overcame him by the blood of the Lamb, and by the word of their testimony: and they loved not their lives unto the death.
>
> Therefore rejoice, ye heavens, and ye that dwell in them. Woe to the inhibitors of the earth and of the sea: for the devil come down unto you, having great wrath, because he hath but a short time.
>
> And when the dragon saw that he was cast unto the earth, he persecuted the woman which brought forth the man child. (Revelations12:7-13)

Any Mormon has been taught that Lucifer is another name for Satan. Lucifer literally means "Light Bearer." Illuminati literally means "Illumined Ones." Interesting similarities. So what did this blue book have to say about Jesus? Well, in the chapter called "Emmanuel," Christ is described:

> There was a Christ figure on the Earth at that time... named Emmanuel. He was a product of the mixture of Mary and a Lyraen descendent. Mary was physically abducted and implanted. She said that she was visited by angels. As a young man, Emmanuel was removed from his mother, and taken to the Great Pyramid on the Giza Plateau. Here, he was taught ancient Lyraen/Atlantean/Egyptian principles for twenty years.

He was also taken aboard the Federation ships and indoctrinated in ways to steer the masses away from the Reptilian influences. His orders were to inculcate the three strains of humanity that had the purest genetics on Earth. These were the Hebrews, created by the Sirians; the Germanic tribes, created by the Aldebarans; and the Northern Indian Arians who now lived in the foothills of the Himalayas. All three people used a lion as their symbol, and were descendents of the original blonde-haired, blue-eyed Lyraens.

So what exactly were "Christ's Orders" that he inculcated into these three strains of humanity? Swerdlow goes on to answer:

The ancient Hebrews have nothing to do with modern Jews. As mentioned in the previous chapter, the Hebrews were Sirian-created in Egypt by combining Sirian and Lyraen genetics. These people were tall and powerful, and spoke the Sirian language, which is the equivalent to the ancient Hebrew language. Scholars agree that the Hebrew language suddenly appeared on the scene...

The Hebrews were actually paid workers in Egypt. They were sent to Canaan to assimilate the native cultures for the Egyptian Empire. They mixed with the local tribes of Sumerian-hybrid descendents, practicing blood-ritual and human sacrifice. All of this was incorporated into the conglomerate religion based on ancient Egyptian/Atlantean/Sirian beliefs. That is how Judaism was born...

The actual translation of how the Ten Commandments, or the Bible codes, were transmitted to the people of the Exodus, states that the people spontaneously started speaking the instructions. This is a demonstration of mind-to-mind communication. In this case, programming was electromagnetically activated, revealing DNA instructions that were then written down. These instructions were designed to keep the experiment/project in line...

It was then that the Torah, or Holy Commandments, was given to this people as a code by which to live. This document is in a code that can only now be deciphered with the use of a computer. The land of Canaan needed to be conquered in order to give development room to the new creations. In effect, the Hebrews were the next sequence of the experiment, and the old versions were to be eliminated or assimilated.

The Hebrews carried the new coded laws in the Ark of the Covenant…that only the priests could touch. When the University of Minnesota in the 1960s attempted to build the Ark as described with instructions in the Bible, it was so electrically charged that it had to be dismantled! This is why the ancient Hebrew priests entered into the Ark area alone, for safety reasons. They also had to wear white linen, as non-conductive clothing, and wore a special breastplate that grounded them electrically and acted as a protective shield. The Ark was really a communication device. This is why the priests had "messages from God" whenever they were in the Ark's presence.

The Ark also acted as a location device for beacons originating outside of this planet. The Ark was originally kept in the Great Pyramid to focalize energies. It was sent with the Hebrews for safekeeping. It has since traveled from Egypt to Canaan/Israel to Ethiopia, back to Israel, and now is located under the pyramid again. However, there are actually two Arks. The second one is in Jerusalem.

This all reminded me of a movie that I'd seen called "Pi" (the symbol) not to mention "Raiders of the Lost Ark." Pi was about a computer geek who was translating the Bible codes and accidentally came upon the code name for God. A group of elite Jews (who went by the name of Cohen) kidnapped him and forced him to give them his research so they could ceremonially activate his name and contact God (as was their mission). I never would have checked out this movie, but a young woman customer at Hollywood Video insisted I watch it. She even spent time helping me find it. This wouldn't have been so unusual had I not at the time been curious about the Cohen family. I'd found in my research that they were an elite group of Jews who were the scribes responsible for translating the Bible codes (and keeping them intact).

It was also around this time that I'd have an influx of Cohens come to me at the Bellagio to be massaged. I searched through my intake forms to find that four of them had come to me during the period between 2/14/05 and 3/09/05. It's very unusual for massage therapists to have a last name repeat that frequently.

I remembered one client who was *very unusual.* His name was Eli Cohen, and when I first encountered him I felt a strange energy coming from him.

He was about 60 years old and had long hair and a beard. As I walked him down the long hallway to the massage room, he looked directly into my eyes and said, "You're reading me, aren't you?" I didn't know what to say. Of course I was reading his energy as I do all my clients to see if they are "safe" or not. His energy was a little weird but I felt he was safe. He then said, "That's good."

When I got him on the table, he immediately relaxed into a deep meditative state. The entire session was silent with a strange sort of energy connection between us. I felt that he was trying to connect with me energetically and to "read me." When I finished, he asked if he could relax for a few minutes on the table to take in the energy. I told him that would be fine. I went into the computer cubicle next to the massage room for a moment to check on my next client's status, but when I returned the door to the massage room was open and Mr. Cohen was gone. I asked some of the other massage therapists if they'd seen a client leave but none had. I looked down the long hallway (which is at least a football field long) and could not see him *anywhere*. This distressed me as it's a rule that we had to walk clients back to the waiting area because the spa is quite large and easy to get lost in. I walked down the hallway, looking for Mr. Cohen, checking the restrooms and each massage area to make sure he wasn't lost. *But no Mr. Cohen!* As far as I knew, Mr. Cohen had vanished into thin air!

About a year later, I was doing more research when I was impressed to read the book, *The Chalice & the Blade* by Riane Eisler where I happened upon another reference to the Cohen family. It read:

> Hebrew tribal society, like that of Kurgans and other Indo-Europeans, was also extremely hierarchic, ruled from the top by the tribe of Moses, the Levites. Superimposed on them was an even smaller elite. This was the family of Konath or Cohen, the hereditary priests in the Old Testament, the men of this clan claimed their powers directly from Jehovah. Moreover, what biblical scholars tell us is that it was this priestly elite that most likely carried out a good part of the job of rewriting myth and history to solidify their dominant position.
>
> Finally—completing and buttressing the dominator society configuration of violence, authoritarianism, and male dominance—is the Old Testament's explicit proclamation that it is God's will that woman be ruled by man. For like that of the Kurgans and the other Indo-European invaders

that wreaked such havoc in Europe and Asia Minor, ancient Hebrew tribal society was a rigidly male-dominant system.

Once again, it is imperative to stress that by no stretch of the imagination is this meant to imply that the religion of the ancient Hebrews—much less Judaism—is to blame for the imposition of a dominator ideology. The shift from a partnership to a dominator reality began long before the Hebrew invasions of Canaan and was going on simultaneously in many parts of the ancient world. Moreover, Judaism goes far beyond the Old Testament in its conceptions of deity and morality, and in the mystical tradition of the Shekhina it actually retained many of the elements of the old worship of the Goddess.

Okay, so I was curious as to what the Cohens had to do with changing the "Bible Codes" so as to eliminate all the feminine "power" aspects in the Bible. What would it do to profit them?

It was the next day that I got into a lengthy debate about all of this Illuminati stuff with my brother, Bruce (who is a Mormon scriptorian). During the discussion, Bruce turned me onto another direction. He had been clipping articles in the paper concerning the fifth anniversary of 9/11. He clipped an article with a picture of a man weeping at a memorial site of the World Trade Center. Bruce related it to a prophecy he'd discovered in Zephenia 1:14-18:

> The great day of the Lord *is* near, *it is* near, and hasteth greatly, *even* the voice of the day of the Lord: the mighty man shall cry there bitterly.
>
> That day is a day of wrath, a day of trouble and distress, a day of darkness and gloominess, a day of clouds and thick darkness,
>
> A day of the trumpet and alarm against the fenced cities, and against the high towers,
>
> And I will bring distress upon men, that they shall walk like blind men, because they have sinned against the Lord: and their blood shall be poured out as dust, and their flesh as the dung.
>
> Neither their silver nor their gold shall be able to deliver them in the day of the Lord's wrath; but the whole land shall be devoured by the fire of his jealousy: for he shall make even a speedy riddance of all them that dwell in the land.

Bruce said that ever since I'd sent him the book, *The Prophet*, by Frank Peretti, he'd been fascinated by the 9/11 event. I'd sent him the book twice (by mistake) for his birthday—once before 9/11 and once afterward—as I thought the whole story reminded me of him and that he'd enjoy reading it. He did, but the astonishing part for him was its cover. It had a picture of two towers with the number 6 on one of them and an airplane flying into them. He thought the event had been prophesied in the scriptures as the beginning of the great destruction and the War of Armageddon. He then said that the line in Zepheniah about the day being "A day of trumpet and alarm against the fenced cities, and against the high towers" was interesting as it was the same day of the Judaic "feast of the trumpets" and 9/11 is the number we call for alarm. He also said that the line "their blood shall be poured out as dust, and their flesh as the dung" was relevant to the aftermath of the collapse of the twin towers.

I thought these were all very fascinating coincidences. I then told Bruce that I thought the whole World Trade Center event was rigged by the powers that be (after seeing the movie *Fahrenheit 9/11* by Michael Moore.) Michael Moore shows how America has been set up for the war in Iraq as a means of controlling the oil reserves and how President Bush is part of all of it showing footage of Bush's unalarmed candor when he first hears about the so-called "terrorist attacks." (This footage is also shown in Al Gore's movie, *An Inconvenient Truth."*) It's obvious by the look on the president's face that they came as no surprise—it's as if he already knew about them ahead of time. Well, if he was really an Illuminatus as indicated by the resource materials I'd uncovered (Stewart Swerdlow names Bush as being part of the 300 supporting families of the Illuminati known as the "Committee of 300"), then this would all make sense.

By then as I was scrambling to find more information on 9/11 I came across an article in the Deseret News concerning a BYU Professor named Steven Jones. He had been placed on leave from the BYU for talking about who might have been behind what he alleged was "government involvement in the 9/11 terrorist attacks." Jones was a physics professor who conducted research into how the World Trade Center towers had fallen. Disturbed by the remarkable speed at which they fell to the ground and by material evidence found at ground zero (molten metal and barium), he developed a hypotheses that the collapse of the towers was aided by pre-positioned demolition charges. He later began to say that the charges must have been set by a group from inside the U.S. government. After naming one of the groups as the "international banking cartel" on a KUER-FM news talk show, Jones was accused of being anti-Semitic. The Anti-Defamation League got involved and sent a letter to BYU complaining about his comments. BYU then relieved Jones of his teaching position while he conducted a formal review of his research and statements.

I thought this was all fascinating, so I went back to find out how the Jews and the Cohen family were involved in the Illuminati. In the book, *The Templar Revelation* by Lynn Picknett and Clive Prince there was this reference in the Appendix entitled "Continental Occult Freemasonry."

> Marines de Pasqually (1727-1779) founded another form of occult Freemasonry, the Order of the Elect Cohens, in 1761. Very little is known of de Pasqually's background, although he was probably Spanish. Some researchers believe that de Pasqually was connected with the Dominican Order—the former Inquisition—and that he was able to draw upon heretical and magical material in their archives. He was also able to produce, for the Grand Lodge of France, a license granted to his father by Charles Edward Stuart, which links him to the Scottish Masonry that was behind Baron von Hund.

It went on to discuss the Rectified Scottish Rite and the Strict Templar Observance influencing a form of "occult" Freemasonry, the Egyptian Rites, created by Count Cagliostro who developed his own system that incorporated alchemical and other ideas that he had learned from German occult groups. The distinctive feature of this system—apart from its use of ancient Egyptian symbolism—was the *equal role of women*. This was an interesting fact considering that Mormon temple rituals all include women. Was this why the Masons were so angry with Joseph Smith when he hijacked their "occult temple rites" and made them his own? Joseph Smith was a 33rd degree mason and it's a well-known historical fact that the Masons were part of the mob who murdered Joseph Smith at Carthage jail.

Just for fun, I decided to google the "Order of Elect Cohens." It brought up the "Elect Cohen Group" which brought up something *very interesting*. It referred me to the "Global Elite" page, which bore the Illuminati symbol of the all-seeing eye on top of the pyramid (like on the back of the one dollar bill), and in the margin was a list of all of the Global Elite groups including: Bilderberg Group, World Economic Forum, American-Iranian Council, US-Egypt Business Council, European Union, European Commission, Royal Institute of International Affairs, Trilateral Commission, Council on Foreign Relations, United Nations, International Crisis Group, International Institute of Strategic Studies, Foreign Policy Association, Nuclear Threat Initiative,

Institute for Science and International Security, Bank of England, Federal Reserve, Aspen Institute, Fabian Society, Human Rights Watch, Rockefeller Foundation, Viacom, News Corporation, New World Order, One World Trust, American Friends of Bilderberg, Open World Leadership Center, etc.

The list went on and on with what I *knew* to be organizations belonging to the Illuminati. Then I saw the "Quote of the Week" by Mikhail Gorbachev: "The threat of environmental crisis will be the 'international disaster key' that will unlock the New World Order." That was a bit alarming to me as I'd recently seen the film "An Inconvenient Truth" narrated by Al Gore. Was Al Gore an Illuminatus? I'd met him years earlier at a Windstar Symposium in Aspen, which took place right next to the Aspen Institute. I'll put it this way—when I shook Al Gore's hand I didn't get any warm fuzzies, but I had been hopeful because he wasn't mentioned by Arizona Wilder as being present during the reptilian shape-shifting blood sacrifice frenzies!

I then clicked onto the Cohen Group that was listed as one of the Global Elite groups. And guess who I pulled up as the Chairman and CEO of the Cohen Group? William Cohen, Secretary of Defense from January 1997 to January 2001. Although Cohen wasn't in office during the 9/11 attacks, he was a major influence in the testimonies concerning the terrorist trials in 2004. I clicked on his entire statements to *The National Commission on Terrorist Attacks upon the United States* and, of course, after scanning through it, he upheld the current Bush administration's way of handling it—putting all of the responsibility on al-Qaida. But then I came across an interesting quote by William Cohen, which states:

> There are some reports, for example, that some countries have been trying to construct something like an Ebola Virus, and that would be a very dangerous phenomenon, to say the least. Alvin Toeffler has written about this in terms of some scientists in their laboratories trying to devise certain types of pathogens that would be ethnic specific so that they could just eliminate certain ethnic groups and races; and others are designing some sort of engineering, some sort of insects that can destroy specific crops. Others are engaging even in an eco-type of terrorism whereby they can alter the climate, set off earthquakes, volcanoes remotely through the use of electromagnetic waves. So there are plenty of ingenious minds out there that are at work finding ways in which they can wreak terror upon other nations. It's real, and that's the reason why we have to intensify our efforts. And that's why this (the war on terrorism) is so important.

I thought this was all *very* interesting and co-incidental (incidents being brought together) after the recent E-coli scare on spinach. (The spirit told me *not* to buy spinach that week for some reason.) And if you've ever seen the recent movie, *The Constant Gardner*, about how a global pharmaceutical company tested unsafe vaccinations on desperate and impoverished African tribes—all of it seemed to make a lot of sense. But my question was how did William Cohen come by all of that information? And exactly which groups was the recent E-coli scare targeting? Health foot nuts? I won't answer that, but I knew spirit was leading me on an intriguing investigation.

Since I was already on the Internet, I decided to google "Montauk Project," to see if the "indoctrinations" that Swerdlow (the blue book author) received from there could be validated. It brought up thousands of sites, so I just clicked on the first one at *wikipedia.org. Very interesting!* It had a photo of the site at Camp Hero in Montauk, New York and the following:

> "The Montauk Project was purportedly a series of secret United States government projects conducted at Camp Hero and/or Montauk Air Force Station on Montauk, Long Island. It was claimed by a small number of conspiracy theorists to be secretly developing a powerful psychological war weapon. The Project is widely regarded by mainstream sources as fictional.
>
> The Montauk Project is believed by a small number of people to be an extension or continuation of the probably fictitious Philadelphia Experiment, which supposedly took place in 1943—also known as Project Rainbow.
>
> According to the myth, sometime in the 1950s, surviving researchers from Project Rainbow began to discuss the project with an eye to continuing the research into technical aspects of manipulating the electromagnetic bottle that had been used to make the USS *Eldridge* invisible, and the reasons and possible military applications of the psychological effects of a magnetic field.
>
> The myth goes on to say that a report was supposedly prepared and presented to Congress, and was soundly rejected as far too dangerous. So a proposal was made directly to the Department of Defense promising a powerful new weapon that could drive an enemy insane, inducing the symptoms of schizophrenia at the touch of a button. Without Congressional approval, the project would have to be top secret and secretly funded. The Department of

Defense approved. Funding supposedly came from a cache of US $10 billion in Nazi gold recovered from a train found by US soldiers in a train tunnel in France. The train was blown up and all the soldiers involved were killed. When those funds ran out, additional funding was secured from ITT and Krupp AG in Germany.

It went on to describe how the site was constructed and installed with a large radar dish. I won't bore you with all the details, but it gets even more interesting.

Various conspiracy theorists claim that experiments began in earnest in the early 1970s. They claim that during this time one, some or all of the following occurred at the site. No evidence has ever been provided that any of the following is true: (It was a long list so I'll just list the points I thought were relevant.)

- Homeless people and orphans were abducted and subjected to huge amounts of electromagnetic radiation. Few survived.
- People had their psychic abilities enhanced to the point where they could materialize objects out of thin air. Stewart Swerdlow (remember the author of the blue book) claims to have been involved in the Montauk Project, and as a result, he says, his 'psionic' faculties were boosted, but at the cost of emotional instability, post-traumatic stress disorder, and other issues.
- Experiments were conducted in teleportation.
- A 'porthole in time' was created which allowed researchers to travel anywhere in time or space. This was developed into a stable 'Time Tunnel.'
- Contact was made with alien extraterrestrials through the Time Tunnel and technology was exchanged with them which enhanced the project. This allowed broader access to 'hyperspace.'
- An alien monster traveled through the time tunnel, destroyed equipment and devoured researchers. The tunnel was shut down and the creature destroyed.
- Mind control experiments were conducted and runaway boys were abducted and brought out to the base where they underwent excruciating periods of both physical and mental torture in order to break their minds, then their minds were re-programmed. Many were supposedly killed during the process and buried on the site.

- On or about August 12, 1983 the time travel project at Camp Hero interlocked in hyperspace with the original Rainbow Project back in 1943. The USS *Eldridge* was drawn into hyperspace and trapped there. Two men, Al Bielek and Duncan Cameron both claim to have leaped form the deck of the *Eldridge* while it was in hyperspace and ended up after a period of severe disorientation at Camp Hero in the year 1983. Here they claim to have met John von Neumann, a famous physicist and mathematician, even though he was known to have died in 1957. Von Neumann had supposedly worked on the original Philadelphia Experiment, but the U.S. Navy denies this.
- Cameron used the mind enhancing system at Camp Hero to manifest a 'Bigfoot' or 'Yeti', which destroyed large parts of the facility.
- Staff from the Camp Hero site traveled to the USS *Eldridge* and shut down the generators, causing the ship to return to Philadelphia navy yard in 1943 and causing the time tunnel to collapse and the Yeti to disappear.
- Metahumans and experiments in special serums to create such individuals were tested there.
- Early work on inventing the Internet and its implementation were undertaken there.
- Black helicopters were manufactured and flown there.
- Nikola Tesla, whose death was faked in a conspiracy, was the chief director of operations at the base.
- Mass psychological experiments, such as the use of enormous subliminal message projects and the creation of a 'Men in Black' corps to confuse and frighten the public, were invented there.
- Early development of Project Stargate was developed from the remote viewing techniques developed by Montauk Project researchers. The lost city of Atlantis was discovered in another galaxy, via the Time Tunnel.

WOW! This project sounded like the inspiration for the scripts of some of my favorite films: The Philadelphia Experiment, Somewhere in Time, A Wrinkle in Time, Back to the Future, Stargate, The Time Machine, Contact, The Matrix, Star Trek, Star Wars, Men in Black, ET, Close Encounters, Independence Day, War of the Worlds, etc. Could some of them have been based on fact? Well, I still wanted more information on Montauk (unedited by the powers that be), so I clicked on the next two sites and printed pages and pages of information. I read them that night and came up with a few insights from the interviews from the three known survivors of the project—Al Bielek, Preston Nichols, and Duncan Cameron. They included some very interesting quotes that I thought were relevant to my research:

As (the book) The Montauk Project was published, further research and events continued that would indeed establish that there was a real scenario behind the wild information Preston was talking about. These were chronicled in Montauk Revisited, but the most spectacular of all these corroborations was the discovery that the Montauk Project was inextricably linked to the most infamous occultist of all time: Aleister Crowley, often described as "the wickedest man in the world". According to reports, Crowley himself had used the practice of sexual magick in order to manipulate time itself, communicate with disembodied entities and to travel interdimensionally. It was even suggested that the interdimensional nature of the Philadelphia Experiment could have been the outward expression of Crowley's magical operations.

Hum, interesting. Aleister Crowley was a name I was familiar with. I'd read about him in a book called *The Most Evil Secret Societies in History* by Shelley Klein as part of my research into the Illuminati. It had an uninteresting chapter concerning their history, but the chapter that followed really piqued my interest. It was Argenteum Astrum—Orgies in Sicily, and referred to Aleister Crowley as "The Beast" or "The Wickedest Man on Earth" because of his involvement with Satanism, illicit drugs and sexual magic. Again, most of the chapter was simply a boring historical review with little food for thought. But the Montauk information had an incredible amount of "food for thought," and I followed the research along the lines of Crowley's sexual magic and the Reptilian Illuminati and found a few more interesting quotes:

Al Bielek and Duncan Cameron were assigned to the psychic division of Montauk and worked with time tunneling and Teleportation. One of these is the famed "Montauk Chair". The Montauk Chair was essentially a mind amplifier. They found that they could easily re-program people when they were put into the orgasmic state of emotion, this would separate the conscious mind, and free up the unconscious submissive mind and allow programming. The chair would pick up this thought. With the help of a psychic and machines, anyone who sat in the chair could simply concentrate and an alternate reality would be created...

Many people tested the tunnels. He explains how he ran his own test to verify that telepathic thought was receivable to unsuspecting subjects. Telepathic brainwashing can now be done without electronic equipment—with only thought.

Another of the lesser known projects was called Project "God Edge." In this black project, Al explains how they were able to manifest objects by using the subconscious mind. They were able to produce physical objects on demand using only the powers of the mind. They thus now had to create formulas for the zero-point vacuum to keep track of alternate realities. These techniques were a result of genetic experiments with humans and the Reptilians...

Al explains how Atlantis was destroyed by created international earthquakes, and after which two humans and one from the Reptilian race formed the early secret societies leading to the ultimate development of the Illuminati.

I went back to the blue book and reread some of the information I'd read about sexual magic:

Another type of ceremony involves sexual magic. This ritual is designed to use the energy produced during heightened orgasmic activation to physically manifest a specific event or object. In other words, whatever thought is released into the ethers at the moment of intense orgasm is then propelled into existence. This is what is meant by the Illuminati when they rewrote the Bible and said, "whenever two or more are gathered in my name."

When two or more people simultaneously engage in intense sexual activity, the energy to manifest the goal of the event is multiplied. This is why group sex and orgies have been promoted for centuries. Because male body energy is more powerful than the feminine body energy, the Illuminati prefer a minimum of two males performing with a single female because of the semen. Symbolically, this represents the finite physical reality and the infinite non-physical. Currently, the drug known as ecstasy, which increases libido, and the so-called "date rape" drugs are the latest catalysts to enhance sexual magic activity.

Because the Reptilians are inherently androgynous, it is unimportant whether sex is with a male or female. To them, it is all the same. They prefer males because of the powerful energy boost from the male body. Female energy tends to draw into itself, and therefore is more desirable for sexual magic. The female represents physical reality, or Mother Earth, accepting the powerful male, non-physical, Father Sun energy, to create something on the planet. This explains the symbolism. For these reasons, bisexuality is the promoted lifestyle in the New World Order.

Of course my next question to the Universe was, "Is sexual magic evil and wrong or is it simply a powerful tool that can be used for good?" I thought back on my previous book, *Heartsong,* and how the last chapter described a ceremony conducted by the White Buffalo Woman for the purpose of opening up a rainbow vortex to the next dimension to bring down angels and resurrected beings from heaven. I felt very inspired when I wrote that chapter as I felt it was part of my spiritual journey to connect these two dimensions together—to create heaven on Earth.

Somehow, after I'd done all my research for this chapter on *Angels and Demons,* I realized that there was more to it than I thought. Could the unified magnetic field I described in my book also be used to contact demonic forces from the astral plane and bring them into our reality? I was now convinced it was possible. But I was also convinced that the same unified magnetic field could create the opposite effect. Used in conjunction with the "God-Mind" or "Christ-consciousness," it could also be used to bring authentic illumination, peace, love, joy and goodness to the planet. And God only knew how much those where necessary to combat the evils now present. This again was validated in the blue book by the author's wife, Janet Swerdlow, who included some of her excerpts from her own book, *Belief Systems Shattered.*

> Sexual energy is the most powerful creative energy available in the physical reality. When properly used by the correct combination of people, the possibilities for creation are endless. The powers that be know this, and they are out to systematically subvert sexual energy to keep it in an animalistic arena.
>
> Blatant sexuality is all around, from fashion to media to everyday speech. This sexuality is a deep, bright red that essentially pulls on your sexual chakras and opens them up. Using color, tone, and archetype (or symbol), these chakras are systematically opened, fed and energized, expanding them out of proportion until they have control over you.

Then, you are controlled and manipulated through these chakras...

Our present system simply produces children as potential workers, as the powers that be see all people. They do not want people that are too aware, too healthy, too stable, or too connected to God-Mind. This kind of person will see their agenda and refuse to be a part of it. A person here or there is not such a problem, but an entire race is.

The reality is that each sexual position has a specific function. Specific positions create specific results. Specific colors, tones and archetypes also create specific results. Sexual energy can be purposefully directed to create whatever you desire in physical reality. Sexual energy can be used to create on the hyperspace level when the couple is linked into God-Mind using specific color codes, archetypes, and sounds.

The Reptilians know all this, except they use sex to create on the astral level, and bring that into physical reality. They do not want the common populace to have or know this information. That is why major religions have so many rules about sexuality, which seems to almost always include instilling guilt.

For example, the Bible tells you basically to use sex only for procreation, and major religions primarily advocate only one position. The powers that be did not want any purposeful sex other than the continuation of the worker line. They did not/do not want people to discover the true nature of sex. They do not want you exploring the higher realms of sexuality because you may discover the true purpose of sex in physical reality.

I feel these were truths discovered and written by a very inspired woman. I desired to meet Janet Swerdlow and her husband Stewart and to discuss these things with them at length. Perhaps there'll be a time and a place for that. I also want to talk to Stewart Swerdlow's ex-wife, Mia, about what he'd written about her. It was the icing on the cake as far as coincidences were concerned.

During this time, I tried unsuccessfully to develop a relationship with (my daughter) Jaime. She was living in Connecticut with her mother. Mia was dating John Denver, and was devastated after his fatal plane crash. I believe that he committed suicide because he was despondent over his relationships and career. His small plane went up without enough fuel. He must have known that when he took off.

I don't believe John Denver committed suicide. And I don't believe that there are *any* accidents. I personally believe John Denver *knew too much* and had to be eliminated. He was too aware and connected to the God-Mind and was downloading too much information to individuals who had ears to hear. When he went up in that airplane that fateful day and ran out of gas—who do you suppose was responsible for making sure the gas tank was full?

If I happen to die in a so-called accident—don't believe that it was one. *I probably know too much and am revealing too much.* But Christ is my Savior and protector, and I am saved by His blood. That makes all the difference in my life as it can in yours. Count on it. I'm afraid that Patrick and John didn't depend on this truth, and now they're gone from this physical reality. It's everyone's sorrowful loss. Pray for me, and I will pray for the awakening of the world to what is real.

This is the true gathering of "Is-real." And you are all part of it if you wish. I quote a favorite scripture from the Bible:

"And ye shall know the truth, and the truth shall set you free."

YOU ARE FREE! In closing this chapter I'm including a song dedicated to my favorite singer/songwriter. You know who, of course. This is from John Denver's *Flower that Shattered the Stone* album.

Raven's Child

Raven's child is chasing salvation
Black beak turned white from the crack and the snow,
On the streets of despair, the answer is simple
A spoonful of mercy can set free the soul.

The drug king sits on his arrogant throne
Away and above and apart,
Even children are twisted to serve him
Greed has corrupted what once was a heart.

Raven's child keeps vigil for freedom
Trades for the arms that once made her strong,
With nuclear warheads and lasers in heaven
Fear does the choosing between right and wrong.

The arms king sits on his arrogant throne
Away and above and apart
Bankers assure him, he needn't care
Greed makes a stone of what once was a heart.

Raven's child is washing the water
All of her wing feathers blackened with tar,
Prince Williams shoreline an unwanted highway
Of asphalt and anger—an elegant scar.

The oil king sits on his arrogant throne
Away and above and apart,
Lawyers have warned him, he mustn't speak
Greed has made silent what once was a heart.

Still there are walls that come tumbling down
For people who yearn to be free,
Still there are hearts that long to be open
And eyes that are longing to see.

Raven's child is our constant companion
Sticks like a shadow to all that is done,
Try as we may, we just can't escape him
The source of our sorrow and shame—we are one.

The true king sits on a heavenly throne
Never away, nor above, nor apart,
With wisdom and mercy and constant compassion
He lives in the love that lives in our heart.

Raven's child is washing the water...
Raven's child keeps vigil for freedom...
Raven's child is chasing salvation...
Raven's child is our constant companion...

Chapter Twenty-five—Ariel's Wedding

There's always something to be said about love and marriage. In fact, there are probably more poems and songs written about love than any other subject. And, of course, this is as it should be, as I believe that love is the most powerful energy in the Universe. It's certainly the greatest motivator as wars have been fought over it, cities have been built around it, religions have tried to control it, and some of the greatest discoveries have been made because of it. Perhaps it's best said in three simple words—*God is love.*

And if God is love, anything we do in the name of love, we do in the name of God. Now that's a powerful thought. But what about marriage? That's where the confusion begins for me (and probably for a lot of other people) because the history of marriage is terribly ambiguous and confusing, and according to my research not always based on God. In fact, historically marriage was designed as a tool for political, economic and social exchanges of power. Historically, it was not based on love as it is today—or is it even now?

As you read the New Testament scriptures about marriage, they're downright depressing. Take for instance, Paul's statements concerning marriage. (I'm not a real Paul fan but we'll go with him anyway.) In I Corinthians chapter 7, he writes, "Now concerning the things whereof ye wrote unto me: It is good for a man not to touch a woman."

Now there's a brash statement if I ever heard one. Does that mean women have a dreaded disease and aren't to be touched by men because they might be contagious? (From a woman's standpoint, you can understand the offensiveness of these words.) Or does it mean that Paul is gay and advocates only male/male touching? (I've always questioned Paul's motives in that regard.) Or is this particular passage another rewrite by the Nicean Council or the Illuminati to again discredit the power and sacredness of sexuality as a means of controlling the masses? I'll vote for that one, thank-you!

Paul went on to say that, "Nevertheless, to avoid fornication, let every man have his own wife, and let every woman have her own husband." That's the first statement in the Bible that advocates monogamy. And I suppose that from these two passages alone came the Catholic and subsequently the entire Christian position on marriage. But think about what God is saying here, "If you can't handle celibacy then fall back to monogamy?" What kind of bullshit is that?

It would certainly also be limiting love and sexuality as being an essential ingredient in contacting God. Perhaps sexual repression and restrictive monogamy are why the Catholics and other Christians no longer receive direct communication with God. Isn't the act of making love the greatest joy and ecstasy possible? If it isn't for you, than maybe you have some early life trauma to overcome or cultural deprogramming to do. I personally feel closer to God while making love than at any other time. In fact, sometimes I even feel like I'm making love directly *to God*. So why would the Christian church limit humanity's ability to contact God directly in this way?

Nevertheless, most people feel safe and secure in a "traditional monogamous marriage." News flash—monogamy has rarely been the "traditional" form of marriage. In a book I picked up at the library called *Marriage—a History* it states:

"In many societies of the past, sexual loyalty was not a high priority. The expectation of mutual fidelity is a rather recent invention. Numerous cultures have allowed husbands to seek sexual gratification outside marriage. Less frequently, but often enough to challenge common preconceptions, wives have also been allowed to do this without threatening the marriage. In a study of 109 societies, anthropologists found that only 48 forbade extramarital sex to both husbands and wives."

So, in other words, over half of all societies don't believe in "traditional monogamous marriage." (Actually, it's probably more than that.) But here I go again standing on my soapbox. I'll get down in a moment, but I just wanted to share a few quips from one of my favorite authors, George Bernard Shaw, as he describes marriage:

"Marriage is an institution that brings together two people under the influence of the most violent, most insane, most delusive, and most transient of passions. They are required to swear that they will remain in that excited, abnormal, and exhausting condition continuously until death do them part."

And in his essay called "Polygyny and Polyandry," Shaw promulgates the theory that "our monogamous nature was a myth invented by inferior and insecure men who were alarmed by the fact that women did not like them. Instinctively, women sought out the strongest and ablest men to impregnate them so they would produce the strongest children. If a woman had to choose between a complete second-rate man and a fraction of a first-rate one, she would certainly prefer the latter. Second-rate and third-rate men created the law of monogamy so they wouldn't be without women."

Quoting Shaw again: "It has been said that in medieval times sexual rivalry and jealousy were a major cause of violence. Loving and sex are life-giving forces of nature. It was the artificial restriction produced by taboos that cause much medieval violence. The Tao Te Ching says, 'The more the taboos, the more miserable the people.' The inevitable result of such prohibition and restriction is violence."

I've always wondered what society would look like if we just followed the laws of "natural selection." Yes, I'm redefining Darwin here, but still what would our world look like if people were able to procreate with whomever and whenever they chose? Can we envision a society with this kind of freedom and love? Yes, love, because if we allow our hearts do the choosing for us, our choices would always be God-directed wouldn't they? If God is love—then let love/God do the choosing and not societal restrictions. And God's love is abundant love and is not bound by humanity's laws or religious institutions. Remember the most creative powers in the universe are love and sexuality—and those two should be inseparable. These are powerful energies and should be handled with TLC (tender loving care). I suppose if there is any reason for marriage it is for the purpose of creating stability for children and society

And so it was that my daughter, Ariel, let God do the choosing and fell in love with Brad. Don't panic—he's a different Brad than mine. Ariel went through a lot of fish to catch this whopper, but she kept her virginity until her wedding night (which I find remarkable in this day and age) as they'd agreed upon a temple marriage. This meant that none of her immediate family could attend the wedding as none of us qualified for a temple recommend. But this was what Ariel and Brad had decided on which was their decision to make

Her Brad's family had also insisted upon it as it was their "tradition" they wanted to uphold. (Kind of like Tevye in *Fiddler on the Roof*, I'd say.) And since they were paying for most of the wedding (I purchased her wedding dress and bridesmaid dresses—Kurt paid for absolutely nothing—but we won't go there) his family got to choose the location for both the wedding and the reception. And since they are quite well-off, the reception was held at their country club in the gated community where they lived.

It was a spectacular reception with dinner, dancing and the works, which took place on January 21, 2006. Ariel looked especially radiant in her "altered for the temple" wedding dress that Aubrey and I had helped her pick out. (That was a delightful experience, I must say.)   Aubrey and Destiny had moved from Montana to St. George to be closer to Ariel and me. (I found out that "Saint George" was a famous "dragon slayer," so I felt like this was a safe place for the three of them to reside.) I paid for Kurt to bring down the rest of the children from Montana along with Deserae and her two children, Emalee and Fisher. (I also paid for Kurt's tux rental and all the kid's clothes, but again we won't get into that.)   We all celebrated in style except for Brad who showed up 12 hours late and in blue jeans and a work shirt. (He got severely scolded the next day.)

I shed a few tears as I drove alone from Las Vegas to the wedding as I listened to an obscure John Denver tape I'd recently purchased. *Forever, John* was recorded after his death and, as its name implies, it's a voice from the past describing the present—and perhaps the future. The song that really got to me emotionally was called "Dance Little Jean."

Dance Little Jean (Jenny)

Played the wedding for the money
And I wish I could have told the bride and groom,
Just what I think of marriage
And what's in store after the honeymoon.
I was rumbling through the verses
Of how men and women ought to live apart,
How a promise never made could not be broken
Or ever break a heart.

Suddenly from out of nowhere
This little girl came spinnin across the floor,
Her grinilins were billowing
Beneath the skirt of calico she wore.
As her joy fell on the honored guests
Each one of them was drawn into her dream
And they laughed and stamped and clapped their hands
And hollered at her, "Dance little Jean."

They said, "Dance little Jean
This day is for you,
Two people that you love
Stood up to say, "I do."
Dance little Jean
A prayer that you had,
Was answered today
When Momma's marrying your Dad.

Well, the cynic's heart just melted
When I figured what this get together meant,
How it ended years of tears and sad confusion
That the little girl had spent.
They told the band to pack it up about the time
The couple cut the cake,
But we stayed and we played all night long
For love that lasts and little Jeannie's sake.

We played dance little Jean
This day is for you,
Two people that you love
Stood up to say, "I do."
We said dance little Jean
A prayer that you had,
Was answered today
When Momma's marrying your Dad.

Yes, this cynic's heart was softened when I heard this song and thought of the possibilities of love. Weddings are definitely the time for celebrating relationships and the love we share. They're also a time to heal the separations that cause us pain and offer a chance once again to return to the oneness we once knew.

And so this other song on *Forever John* is dedicated to the men in my life I once loved (and continue to love) but who aren't with me any more. It's a bittersweet song—the song of true love.

The Game is Over

Time, there was a time
You could talk to me
Without speaking
You would look at me
And I'd know
All there was to know

Days, I think of you
And remember
The lies we told
In the night
The love we knew
The things we shared
When our hearts
Were beating together

Days that were so few
Full of love
And you

Gone, the days are gone now
Days that seemed so wrong now

Life won't be the same
Without you
To hold again
In my arms
To ease the pain
And remember
When our love
Was a reason for living

Days that were so few
Full of love and you

The game is over…

My dearest John. My question for you…is the game of love *ever* over?

Chapter Twenty-six—Jared's Wedding

My oldest son, Jared, got married the same year on June 8, 2006. I hope he doesn't mind me telling about his wedding, as it's a bittersweet story for me.

Jared's first marriage to Holly had ended up as a complete disaster after they had two of the cutest, sweetest children I ever saw—Kiley and Anthony. Holly ended up having an affair with a Black guy (no, I'm not prejudiced) and got pregnant. It had really devastated Jared, and I was glad when he told me he'd found Krista who was very sweet and treated him well.

Jared received custody of the children (which was a real blessing), but I knew it would be quite a handful for him to take care of his two children alone. Krista had a son, Caleb, from a previous relationship with an African American (again, I'm really *not* prejudiced) who had skipped out on her. Caleb was a year older than Kiley. When I heard that Krista was already pregnant with Jared's child, I knew they'd really have their hands full with four children under the age of four. I tried not to judge the situation, but coming from a mother's perspective, I wished Jared had taken things a bit slower after the divorce. I realized that he was desperate for help even though Krista was certainly not the partner I'd envisioned for him. Jared was tall and lanky; Krista was more on the short, stocky side.

After I got to know her, however, I couldn't help but fall in love with her. She had a great attitude about life and was a conscientious mother to all of the children. I knew God had brought Jared just who he needed. Jared started building his broken life back together, and in no time he was the owner and operator of a framing company at only 26 years of age. He makes a mother proud.

But the difficult part of the story for me was the wedding. Kurt had told Jared that he was only going to let his two brothers, Jordan and Jonathan, come because he didn't want the younger ones—Kelsey, Jenny and Andrew—there for some unknown reason. I figured out what that reason was after Kurt had asked me to give him $3,000 so that he could pay for the property taxes that were due. I told him I didn't have the money to give him but was sure Brad would be hysterical over the proposal. I realized Kurt was holding the younger children's wedding attendance as "ransom" unless I came up with the $3,000. It was a real "below the belt" shot but typical of Kurt.

A few days before the wedding, I went to Montana for my monthly visitation and to try to talk some sense into Kurt. He would not make himself available, so in desperation I prayed to God to show me what to do. I was directed to not play along with his control games and simply to load the children into the car and drive them to Salt Lake with me. Kurt would be coming down for the wedding in a couple of days anyway, and he could take them all back. I was going to play the game my way—and God's way—for a change.

I called Deserae as I was headed out of town so she'd know what had happened and in case Kurt got worried when I didn't bring the children back on the designated day. She and the children all thought it was a wonderful game to play on their dad as we were all tired of his constant control dramas. It felt like we were finally liberating ourselves from a tyrant who had controlled us once too often. Of course, Kelsey was concerned we might cause her dad to have another heart attack (he'd suffered two since I'd left him). They said the excuse he'd given them for not letting them go to Jared's wedding was that it was too close to 6/6/6—the day of the beast. He believed the world would come to an end on that day just as he'd told everyone it would at the beginning of 2000. I told them it was all a bunch of bullshit, and the only "beasts" they needed to worry about were those who controlled other people's lives. (I didn't mention any names.)

We all had a great time going to Lava Hot Springs and Lagoon (a local amusement park) while in Utah. Even Ariel joined us at Lagoon after being verbally ripped apart by her father. Kurt told her he was going to call the cops and have me arrested for kidnapping. She calmed him down (after the cops showed up), and I told her to tell him to go ahead and have me arrested—it would make great Oprah material. Besides, being in jail would give me some nice, quiet time to write my next book (the one you're now reading). Hey, I've been arrested before, and it's not a big deal anymore. Prisoners don't have such a bad life—free room and board and all the TV they can watch. Plus lots of time on their hands to write.

Jared, however, was upset by all the drama and chewed me out royally for taking the kids just two days before his wedding. He didn't want all the drama during this special time. I cried that night because his words cut so deeply and painfully. I remembered all the times that I *had* caused drama in others' lives. But this time I'd done it for him and Krista as they'd expressed

how they *really wanted all of Jared's brothers and sisters in the wedding line.*
I knew "kidnapping" them was the only way I could get them there, and I
honestly thought I'd be appreciated for my efforts. Instead, I felt rejected
by my oldest son. I felt like such a failure, and I said perhaps I should turn
myself in and spend his wedding day in jail for doing what I thought would
make him happy. I knew I was playing the PLOM (poor little ol' me) role and
determined to drop it ASAP so we could all enjoy the wedding celebrations.
And so I did.

But others weren't as flexible as I was. Jared told me he'd talked to his
dad and had calmed him down somewhat, but Kurt was still consumed by
rage in the situation that was out of his control. Still full of anger at the
wedding, Kurt made an obvious scene by standing up during the middle
of the ceremony to find a seat that was *not* next to me. Guests commented
about how rude and obnoxious he was—but he didn't care. He was making
his point. But we did get a family picture of all of us together with Kurt and
me standing side by side. He made a lewd remark, asking me if I was wearing
any underwear, so I knew things hadn't changed much.

But the real heartbreak came at the end of the reception during the
traditional father/daughter and mother/son dance. Jared wouldn't even look
at me let alone ask me to dance. I was crushed and shed silent bitter tears over
it. Jared, who I thought would wake up and see things as they really were,
was turning out so much like his father.

The reaction of others made me wonder if the world would ever have
a chance at reconciliation in the battle between the sexes as even Brad was
disappointed by my "impulsive behavior" and sided with Kurt and Jared. This
was the final blow to my female "ego" that simply wanted peace, happiness,
oneness and joy. Who could deny the joy radiating from my sweet little
ones' faces—Kelsey, Jenny and Andrew—as they promenaded with their
cousins arm-in-arm down the aisle? And who could deny the joy inside of me
erupting into smiles of jubilee watching my darling children all dressed up for
the grand wedding parade? Was this too much for a mother to ask? But after
everything was said and done, I decided to put my sword down and not go to
battle any more with men—except in my writing. So please be patient with
me as I express my suppressed e-motions (energy in motion). I hope someday
we can all freely "emote" without taking it too personally.

To top it all off, a week after the wedding I received a letter from the
District Court of Missoula with a motion for the return of my five abducted
children and an amendment to the parenting plan for child support. I shook
my head as I stuck the letter in my desk drawer, amazed at how far Kurt would
go in this melodrama. A month later, to my surprise and delight, I received

Chapter Twenty-seven—Black Sheep

By June, Brad and I had moved our furniture from Las Vegas to Salt Lake and into Jared's new house, which had four bedrooms, two living rooms, and a large bedroom, den and bathroom in the basement. Our storage unit stuff went into the large shed in his backyard. I'd helped him financially with the wedding and his honeymoon and he was using our furniture, so we decided to call it even. We moved in with Mom who was 83 and appreciated the company and the help.

My niece, Danielle, and her husband, Joel, and their two children, Ethan and Bryce, had moved into Mom's basement after my sister, Marsha (Danielle's mom), had remarried and moved out. Joel had been out of work and was paying nothing for rent or utilities (I won't even go there), so I wanted to make sure Mom's needs were being taken care of.

I knew this would be a temporary situation until we got our five-bedroom modular home set-up on the fifteen acres in Indianola. But given Brad's "pokeyman" mentality, I didn't know how long this "temporary situation" would be. I was hopeful despite the fact that my children had nicknamed Brad "The Sloth." I thought that might motivate him, but all he said was "A sloth is a wonderful creature." But try being married to one!

After Jared's wedding, we went to Indianola to sheer the six Cherro sheep that survived the winter. There were the three older ones—Zeus, Ramses, and Aphrodite—but the older female, Athena, had died after Brad fed them a bucket of raw wheat. He didn't know that that would give them scours, so Athena passed on to Mt. Olympus before I could tell him. She had a black yearling ram, which I hadn't named, and Aphrodite had two black lambs that had been born that spring—a male and a female—which I named Sambo and Samantha. I was excited about the black lambs as black wool was hard to come by. Ramses was the only black sheep of the bunch, so obviously he had some dominant genes. As I was holding the sheep down while Brad struggled with the electric sheers (he definitely wasn't a professional Aussie sheepsheerer), I thought about a comedy monologue I'd written and performed for Patricia's acting class. I had a good chuckle thinking about it.

Black Sheep

Ya know black sheep have really gotten a bum rap. I mean, what does it really mean when someone says, "Oh, she's just the black sheep of the family?" Is that supposed to be derogatory or something? Like a polite way of saying, "Oh, she's *really* out there!" or "She's *really* gone off the deep end!" Well, I've always been known as the black sheep of my family. And ya know what? I'm damned proud of it!

It reminds me of one of my favorite cartoons. I had it enlarged and stuck it to my fridge for months. It was a picture of a flock of sheep going over a cliff in mass. Picture it—a big flock of white sheep following the leader over the edge into a great abyss. Stupid, huh? But you also see a little black sheep moving in the opposite direction with a caption that reads, "Excuse me, excuse me."

You might think the black sheep was just being polite as he moved past the others. "Excuse me, excuse me—so sorry, didn't mean to nudge you." A "just let me get by, please" kind of thing. But I don't think that's really what he's saying here. It's more like, "*Excuse me*, you idiots! But up ahead there's a big, damned cliff, and if you don't turn around you're all gonna fall off and break your sweet little necks!" Or, "Excuse me, brothers, but this little ol' black sheep may look a little weird …but I sure ain't *stupid!*" Or, "You'd better get your white asses turned around and follow this black ass, or you're all gonna be dead as lamb chops!"

I think you'll realize that it's always been the black sheep who've been the enlightened ones. They've always been asking the really tough questions like, "I have to do *what* to get into the Celestial Kingdom? Says who?" Or, "What keys of authority did you say you have? Ones to *force me* into the Celestial Kingdom?" Or, "Maybe I'll just get *my own* keys?" Or, "Who needs keys anyway? I think I'll just hot-wire this old jalopy and get there myself!"

Or here's a question to ask your bishop (if you still have one) the next time you go for an interview. "Say, bishop, didn't the enlightened prophets of the Old Testament have lots of lovers, drank wine, and celebrated by dancing naked and singing praises to God for *all* things? Now that's *my kinda* prophet! I don't want a prophet who says I gotta wear this funny underwear that covers my entire body even when it's 100 degrees. And if you're a fundamentalist the "prophet" would also have you believe that you have to wear it even when you have sex! Can you imagine it? And, by the way, you only get to have sex to procreate.

Can you imagine one of King David's 365 wives waiting in line for an entire year for her turn to…procreate…and then realizing, "Damn, I'm on the rag!"

What is it about polygamy anyway? Is it male ego totally out of control or what?! I mean what person in their right mind could possibly think that one man could satisfy the needs of more than one woman? *Get real!* I mean, if you're going to do polygamy you may as well make it fair. What's good for the goose is good for the gander, right? None of this, "The scriptures say a man has to have more than one wife to make it into the Celestial Kingdom." What bullshit! Of course, on second thought—maybe it does take four or five women bitching at a man for the same thing just to get him to listen!

But seriously, what man on the planet would put up with the reverse scenario. "Sorry, sweetheart, tonight's your night to sleep in the other room by yourself. Close the door *real tight* so you don't have to listen to me in the next room screwing Tom. Or was it Dick tonight…or maybe it was Harry? I can't remember.

Or then there's Joe Smith going to God with his dilemma. "Hey, God, I got this problem. You see I'm in love with two babes. One's Edith and the other is Kate. I just can't decide between the two of them, God. What should I do?"

And God replies sympathetically, "Silly Joseph, you don't have to choose. You can have your Kate and Edith, too!"

But then Joseph's wife, Emma, goes to God with her problem. "Hey, God, I'm getting kinda tired listenin' to Joseph in the other room having his Kate and Edith, too. So when is it my turn, God, when is it my turn?"

Could you imagine God saying, "Be patient Emma, you'll get your turn. All you get for now is Joe Pie!"

Or then there's Brigham going to God with his problem. "Hey, God, I got this *real* problem. I've fallen in love with my best friend's 14-year-old daughter. Is it okay to screw her? I mean you screwed Mary when she was only 14 didn't you? It must be okay, then."

And God replies, "Breed 'em young, Brigham, breed 'em young."

But then Brigham's over-the-hill wife, Melba, takes her problem to God. "Hey God, Brigham's got all these young babes lined up for the month. When's it my turn, God, when's it my turn?"

And God replies, "Sorry, Melba, so sorry. You're too old to breed any more. What's the point? The point is we like to breed 'em young."

Well, if that's someone's idea of God and how to get to heaven, I'll take hell, thank-you! Maybe it's just the black sheep in me that has a hard time with *any* organized religious bullshit. That's probably why they kicked me out of the Mormon Church without even notifying me. But you know what

I got when they kicked me out? A 10% raise, Sundays off and…best of all…I get to pick out my own underwear!

When I became an outcast, I started thinking that it might not be a bad idea to start my own church—the Church of the Black Sheep. Wanna join? The Black Sheep are those who question authority, don't swallow the bullshit and believe only what's real. Hey, maybe I'll call it the Church of the Gathering of What Is Real.

Speaking of what's real. The other day I was talking to an old farmer who raises sheep. He told me that the black sheep are the most valuable of the flock. For every hundred white sheep, they put in one black one. That way they only have to count the black sheep and multiply by 100 to determine how many sheep are in the flock. In other words…the black sheep are the only ones that count!

Forgive me for my cynicism, but thinking about that story passed the time as I held the sheep down. Brad finally finished sheering Zeus, Ramseys, and Aphrodite. He was left with No-Name whose wool had turned gray and hairy after the first year—which is not a good quality for wool. As Brad tried to corral No-name, he got butted right in the butt. I laughed, but Brad didn't think it was very funny.

"You damned sheep! You're going to the butcher if you keep it up!" he yelled. Again No-Name went after Brad, but he quickly dodged out of the way. "That settles it! I'm taking you to the butcher!" I didn't put up an argument as we loaded No-Name into the pickup. We were both sweaty and tired and covered with sheep shit, and I was glad we didn't have to sheer her.

As we got ready to leave, we noticed Zeus and Ramseys butting heads vying for Aphrodite's attention. She was busy grazing and ignored them. "See," Brad said, "Males can never get along if they have to compete for a female." Perhaps he was right, but I wanted to believe that humans were different—that they could evolve beyond their jealousies and competitiveness and learn to get along.

Just then I had an epiphany and came to peace with the idea of war. Maybe it was God's way of getting rid of those who can't get along with others like Brad had done with No-Name. War might be a way to rid the world, for a time, of warmongers who kill themselves off which makes the planet a more peaceful place for others. Those who don't choose war—the peacemakers—could live in joy and love by following the ways of peace. It all made sense to me—it was all about choice.

The only problem with this revelation is that governments often force peacemakers to go to war against their will. This, I thought, was *frong* (fucking wrong). We should just divide the planet in half and give half to the warmongers and half to the peacemakers. Of course, everyone would have to agree not to use weapons that might destroy the entire planet. Those would all need to be eliminated. The peacemakers would also need to source safe and sustainable energy resources so the need for fossil fuel (the major cause for war these days) would be eliminated

As we drove away, I looked across the desolate 15 acres and envisioned Heartsong Living Center surrounded by beautiful ponds, gardens and green foliage. I silently dedicated the land to building an intentional community for peacemakers. That would be *my* contribution to World Peace.

Chapter Twenty-eight—Emerging

A week before the Fourth of July, Brian e-mailed me regarding a party at "April's house." I didn't have a clue as to who April was, having been out of the party circuit for nearly two years, but Brian (who was the networker of the group and the sweetest hunk you'll ever meet) always kept us abreast of the goings on of the "Cottage Crowd."

As usual, I was excited to go to the party—and, as usual, Brad was resistant. We always played a silly little game whenever I wanted to go somewhere and he didn't. I told him he was free to stay home if he wanted, but I was free to go with or without him. In the end (about five minutes before I was ready to leave) Brad would always concede and come along. Of course, We played the game for April's Fourth of July party, even though it was getting rather boring. I played along out of love for Brad—or so I thought.

All day long I anxiously anticipated seeing old friends and perhaps meeting a few new ones. But that evening when we arrived at April's house and watched as stranger after stranger entered through her backyard gate, we both became somewhat apprehensive. I said I'd go in and check to see if there was anyone we knew while Brad sat in the car. In the backyard, I ran into a few old friends, so I went back for Brad. He resisted, as usual, but I told him that if things turned stale we'd leave.

A few guys were playing bocce-ball while the rest of the crowd was sitting around socializing. I grabbed a plate of food and a drink and found an empty chair by a gal who I knew only vaguely. Debbie, along with her husband, Tim, had taken a six-week seminar with us from a mutual friend, Robert, the previous summer. We hadn't really connected in class as Brad and I had kept mostly to ourselves, but I did run into Tim at Robert's office one day after I'd had a spinal adjustment.

Tim was all aglow as he recounted his recent experiences with Debbie and polyamory. They said they'd started a healing center and were conducting what they called "Alchemy of the Soul" classes and also couples' Tantric weekend workshops. The word "tantric" piqued my interest, and I asked Tim for a business card so I could visit their website. He said they were holding a weekend retreat in a few weeks at Gary's, a mutual friend's cabin, and I told him I'd check it out. (It turned out that the weekend for the couple's retreat didn't work for our schedule.)

However, at April's party as Debbie and I talked, catching up on what's been happening, I felt an immediate connection with her. I shared things I'd never told any of my friends before—things about Patrick and the whole White Buffalo Woman story. I even slipped off my flip-flop and showed her my birthmark of the white buffalo, which she immediately recognized and related to.

Debbie told me she did a lot of Native American ceremony at her healing center in Draper as Shamanism had always interested her. She also said me she was in a three way relationship with Tim and another man, Alan, from Montana. I told her I'd spent many years in the Bitterroot Valley and missed my home and family up Ninemile near Missoula. We talked for over two hours as if no one else was around. Brad kept coming over, interrupting us and asking if we could leave; but I brushed him aside and told him to find someone to socialize with. For me, this was much too important to drop.

As most of the crowd started to leave, Debbie and I went into the kitchen where Tim, Alan and Brad were talking. Brad hadn't quite put the three of them together, and when they asked me to come with them to Montana to Tim's high school reunion in Alberton (Tim was also from Montana), I was ready to jump at the chance for a free ride to visit my children. But after Brad figured out the whole threesome thing, he got defensive and insisted that this was totally out of the question.

I pouted as I allowed Tim and Alan to give me a warm hug before the three of them left. I got scolded all the way home from Brad for my "indiscretions." He wasn't about to let *his* wife venture all the way to Montana with an imbalanced threesome of two men and one woman. In the back of my mind I envied Debbie and knew I hadn't heard the last of her polyamory adventures.

When Tim, Debbie and Alan returned from Montana, Debbie called and invited me to attend a "full-moon ceremony" at their house. I dragged Brad along with me after Jonathon's birthday celebration and, of course, we were late. But we still got to join in the ceremony of burning our list of "releases" into the warm night air under a full moon. The next day I called Debbie and told her I really wanted to go to her upcoming *Alchemy of the Soul* classes, but I couldn't afford the thousand dollars tuition. I asked if she would be interested in trading for massages. She said that that would work because her regular massage therapist had moved out of state. I told Brad, and he nearly flipped out. He said he felt threatened by the whole situation and that if I was going to attend, he'd need to come with me to "protect his territory." What bullshit, I contended, as the visual of a dog urinating on me came to mind. I deeply resented the fact that Brad thought of me as "territory," but I knew we were Both in for some alchemical shifts of consciousness.

The *Alchemy of the Soul* classes were extraordinary, especially the weekend retreat at Gary's cabin near Bear Lake.   Each student had been assigned "stretches" designed to enlarge the soul.   One stretch was a presentation by groups of three on a specific word; the other was a skit with a partner to a particular song. Brad and I were assigned to do the skit on the song, *Along Came John*. I thought it was perfect synchronicity as Brad dressed up as a "damsel in distress" and I dressed up as John Denver wearing Brad's wire-rimmed glasses, playing his guitar as I rescued him…errr…her. Brad looked fabulous in pigtails, mascara and plaid skirt. Everyone cheered at the end of the skit.

My other stretch was with Alan and Katie (Debbie and Tim's daughter-in-law), and we had been given the word "emerging" as our presentation word. My mind was filled with inspiration the entire week before as ideas flooded my brain.   I decided to use the theme of the butterfly through its stages of metamorphosis—ending with my own metamorphosis into the archetype of the White Buffalo Woman. It was a huge stretch for me to take a giant step forward and reveal my true self—and I wondered if I was ready for it.

For our introductions Katie (a ballet instructor) led the group in dancing out each of our own personal metamorphosis. It was fabulous and freeing. Then we all sat down, and as I began my own speech, I grew a bit nervous sensing butterflies inside my stomach.   I suppose that was appropriate considering the metaphor we were using, but I still questioned my own abilities to perform. I began with a quote from Trina Paulus:

"How does one become a butterfly?" she asked pensively.
"You must want to fly so much that you are willing to give up being a caterpillar."

I then shared my own experiences of having been fascinated by butterflies all my life. As a child I had always chased them even to my own near destruction. Once, at a family reunion in Idaho, I'd been chasing butterflies near a brook when suddenly I was swept away by firm hands. I looked back in terror as a huge brown bear crossed the bridge to where I'd been playing. An attentive relative had seen the situation and had rescued me by risking his own life. Later that day the bear was hunted down and killed. It was one of my distinct memories as a child.

A more pleasant memory of butterflies was when I had attracted a "pet" butterfly that would come and light on my finger each day. It was a Morning Glory that I named "Brownie," and I was sad the day it didn't return. I told myself it had flown away somewhere as I couldn't bear the idea that it had died.

Years earlier, I'd written a poem describing my fascination with the process of metamorphosis—something we each go through to reach enlightenment.

Metamorphosis

Caterpillar, caterpillar, consuming all in thy path
Nourishing body, mind and spirit with all that the world has.

Caterpillar, caterpillar, spinning the web of time
Can't you see the web you weave are memories gone by?

Caterpillar, caterpillar, trapped in your cocoon
Struggling against the energy veil that you alone have spun

Caterpillar, caterpillar, look within your heart
And break the bonds, which hold you bound...
to fly on wings of fire!

Annalee Skarin in her book, *Book of Books*, shares insights concerning the metamorphosis of the caterpillar into the butterfly.

"Scientists have discovered an infinitesimal gland in the brain of a caterpillar, that if removed or injured, the worm can never develop into a butterfly. It may go into its cocoon and fulfill the outside laws of its own perfecting yet fail to bring forth the actual inside achievement. In order to fulfill its promised destiny it has to put the outside flesh aside and let that inner-knowing take over. And only as that tiny gland is developed can that full functioning of a brilliant, evolved caterpillar be accomplished.

"There is also within the caterpillar another gland, infinitely tiny, located in the center of its body. And man has both of these glands also. They are right within himself. The one in the brain changes the thinking, being personality of the worm conscious, which transforms the mortal conscious man into a new being as far above his mere mortal conscious man into a new being as far above his mere human condition as the butterfly is above the worm. The change in the caterpillar lifts it above the drab, ugly earth into new heights and realms of vision and grandeur. It has a new heightened awareness of itself and its surroundings.

"The central gland develops the very wings needed to match the advancement in thought and comprehension. The caterpillar is no longer a crawling insect pushing and dragging itself along over every obstacle in its path. It can fly above the clods and sticks and stones and mountains of grass.

It can travel in a minute the distance that would have required a full day of grinding effort in its previous condition.

"The caterpillar is the perfect symbology of man in his unawakened state of mortal, worm consciousness."

The butterfly, on the other hand, is the perfect metaphor for humans who break through the illusions of separation or veils of darkness they have created for themselves, and look within their own hearts and realize who they truly are—GOD. But this can only happen when, as in the symbol of the emergence of the butterfly, all the energies of our entire being are committed to that emerging out of the darkness and into the light. These energies must come from within; for if anyone tries to release us from our own cocoon, it inhibits the strength necessary to produce the wings to fly us to God.

My next intention was to play John Denver's song "It's the Fire and the Wings that Fly Us Home," but I couldn't find a copy of his *Spirit* album that contained the song. Instead I put on Carlos Nakia's *Earth Spirit* flute music as I disappeared into the bedroom to change into my White Buffalo Woman costume. As I emerged from the bedroom carrying my sacred peace pipe and holding a picture of the White Buffalo Woman emerging from a beautiful white buffalo, Alan began reading my poem:

Gift of the Sacred Pipe

Amber sunset over the Great Plains—
Two warriors from the Lakota tribe
Warm themselves by campfire flames,
One in quiet rapture, one in pride.
"How's the hunt," booms a boisterous voice.
"Not so good," whispers the quiet one.
"I shot a doe, I had no choice,
Its leg was broke, it couldn't run."
"You call that hunting?" the voice demands.
"I shot two buffalo on a full run."
Firelight reflects on bloodied hands,
And moonlight replaces the light of sun.

Moving in silence, the spirit seeks
The honor of each of their victories.
One who sees much, but rarely speaks,
One who speaks much, but rarely sees.
In the east, Orion's arrow

Pierces through all false pretense.
One whose path is straight and narrow,
The other crooked, filled with nonsense.
Yonder horizon, a glowing specter
Silently walking, its form draws near.
Traveling through the darkened sector,
The illumined figure is brightly clear.

A beautiful woman surrounded by light
Appears before the astonished braves.
Clothed in buffalo skins of white,
Her hair cascading in rippling waves.
Ageless eyes search deep the center
The soul of each brave's true intent.
One heart pure and holy to enter,
The other one filled with vile contempt.
The dazzling oracle perceives their wonder,
Extends her arms to be embraced.
One is fearful to gaze upon her,
The other is evil and carnally based.

One rushes forward in lustful desiring,
Seeking the thrill of her physical form.
His rugged hands are never tiring
Of feeling the flesh of a body warm.
Suddenly, dark clouds descending,
Surround him in blackness and breathless cold.
Lightning flashes and thunder crescending,
The destroying angel's wings unfold.
Shadows lift, light no longer dim,
Exposing the evil man's heart of lust.
His malevolence has turned upon him,
His flesh and bones now whirling dust!

The honorable man falls to his knees,
Questioning his own heart's desires.
Fearing the angel through him sees
If he'll pass through the discerning fires.
Dawn breaks forth in brilliant rapture,
Shining forth a celestial glow.
Gazing down, her vision captures

The honor of his intent she knows.
Reaching out, she beckons the penitent
To arise and step forward from bended knee.
Her hands upon him, his soul contented,
Purity of heart she can clearly see.

With tender words, a divine message told,
Describing the mission the two shall share.
The bundle she carries, she now unfolds,
Revealing the sacred object she bears.
Carefully she lifts the precious item—
A distinctive pipe of exquisite beauty.
Its purpose to unite the children of men
In peace and love and prosperity.
Together they travel to carry the pipe
To all the villages far and near
With minds that are open, hearts that are ripe
"Love is the way"—the message is clear.

"We are all one," the messenger sings,
"Connected to God," chants the resonant voice.
"And to the Sacred Circle the Spirit brings
All of His children who make this choice—
To live in peace and love one another
And build His kingdom here on earth.
For each is your sister or your brother,
This is the truth withheld from birth.
In sacred ceremony we'll remember
The precious truths about who we are…
As God's children, we've been sent here
Like seeds within a bright, shining star."

The message is given, the woman departs,
Leaving them wondering when she'll return.
And the Holy Spirit enters their hearts
Revealing the lessons they must learn.
When the children of God can love one another,
Singing songs of oneness, songs of peace,
Then Heaven and Earth will dwell together—
The Spirit of God will then increase.
To all Four Corners, she bows in silence,

The smoke from the peace pipe fills the air.
And when it clears, in divine benevolence—
A white buffalo calf remains standing there.

Numerous centuries have come and gone
But the legend remains the same.
The Pipekeepers have kept the vigil long
From the moment when she came.
The prophecy says—she will return
When the long shadow covers the earth.
The sign is—a white buffalo born
And the whole world reveres its birth.
Then God will move upon her heart,
The Holy Spirit within her burns.
The strange act of which thou art
When the White Buffalo Woman returns.

She will open the hearts of men
Like a flower that shattered the stone,
Peace, love and joy will return again
And the many will live as one.
So if you believe the story told
And the gathering of what "is real."
Then listen to me, young and old
And together we'll begin to heal.
When you surrender your hearts to each other
And the Spirit within you burns,
Then Heaven and Earth will dwell together
And to her hands the Sacred Pipe returns.

I then sat down and shared with everyone my favorite butterfly story—the Introduction and Chapter One of this book, *Heart Wide Open*. I ended with two quotes from one of my favorite books, *Buffalo Woman Comes Singing* by Brooke Medicine Eagle.

These questions are asked of all of us as we move into the New Age of Enlightenment.

Am I willing to *have* absolutely everything? Am I willing to be truly whole? Am I willing to walk in a holy manner?" lies at the back of my mind, and moves me to seek a whole new way of being inside myself. It moves me toward a place of power, where I am in flow with the river of life, rather than struggling upstream or across it in a tipsy unstable canoe. I know that this flowing river of life is akin to the experience of oneness of which White Buffalo Calf Pipe Woman and Dawn Star spoke.

When we are at one with things, we will enjoy not so much a sense of power, but a sense of ease; not so much a sense of good timing, but of synchronicity; not so much of conquering our weaknesses as of bringing forward our most wonderful gifts. So I am called again and again to the question of wholeness, of holiness, of unity, of oneness. It is exactly what White Buffalo Woman prescribed—good relationship. And the way to create this lies in unity, in cooperation, in the breaking down of barriers, in the release of fear and constriction…

And so White Buffalo Woman comes singing into our world her ways of unity, oneness, harmony, and cooperation. I hear her song, as I move forward in my ability to use these principles in my own life and in my work with others. I hear her words in my mind, 'Carry forward this pipe, this way of unity and oneness. With it you will be able to go through this time, into the new time, and on until the end of time. And I will meet you there."

Everyone's heart, I could feel, was blown wide open. And that was the intention as a practical application of the word—emerging. Together we had emerged from the darkness of our own limitations into the illumination of our unlimited creative potential. We had let go of the caterpillar mentality and had emerged out of our own cocoons to fly on our own wings of fire.

Finally, I wish to share John's song, *It's the Fire and the Wings that Fly Us Home.*

> There are many ways of being
> In this circle we call life,
> A wise man seeks an answer
> Burns a candle through the night.
>
> Is a jewel just a pebble
> That's found a way to shine?
> Is a hero's blood more righteous
> Than a hobo's sip of wine?

I dreamed of you one morning
On some distant world away,
Were we broken by the water?
Did I lie you in the grave?

Were we brothers on a journey?
Did you teach me how to run?
Did I pierce you with an arrow?
Did I lay with you in the sun?

I dreamed…
You were a prophet in the meadow.
I dreamed…
I was a mountain in the wind.
I dreamed…
You knelt and touched me with a flower,
I awoke with this…a flower in my hand.

I know that love has seen
All the infinite in one,
In the brotherhood of creatures
Through the Father, through the Son.
The vision of your goodness
Will sustain me through the cold,
Take my hand now to remember
When you find yourself alone…
You're never alone…

For the Spirit fills the darkness of the heavens,
It fills the endless yearnings of the soul,
It lives within a star too far to dream of,
It lives within each part and is the whole.
It's the fire and the wings that fly us home…
Fly us home…Fly us home.

Epilogue

It was Monday morning, October 2, 2006, as I walked into Mom's kitchen and noticed the newspaper on the kitchen table. She always left it there for Bruce to read when he came "home" for lunch. I glanced at the front page headlines, noticing a large photo of LDS President Gordon B. Hinckley raising his hand with the caption "At 96, 'I feel well'." Could *he* be a shape-shifter? I laughed to myself, as his profile admittedly looked reptilian. Those reptilians can live a long time, I thought, as I recalled the life span of certain turtles and lizards. David Icke, in his book, *The Biggest Secret,* mentions that there are reptilian blood-sacrifices that occur beneath the Mormon temples. I thought it best not to mention any of that to Mom or Bruce who I'm sure listened to the entire General Conference that weekend.

Brad and I had spent our Sunday (yesterday) at sunny Diamond Fork Hot Springs with the usual "Church of the Hot Springs" crowd. It was a glorious day and our friends, Jodi and Eldon, showed up for an interesting discussion on polyamory. Jodi promised to send me a download of the radio interview she did on the subject. I was anxious to get to my e-mails to hear it.

As I prepared my morning brew of fresh lemon and warm water, I sat down to read the *Morning News.* Next to Hinckley's picture was a picture of Defense Secretary Donald Rumsfeld with the headline, "I won't resign, insists Rumsfeld." I started to read the Associated Press article:

"Defense Secretary Donald H. Rumsfeld, coming under renewed fire for his management of the Iraq war, said Sunday he is not considering resigning and said the president had called him personally in recent days to express his continued support."

I skimmed through the rest of the bullshit article, recalling a famous quote from Mark Twain: "Those who *do not* read the newspaper are uniformed. Those who *do* read the newspaper are misinformed."

But another front-page article caught my interest. It was captioned "Utah urged to get ready for disaster." Now that was an article I could relate to, so I read it in its entirety. It was a recap of the 2006 Preparedness Symposium, which referred to a survey that showed that most people aren't taking the proper steps to prepare for a disaster such as a large scale earthquake or pandemic flu, the two scenarios discussed most often at the Symposium. It was frightening how unprepared Utahns were concerning food and water storage. Less than 50 per cent even had a 72-hour emergency kit. I admit that my own time and efforts had been directed toward developing my 15 acres into a safe haven, but if a disaster hit unexpectedly, I'd simply be SOL (shit out of luck) just like most people. I promised myself I'd get some food and water storage for Mom's house—just in case.

After finishing the lemon water, I went to the library/therapy room to check my e-mail. Jodi's hadn't come in yet so instead I forwarded her Brian's humorous e-mail concerning "Men" thinking she'd get a chuckle out of it.

Subject: MEN

For all those men who say, Why buy a cow when you can get the milk for free? Here's an update for you: Nowadays, 80% of women are against marriage. WHY? Because women realize it's not worth buying an entire pig just to get a little sausage.

Men are like…

1. Men are like Laxatives…They irritate the crap out of you.
2. Men are like Bananas…The older they get, the less firm they are.
3. Men are like Weather…Nothing can be done to change them.
4. Men are like Blenders…You need one, but you're not quite sure why.
5. Men are like Chocolate Bars…Sweet, smooth, and they usually head right for your hips.
6. Men are like Commercials…You can't believe a word they say.
7. Men are like Department Stores…Their clothes are always ½ off.
8. Men are like Government Bonds…They take sooooooooo long to mature.
9. Men are like Mascara…They usually run at the first sign of emotion.
10. Men are like Popcorn…They satisfy you, but only for a little while.
11. Men are like Snowstorms…You never know when they're coming, how many inches you'll get, or how long it will last.
12. Men are like Lava Lamps…Fun to look at, but not very bright.
13. Men are like Parking Spots…All the good ones are taken, the rest are handicapped.

Now send this to all the remarkable women you know, as well as to any understanding, good-natured, fun kinda guys you might be lucky enough to know!

You Got Served!
Brian

I laughed at Brian's warped sense of humor, admiring his courage for exposing himself as a man. I then noticed that Debbie had sent me an e-mail. It read:

Lakota Spiritual Leader Issues Call to Sacred Pipe Carriers and to Humanity

David Swallow Speaks on the Birth of Wisconsin White Buffalo Calf

By Stephanie M. Schwartz, Freelance Writer—Member, Native American Journalists Association

September 18, 2006   Brighton, Colorado

To nearly all the American Indian Nations and Canadian First Nations, white buffalo calves are considered highly sacred. To the Lakota, Dakota, and Nakota Siouxan Nations, they play a primary role in their traditional beliefs and prophecies.

Since the rare birth of the white buffalo calf, Miracle, on the Heider Family farm in Janesville, Wisconsin in 1994, numerous white buffalo calves have been born across the country. Interestingly, like Miracle, most of these calves have been born on farms owned by non-Native American people. Additionally, as a symbol of hope for peace, people from many cultures have come to know about and honor these creatures.

Miracle died unexpectedly in 2004 of natural causes at only ten years of age; an event which created shock across the indigenous nations and around the world.

Now, another sacred white buffalo, named Miracle's Second Chance by Valerie Heider, has been born on the same farm in Wisconsin during a lightning storm on August 25, 2006.

David Swallow, Teton Oglala Lakota traditional spiritual leader from the Pine Ridge Reservation, spoke today on the significance and message he sees in this calf's birth.

He clearly believes that the name for this calf was actually part of the message. He said, "The name is right, it is no accident, the birth of Miracle's Second Chance is yes, a second chance for all humanity." And since, to his people, lightning represents the destruction of evil, Swallow feels the message is the strongest yet.

Swallow went on to explain that, "It is not the normal average person or even the normal government people who bring such danger and destruction to the world. It is those who walk in greed and envy who feed the prophesied many-headed serpent who is foretold to consume its supporters."

Swallow explained that the traditional stories of his people tell that the Sacred White Buffalo Calf Woman came at a time of great need and great strife and war to bring the people back to peace, to living in a good way. She initially appeared to two men. In this first encounter, one of the men was honored, the one who showed respect and right spiritual action. The other was consumed and turned to dust because of his evil intentions.

Swallow believes so it will happen in our world again today. "The birth of this calf symbolizes this, that evil will be destroyed." he said.

His words spoke that, "It is time that the white nations and all mainstream cultures return to living in a good way, in peace and harmony with each other and with Grandmother Earth. Only by doing so, will life continue in our world."

But Swallow was clear that there was also a message for the indigenous nations as well. He pointed out that the Sacred White Buffalo Calf Woman had brought the sacred c'anunpa, the sacred pipe, to his people that they might use it to pray in a good way so that their sincere prayers might be heard by the Divine.

Swallow issued a call to all those who carry a c'anunpa. He said, "The Sacred Pipe carriers, whether they are Native American or not, need to get their sacred c'anunpas out and use them every day to pray for peace and harmony to return to our world in a good way. Pray that the "money" people will wake up and stop destroying Grandmother Earth for profit and that her health will return. You can make a difference, a very real difference. The c'anunpas need to be used for this purpose by all who carry them. They need to do this every day and to walk with these prayers in their hearts."

Swallow continues, "My English is not good. I have to be careful because sometimes I use the wrong words and am misunderstood. But everyone needs to understand this clearly: We all need to pray, whether you have a c'anunpa or not, whether you are American Indian or not. We need to pray because it will only be by prayer that the world will be saved. It will only be by prayer that the hearts of those who are destroying the world can be changed."

Swallow ended by saying, "I have said this is our second chance for humanity. I pray that people will wake up and hear the message. Our lives and our world depend on it. Ho hecetu yelo, I have spoken."

I cried as I read these words and immediately sent a reply e-mail to Debbie thanking her for sending me the article. I also requested that we all get together for a pipe ceremony to pray for peace and the opening of people's hearts. Debbie had copied the following quote and had given it to all of us during one of her classes. I admired her dedication and truly loved her, Tim and Alan for their sincere honesty in open relationships. I struggled with my own honesty in mine but still had the faith that things would change.

"Prayer is not an old woman's idle amusement. Properly understood and applied, it is the most potent instrument of action." Mohandas K. Gandhi

I know the value of prayer as I've seen it work miracles in the lives of my loved ones. For example:

Kurt's heart has been recently opened to the point that we are now having intimate conversations on the phone. Christy and I have returned to a friendship and we, too, have long talks.

My children are secure, healthy and happy, and I know that a multitude of guardian angels are watching over them. (Debbie has confirmed this to me through a revelation she received from *her* angels.)

Pam and Joe have stopped smoking and using drugs along with most of our "Family of Friends." Many of them have gone on a cleanse this spring to get rid of toxins that have built up in their bodies. I am proud of all of them.

Ed and Trish are happily married after Trish got divorced from Ray. Ray is having some alone (all one) time to figure out what relationship means to him. I pray for his enlightenment.

Brad and I are listening to each other more and trying to acknowledge each other's true feelings concerning relationship and community. I am pushing less, and he is resisting less. We still get into "our shit" every once in a while when I act on my *real* feelings. In my life there are many men who I truly love and would like to get to know on a more intimate basis. I continue to wait on God's timing, however.

During the last class in Debbie and Tim's Alchemy of the Soul class we all had our aura's photographed by a kirlian photographer. As we set our intentions for the photo, mine was to see the aura Patrick saw which caused him to believe I was the White Buffalo Calf Woman who had returned.

Although at the time I couldn't wrap my mind around the implications of the photograph (featured on the back book cover) I could immediately recognize the white dove descending from a doorway to heaven and the outline of the Buddha laying above my head. The symbols were astonishing to me but it still doesn't change the fact that I am not the only "chosen one" who is commissioned to save OUR planet. We are *all* chosen for this purpose. So let's get going—ALL OF US!!

In the *Course on Miracles* a miracle is defined as "A sudden change of perspective." Perhaps my perspective about who I am and what my purpose is here on Earth may change over time. I pray for a "God perspective" in all things so I'll not be guilty of being shortsighted. I remain open to the Spirit to guide me on my own path to enlightenment.

Writing this book has had a tremendous healing effect, as I've been able to give voice to my most intimate feelings and experiences in life with my "heart wide open." I hope it has helped to open your heart as well. If I've offended any one, in any way, it was never my intention, and I ask for your forgiveness. And if any of the things written need editing for the sake of clarity, please let me know at heartsong@webpipe.net

As always, my heart is wide open to you in love, peace and grace. I look forward to the creation of a Zion (pure in heart) community that will represent Heaven on Earth...or the gathering of what is real. This is *my* work and *my* glory. Amen and Aho.

Books and Authors

Books by Tom Crum:
The Magic of Conflict
Journey to Center
Published by Simon & Schuster
Rockefeller Center, 1230 Avenue of the Americas, New York, NY 10020

Books by Wayne Dyer:
You'll See It When You Believe It!
The Power of Intention
Change Your Thoughts—Change Your Life
Published by Hay House, Inc.
P.O. Box 5100, Carlsbad, CA 92018-5100

Books by Patrick Quirk (Speaking Wind):
When Spirits Touch the Red Path
The Message
Season of the Long Shadow
Spirits of the Flame
Watchers of the Shadow and the Light
The Brotherhood
Lumen
Published by iUniverse
2021 Pine Lake Road, Suite 100
Lincoln, NE 68512

Books by Dan Brown:
The Da Vinci Code
Angels and Demons
Published by Double Day, a division of Random House, Inc.
New York, NY 10020

Books by Edmond Bordeaux Szekely:
The Essene Gospel of Peace
The Unknown Books of the Essenes
Lost Scrolls of the Essene Brotherhood
The Teachings of the Elect
The Essene Way, Biogenic Living
Published by IBS International
Box 849, Nelson, BC, Canada

Books by Elaine Pagels:
The Gnostic Gospels
Beyond Belief: The Secret Gospel of Thomas
Published by Vintage Books, a division of Random House, Inc.
New York, NY 10020

Books by Margaret Starbird:
The Woman with the Alabaster Jar
The Goddess in the Gospels
Published by Bear & Company
One Park Street, Rochester, Vermont 05767

Books by David Icke:
The Biggest Secret
Infinite Love is the Only Truth—Everything Else is Illusion
Published by Bridge of Love Publications USA
1825 Shiloh Valley Drive, Wildwood, MO 63005

The Nag Hammadi Library
By James M. Robinson
Published by HarperCollins Publishers
10 East 53rd Street, New York, NY 10022

The Temple and the Lodge
By Michael Baigent and Richard Leigh
Published by Arcade Publishing Inc.
New York, NY 10020

The Chalice & The Blade
By Riane Eisler
Published by HarperCollins Publishers
10 East 53rd Street, New York, NY 10022

On the Kabbalah and Its Symbolism
By Gershom Scholem
Published by Schocken Books Inc.
New York, NY 10020

Jesus Was Married
By Ogden Kraut
Published by Pioneer Press
3332 Ft Union Blvd., Salt Lake City, Utah 84121

The Second Messiah
By Christian Knight & Robert Lomas
Published by Barnes and Noble Books
New York, NY 10020

The Templar Revelation
By Lnn Picknett & Clive Prince
Published by Touchstone
Rockefeller Center, 1230 Avenue of Americas, New York, NY 10020

Blue Blood, True Blood—Conflict & Creation
By Stewart A. Swerdlow
Published by Expansions Publishing Company, Inc.
P.O. Box 12, St Joseph, MI 49085

The Most Evil Secret Societies in History
By Shelley Klein
Published by Barnes and Noble
New York, NY 10020

Author's Note

Perhaps the world does need just one more prophet—you! What would you do if you felt you were called by God to save the planet?! Guess what? You are!! You are now being called by God (through me) to help save the planet! I can't do it myself even if I were the legendary White Buffalo Woman (not a calf anymore) whose been prophesied by all of the Native American tribes to heal the planet from all of the destructive behaviors of mankind. It's up to you to create the miracle—the miracle of change. Or as the Course in Miracles calls it—a sudden change of perspective. I simply call it a change of heart.

I made a commitment to myself and others to finish this book and get it published. But unlike Heartsong I now feel the need to heal the planet. The planet isn't perfect just as it is. It is still a playground allowing us to create whatever reality we wish to create. All of our choices are still here. This has been its purpose—to give us choice. We can choose to create good things or bad…and we do.

Now I am not only choosing to create my own reality for good, but I am asking you to choose wisely, too. I am currently the owner and manager of Heartsong Healing Center in Holladay, Utah where I indulge in my life's passion—bodywork and water therapy—to help heal others of their separations within (sins). This, in my mind's eye, is the at-one-ment or the coming into oneness. You are welcome to come visit me here at Heartsong and play. I also purchased land in Central Utah where I'm currently developing Heartsong Living Center—a sustainable eco-village. Together let's build a life—and a planet--that is good.

Life is so good
Life is so good these days
Life is so good these days…
Life is so good.

Let's sing this song of John Denver's and build a life for all of us living on planet Earth that is so good. Perhaps when I complete my Heartsong Living Center you can come out and visit me there and we can sing songs, share massages or waterdance, and come together in heartfelt communion. I look forward to that. Blessings—Janae aka Jesse aka J. Bird (naked as a)